THE GREAT EDUCATION
DEBATE

THE GREAT EDUCATION DEBATE

WASHINGTON AND THE SCHOOLS

By

BENJAMIN D. STICKNEY, Ed. D.

University of Colorado
Colorado Springs, Colorado

and

LAURENCE R. MARCUS, Ed.D.

New Jersey Department of Higher Education
Trenton, New Jersey

CHARLES C THOMAS • PUBLISHER
Springfield • Illinois • U.S.A.

Published and Distributed Throughout the World by
CHARLES C THOMAS • PUBLISHER
2600 South First Street
Springfield, Illinois 62717

© 1984 by CHARLES C THOMAS • PUBLISHER
ISBN 0-398-04959-9
Library of Congress Catalog Card Number: 83-24129

Library of Congress Cataloging in Publication Data

Stickney, Benjamin D.
  The great education debate.

  Bibliography: p.
  Includes index.
  1. Education and state—United States. I. Marcus, Laurence R. II. Title.
LC89.S67   1984   379.73   83-24129
ISBN 0-398-04959-9

Printed in the United States of America
PS-R-3

PREFACE

When attempting to come to grips with the varied issues encompassing Washington's involvement in education, one may be less struck by the trends of today than by the uncertainties of tomorrow. Despite the fact that the early sixties to late seventies was marked by a substantial strengthening of federal influence and that the eighties has, thus far, been witness to the curtailment of this growth, it may be unclear whether decentralization of government, deregulation of programs, and the inactivism of the courts are more indicative of some enduring change in national consciousness or more a respite for a people who had grown tired, frustrated, and confused by the educational order. In the years ahead, will the federal role in education be reversed, renewed, or redefined? Will the current discontent and demand for excellence in education be an avenue for an even greater increased state and local control of schooling, lead to no more than a lethargic maintenance of the status quo or be the impetus for an invigorated federal presence in education? If there is any meaningful contemporary agenda in the federal education arena, it is to develop dialogue and entertain examination of these questions.

The current debate involving Washington and the schools has been precipitated principally by the leadership of Ronald Reagan. The President himself has pushed a reversal and has indeed questioned whether there should be *any* role for the federal government in education. Nine days after taking office, he informed the press that he had requested that the Secretary of Education "look at the appropriate role of the federal government in education, *if there is one,* and to report back" (emphasis added).

In so doing, Secretary of Education Terrell Bell has overseen— whether by coincidence or by design—several initiatives that define and redefine Washington's educational role, including replacing the Department of Education by a foundation, consolidating twenty-nine categorical programs, and creating a critical and influential Commission on Excellence in Education. The Commission's often inflammatory indictment of educational status quo, while not principally addressing federal involvement per se, has engendered national attention on our national interests and their association with education.

In *The Great Education Debate: Washington and the Schools,* we have attempted to shed light on the appropriate role of the federal government in education by reviewing the emergence of Washington's growing involvement prior to the election of Ronald Reagan, summarizing the recent trend challenging federal influence, outlining the processes and products of educational change prompted by the Reagan Administration and discussing the influence of the courts on the educational order. Hopefully, this exercise has integrated the many issues, both historic and contemporary, in a manner that will give greater meaning to the national dialogue on education from a federal perspective.

Our interest in offering a chronicle of federal issues in education is, in part, the product of earlier attention to the subject of equity and education. In our earlier volume, *Race and Education; The Unending Controversy,* (Charles C Thomas, Publisher, 1981), we focused on the relationship of the schools to the problems associated with racism in America. Because principal attempts to remedy racial inequality and other domestic inequities centered around federal educational initiatives, we wished to be more than passive witnesses to the recent attempts to fundamentally change the federal education order.

In preparing this volume, we received invaluable assistance from many sources. We extend our particular appreciation to Dr. Hannah Levin for her review of the chapter, "The Constitution and the Schools"; to Edwin L. Dale, Jr., Assistant Director for Public Affairs from the Office of Management and Budget for his review of the chapter, "Cuts, Consolidation, and Compromise," to Christina Martinez and Cindy McClure of the University of Colorado at Colorado Springs Library for their work in collecting a variety of materials; to Julie Eddy and Yem Michali of the Colorado College

Library for their help in gathering federal documents; and to Mae Smith, Verna Bobko, Sheila Tkacs, Connie Wroten and Cindy Burzlaff for their assistance in the preparation of the manuscript.

BENJAMIN D. STICKNEY
LAURENCE R. MARCUS

CONTENTS

Page

Preface v

Chapter

1. The Growth of the Federal Role 3
2. The Winds of Change 60
3. Cuts, Consolidation, and Compromise 88
4. The Constitution and the Schools 128
5. In the National Interest 168

Index 187

THE GREAT EDUCATION
DEBATE

THE GROWTH OF THE FEDERAL ROLE

I n 1979, arguing in support of President Jimmy Carter's proposal for a cabinet-level department of education, Vice President Walter Mondale noted that the United States "is the only major industrial democracy in the world that does not have a department or a ministry of education."[1] That fact provides symbolic represent-ation of that which all Americans are aware: for better or worse, education is a responsibility of the states and is carried out under the auspices of local authorities. The states spend more on education than they do on any other activity. Similarly, local governments dedicate more of their tax dollar to education than to any other service. In fact, in most cities and towns, the school budget accounts for the majority of municipal expenditure.[2] While the federal contribution to public and private institutions at the elementary, secondary, and postsecondary levels (as well as to their students) has grown to such proportions that major chaos would result if the aid were withdrawn, the federal government remains the junior partner in the educational enterprise.

The Basis for Our Pluralistic Approach to Education

The pluralism that our system promotes was probably less planned than acquired. English common law gave parents a great degree of authority over their children. Transported to the Ameri-can continent and placed in the frontier situation, this tradition gave parents the responsibilty for providing for their children's educa-tion.[3] Given the distances between settlements and the difficulty in getting from one place to another, parents or local clergy provided reading and arithmetic instruction. As towns grew, parents joined to hire and pay for a teacher. As early as 1642, and again with the "Old Deluder Act" in 1647, Massachusetts required such collective

3

action. The law insisted that

> every township in this jurisdiction, after the Lord hath increased them to the number of fifty householders, shall then forthwith appoint one within their town to teach all such children as shall resort to them to write and read, whose wages shall be paid either by the parents or masters of such children or by the inhabitants in general . . ..[4]

Thus, by 1783, when Britain finally recognized American independence, the local school district had been a fact of American life for nearly a century and a half. This is not to say that all states and municipalities felt their responsibility equally. Massachusetts, New York, and Connecticut were unique in providing land grants to local citizens for the purpose of education. The common (or public) school movement did not gain hold until the 1830s. The democratic urges spawned by the presidency of Andrew Jackson led to the belief that public education was the foundation of a strong democracy: it would permit citizens to be conversant with the issues facing the new country and to make wise judgments; it would also be a guard against oligarchy and corruption. The South was at least twenty years behind the North and West in developing public schools, and restricted educational opportunity only to white children.[5]

By the midnineteenth century, there were only a few thousand public schools. A hundred years later, there were 25 million children enrolled in public elementary and secondary schools across the country.[6] By the time that the nation celebrated its bicentennial, there were more than 44.3 million public school students, down 1.57 million from the peak year of 1970.[7]

Promoting the State Role

The federal role grew slowly during the first two centuries. Nevertheless, approximately two hundred laws to provide federal aid to education have been enacted by Congress.[8] The debate concerning the proper role of the federal government extends back to the period when the Articles of Confederation provided the framework for national governance. The proposal, made in 1783 by Colonel Timothy Pickering, regarding the dedication of surplus land in the Ohio Territory, provided the concept for a later law that led Daniel Webster to proclaim

> I doubt whether any one single law, or any lawgiver, ancient or modern,

has produced effects of more distinct, marked and lasting character....It
set forth and declared it to be a high and binding duty of government to
support schools and the means of education.[9]

Pickering proposed that the Ohio Territory be opened to Revolutionary War veterans and that "all the surplus lands shall be common property for the State and be disposed of for the common good; as for laying out roads, creating public buildings, establishing schools and academies."[10]

This idea was ahead of its time by two years, at which time the Land Ordinance of 1785 divided the Ohio Territory into townships consisting of thirty-six sections, each 640 acres; the sixteenth section in each township was reserved for the construction of public schools. In 1787 came the measure that was later to be the object of Webster's praise. While it did not provide any additional land for schools, the Northwest Ordinance declared, "Religion, morality and knowledge being necessary to good government and the happiness of mankind, schools and the means of education shall forever be encouraged."[11]

Subsequent Congresses took this change seriously. No state was ever admitted to the Union unless it made educational provisions.[12] The intent of Congress was made clear in 1802 through the Ohio Enabling Act, which required that territory to include in its proposed constitution an education system. Congress acted similarly with Tennessee and the entire Louisiana Territory. Beginning with the enabling legislation for Oregon, two sections of land in each township were to be used for education.[13]

In all, thirty states received federal land grants dedicated to the public schools. The original thirteen and their offshoots (Vermont, Maine and West Virginia) as well as Kentucky, which became a state prior to the 1802 Ohio Enabling Act, all preceded the policy. Texas (which joined the Union after a brief period of national sovereignty), Alaska, and Hawaii did not receive land grants either.[14] The Ohio legislation established the precedent that 5 percent of the profits from the sale of public lands would be dedicated for "internal improvements," including education. Beginning in 1860, this provision was changed to earmark a full 5 percent to education.[15] These measures make apparent the thrust of our early national education policy—to insure that each state provided for the education of its citizens.

Early Support for a Broader Federal Role

Such a policy did not have unanimous consent. Many prominent Americans, including Benjamin Rush, Noah Webster, and Samuel Knox, wanted the federal government to oversee a national system of education.[16] However, it became the prevailing belief that since the Constitution and the Bill of Rights did not expressly mention education, that function would be reserved for the states under the provisions of the Tenth Amendment.

Had James Madison's journal of the Constitutional Convention been made available prior to its publication in 1840, the educational politics may have developed differently. Madison's record indicated that the framers of the Constitution clearly understood education to be included under Article 1, Section 8, (the "Welfare Clause"), which gives Congress the power "to pay the Debts and provide for the common Defense and general Welfare of the United States." Alexander Hamilton's accounts point to the same conclusion. In his "Report on Manufactures" issued in 1791, he noted that "[t]here seems to be no room for doubt that whatever concerns the general interests of learning...all are within the sphere of the national councils, as far as regards an application of money." He cited the Welfare Clause as the basis for his statement.[17]

In his Farewell Address, most famous for setting the policy of international neutrality that was to last for over a century ("beware of entangling alliances"), George Washington joined the cause of a federal education role when he urged the nation to "[p]romote, then as an object of summary importance, institutions for the general diffusion of knowledge" on a national basis as a guard against sectionalism.[18]

To resolve any ambiguities regarding the authority of the federal government regarding education, Presidents Jefferson and Madison supported consitutional amendments enunciating an active federal role at the elementary and secondary levels and providing for a national university. Similarly, in support of a national higher education system, James Monroe called for an amendment to provide "seminaries for all-important purpose of diffusing knowledge."[19] Both John Adams and John Quincy Adams also favored the establishment of a national university.[20]

HIGHER EDUCATION

However, with the exception of the military and naval academies, none of the aforementioned presidents was to see a national university. Perhaps the closest that such a proposal came to being enacted was during the presidency of Martin Van Buren, who, in 1839, recommended that the immense fortune left to the government in the Smithson bequest be used for such a purpose. Congress did not support the idea and, instead, waited until 1846 before dedicating the money to the establishment of the Smithsonian Institute[21] (an investment that still provides both enjoyment and valuable research opportunities to millions of visitors and scholars each year).

The Morrill Act of 1862

While a national university was never established, sentiment grew for the application of federal resources to promote higher education. In 1857, Congress passed an act, sponsored by Senator Justin S. Morrill, that would provide each state with land grants of 20,000 acres per senator and member of Congress. The proceeds from the sale of these lands would be dedicated to supporting agricultural and mechanical colleges. President James Buchanan, in vetoing the bill, stated that it was "both inexpedient and unconstitutional." He believed that "Congress does not possess the power to appropriate money in the treasury...for the purpose of educating the people of the respective states." Further, he did not think it legally possible for the federal government to require a specified use for land it had given away.[22]

What may have been more a telling factor in his decision to veto the bill was the opposition that it faced from the South and the West.[23] The Union, it must be remembered, was under great stress at that point, and Buchanan, a Democrat, sought accommodation with the South, particularly with the Democrats who represented that region in the Congress. Five years later, with Lincoln in the presidency and the South in rebellion, the Morrill Act was again passed by Congress and enacted into law. This version included a stipulation that military training be provided at the colleges benefiting from the act (which granted 30,000 acres per senator and representative) for "the liberal and practical education of the industrial classes in the several pursuits and professions of life," specifically agriculture and mechanic arts.[24]

As has been noted by William V. Mayville, implicit to the focus on the industrial classes was

> a distinction between the professional classes, whose education was presumed to have a different social function (the training of leaders), and therefore a different curricular focus (literary), and the working classes, i.e., the urban and rural workers, whose curricular needs were delineated in the act to be "practical."[25]

Mayville pointed out that the proportion of the industrial class able to make use of the act in the third quarter of the nineteenth century was miniscule. Only 2 percent of those over seventeen had graduated from high school by 1870. One indication of the paucity of eligible clientele was the fact that the 9,593 males graduating from college in 1874 outnumbered the male high school graduating class of four years earlier by over 2,500. Thus, a quarter of the 1874 college graduates did not hold a high school diploma.[26]

The Morrill Act was precedent-setting in four important respects.[27] First, it permitted the use of the land grants at both public and private colleges. It also initiated the policy of focusing federal resources on areas of manpower shortage. (An 1864 proposal to extend the benefits of the act beyond the agricultural and mechanical colleges was defeated.)[28] Further, this thrust established the principle of categorical aid. Finally, it recognized that the colleges receiving the aid should be able to maintain their autonomy from the federal government. According to Paul R. Mort, writing in 1936, there was "no indication that the Morrill Act grants have resulted in any accumulation of federal control in the three-quarters of a century in which they have operated." He cited a 1930 survey of land grant colleges that did not reveal "any disposition [on the part of the federal government] to restrict state control over the offerings of its own higher educational institutions in the fields of arts and sciences."[29]

Despite the accusations that many states mismanaged their land grants,[30] Andrew D. White, the first president of Cornell University, one of the land grant institutions, posited that

> Since the Romans quietly bought and sold lands on which the Carthaginians were encamped in the neighborhood of the Eternal City, there has been no more noble exhibition of faith in the destiny of a republic.[31]

When the land grants for all of education are totalled, they include an area larger than the combined area of Alabama, Indiana, New York and Pennsylvania.[32] The Morrill Act provided over 11 million acres for agricultural and mechanical colleges.[33] Fifteen states used them for existing public institutions; several designated a private college as the land grant institution; twenty-eight established new institutions.[34] Most of the flagship campuses of the major state universities are land grant institutions; many are among our nation's finest institutions of higher education. One must concur with White's judgment and Morrill's foresight.

The Laissez-Faire Years

A decade after the enactment of his milestone Land Grant Act, Senator Morrill proposed additional aid to the agricultural and mechanical colleges. This time, however, he was not successful. He failed again in three of the following four years.[35] Next, it was Senator Ambrose Burnside of Rhode Island who tried. Introduced in 1879, his bill geared the land grant concept toward the support of science and industrial education at the collegiate level (and also sought support for the common schools). During the Senate debate, the bill was amended to include aid for teacher training and to provide at the land grant colleges "schools for the instruction of females in such branches of technology or industrial education as are suited to their sex." In 1880, the Senate overwhelmingly passed the bill. Unfortunately, it died in the House without a vote being taken.[36] Burnside was equally as unsuccessful in 1881 and 1882.[37]

In 1887, Congress finally passed another higher education measure. Limited in scope, the Hatch Act allocated money to the states in order that their land grant college might establish and operate an agricultural experiment station. This was the earliest federal measure designed to promote research at colleges and universities. The program has been funded annually since its inception.[38] (In 1935, Congress passed the Bankhead-Jones Act that authorized nearly a million dollars to be used by the land grant colleges to extend the work of the agricultural experiment stations to include resident instruction. Within five years, the budget had grown by 150 percent.)[39]

After failing again in 1888, Senator Morrill was finally able to see another of his higher education proposals enacted into law. The 1890 bill, known as the Second Morrill Act (or Morrill II), authorized annual appropriations beginning at $15,000 and increasing to $25,000 by annual increments of $1,000. (In 1907, the Nelson Amendment set the annual allotment to each state at $35,000, escalating by $5,000 each year until the total reached $50,000 per year.[40] The allocation continued to be gradually increased by future Congresses.) Morrill II also required those states that practiced segregation to establish separate land grant colleges to serve their black citizens. The Secretary of the Interior was empowered to withhold funds from any state that failed to meet the requirements of the law.[41] As a result of the Second Morrill Act, black land grant colleges were instituted in the seventeen states that required or officially permitted segregation.

The next piece of new legislation affecting higher education was the 1914 Smith-Lever Act, which established the agricultural extension service, an effort to disseminate to farmers the research being conducted by the land grant colleges. Originally a modest program that annually provided $10,000 to each state, the extension service budget was increased by successor acts; by 1949, $31.5 million per year was supplied to the states based on their agricultural population.[42] One different and controversial aspect of the Smith-Lever Act was the requirement that states provide funds to match the federal appropriation.[43] This not only accorded the federal government an element of control over the funds that it allocated, but it also provided a policy direction the states were obligated to support with their own money in order to participate. Poor states and states that either did not agree with the thrust of this program (and others that later used the matching approach) or did not agree with the matching concept based on a "states' rights" position, balked. Nevertheless, the matching concept remained as a powerful tool to promote national policy.

In the National Defense

Other than the 1925 act that established the Reserve Officers Training Corps (ROTC)— and thus provided the first federal scholarships to students [44]— and the establishment in 1935 of the National Youth Administration that allowed financially needy students between ages twelve and twenty-four to engage in "socially desirable" work in order to be able to remain in school (including college),[45] there was little new in the way of federal higher education legislation until World War II, and what came was related to the national defense. In 1940, Congress authorized $9 million to be used by colleges and universities to support courses for engineers, chemists, physicists and production supervisors for the various war-related industries. By 1943, the authorization had risen to $25 million.[46] In 1942, Congress provided draft deferments for science and engineering students, as well as those in medical, dental, and pharmacy school. Such students who were within two years of graduation and who would agree to accept employment determined by the War Manpower Commission were eligible to receive loans of up to $500 at 2.5 percent interest. Five million dollars was provided for this purpose, and between 1942 and 1944, over 1,100 students in 286 colleges made use of the program.[47]

Perhaps the most far-reaching legislation of that era was the Servicemen's Readjustment Act of 1944—the G.I. Bill—which provided financial support for returning veterans who sought to continue their education. In 1947, half of those enrolled in college were supported by this program.[48] Compared to 1940, college enrollments had increased by 100 percent. In all, 7.8 million World War II veterans made use of the educational benefits of this program at a cost of $14.5 billion.[49] They were followed by 2.275 million Korean War veterans.[50] Most important is the precedent that the G.I. Bill set regarding federal support of higher education through the provision of broad-based student aid. Changed by successive Congresses, a descendant version remains as a major source of financial assistance to today's postsecondary students.

The decade of the fifties saw the deepening of the Cold War between the American-led alliance of western nations and the Communist bloc countries of Eastern Europe and Asia. One early response was the passage of the National Science Foundation Act of 1950 that was intended to "promote the progress of science" and provide graduate scholarships and fellowships in mathematics, the sciences and the biomedical fields.[51] The launching of the Russian Sputnik in 1957 shocked the West. The military applications of the Soviet space technology were obvious to a world still having nightmares about Nagasaki and Hiroshima. Americans sought a speedy rise to the Soviet challenge. One proponent of a federal response that would include the bolstering of education told Congress, "The Cold War has been shifted by the crafty leaders of the Kremlin from a competition in physical strength to a competition in brains."[52] Speaking before his Senate colleagues on a bill before that body, Majority Leader Lyndon B. Johnson prophesied that

> History may well record that we saved liberty and saved freedom when we undertook a crash program in the field of education... I hope this bill is only the forerunner of better things to come.[53]

The "crash program" was the National Defense Education Act (NDEA) of 1958; it was the forerunner of greater federal support for education, particulary higher education. The defense orientation of the effort was clear through the bill's language:

> the security of the Nation requires the fullest development of the mental resources and technical skills of its young men and women. The present emergency demands that additional and more adequate educational opportunities be made available. The defense of this Nation depends upon the mastery of modern techniques developed from complex scientific principles. It depends as well upon the discovery and development of new principles, new techniques and new knowledge....[54]

The NDEA included a number of thrusts: it strengthened academic programs in the sciences, mathematics, and the foreign languages; it provided student loans and graduate fellowships; it sought to identify capable students for collegiate programs by supporting guidance, counseling and testing; it assisted the development of new instructional technology and educational media; it provided a science information service; it provided the states with educational statistical services. In its first five years, nearly half a million students borrowed $330 million under the NDEA. The guidance and counseling effort reduced the student/counselor ratio nearly in half from 1:900 to 1:540.[55] An accounting of the impact of the NDEA's first decade revealed that the nation's schools and colleges had received approximately $3 billion from the effort. Loans had been made to 2.5 million undergraduates, while fellowships had been awarded to 25,000 graduate students. The science, mathematics, and foreign language departments had been the beneficiaries of half a billion dollars for modernizing facilities and equipment, for upgrading their curricula, for developing their research capacities, and so forth.[56] In 1963 and 1964, the act was extended by Congress. Its authorized expenditure level for 1967 was set at $150 million.

The NDEA broadened access to higher education in the name of the national defense. The Higher Education Facilities Act (HEFA) of

1963 sought to assist the colleges and universities in making classrooms and other educational facilities available to these students. Originally proposed in 1961 by President John F. Kennedy, the bill was bottled up for a time by the House Rules Committee after different versions were passed by the House and Senate, and was subsequently killed when the House refused to accept the compromise version suggested by a House-Senate Conference Committee. It was filed again in 1963 as part of an omnibus education bill that Congressman Adam Clayton Powell, Chair of the House Education and Labor Committee, wisely divided into discreet bills. As a result, the higher education facilities portion was enacted into law in the early days of the administration of President Lyndon B. Johnson. The HEFA provided $230 million for undergraduate academic facilities between 1964 and 1967; approximately one-fifth of the money was for public, community, and technical colleges. Grants totalling $85 million were provided on a two-thirds matching basis during those three years for use in the construction of graduate education facilities. This matching principle was also used in the loan provisions of the bill. Colleges were required to provide a one-quarter match in order to qualify for 3-5/8 percent, fifty-year loans for new academic facilities; $120 million was authorized for this purpose. Precluded from the benefits of HEFA were athletic and recreation facilities as well as medical and public health buildings. Religious institutions were eligible to receive federal funds as long as none of the funds were used for buildings for religious instruction or observance.[57]

Higher Education and Equal Opportunity

In 1964, President Johnson declared a war on poverty and set in motion a number of major initiatives intended both to provide the poor with greater economic opportunity and to reduce racial discrimination. With this, the basis for the federal support for higher education began to shift somewhat from national defense to social justice. Said Johnson in support of the Higher Education Act of 1965, "[E]very child must be encouraged to get as much education as he has the ability to take . . .. Higher Education is no longer a luxury, but a necessity."[58]

In those days of great hope for a Great Society, Congress readily went along with the president in enacting a seven-part higher education bill. Title I sought to encourage community service by the colleges and universities and to encourage their development of continuing education programs for out-of-school adults; $25 million was authorized for expenditure in 1966, while $50 million was authorized for the two succeeding years. Title II provided $50 million for library materials and $15 million to train library personnel. Title III provided $55 million in aid to developing institutions, approximately four-fifths of which were to be four-year colleges. (As this program developed, it served as the federal government's primary tool for assisting the nation's traditionally black colleges, and subsequently became an item of controversy as better financed, predominantly white public institutions began staking a claim on Title III funds.)

Title IV established the first broad-based federal scholarship program for needy undergraduates. It authorized $70 million to institutions for student grants of $200 to $800 (which needed to be matched by the institution through grants or loans). Those students in the top half of their class were to be granted an additional $200 for this achievement. To complete a student's financial aid package, subsidized loans of up to $1,500 and work-study programs were made available. Coming at a time when the postwar baby boom generation had reached the traditional college age, this program served to broaden dramatically access to higher education.

Title V established a teacher corps intended to support master's degree programs for the training of teachers for inner-city elementary and secondary schools. Title VI provided $145 million in matching funds for educational equipment and minor remodeling. Title VII broadened the 1963 HEFA.

Thus, the Higher Education Act of 1965 provided an all-encompassing aid package with federal funds being reserved on a categorical basis for student and institutional aid. Congress did some broadening of this foundation in 1966. By 1968, federal expenditures for higher education totalled $4.4 billion, approximately a quarter of the total national effort.[59] Along the way, Congress had passed several other acts of importance to higher education. In 1966, the International Education Act was enacted. The following year, the Education Professions Development Act came into existence. It was the Higher Education Amendments of 1968 that attracted the most attention. An update of the 1965 Higher Education Act, this bill increased the level of the federal student aid grants to $1,000 for the neediest students. It also added several new programs, including "Upward Bound" and "Talent Search" (efforts to broaden access to college by educationally and economically disadvantaged precollege youngsters), and a program to provide special support services for high-risk students attending college in order to encourage their retention and graduation.

A controversial element of the 1968 Amendments resulted from the anti-Vietnam War protests that were occurring (sometimes violently) on campuses across the country. The House passed (306 to 54) an "antidisruption" provision proposed by New Hampshire Republican L. H. Wyman. Students who refused to obey lawful regulations of the college were to be denied financial aid if such refusal was "of a serious nature and contributed to the disruption of the university or college administration." Since the Senate accepted a different version, a compromise was reached that removed financial aid for a period of two years if a student were convicted by a court or found by a university hearing body to be guilty of a serious act of disruption. [60] Needless to say, there was student opposition to this provision. Those were the days, however, before the revelations of the Pentagon Papers, and the mass questioning of American foreign policy in the time of war was still not a wholly accepted concept.

The Vietnam War cost Lyndon Johnson his presidency. During the 1968 presidential campaign, Richard Nixon delivered only one major speech on the topic of education. His promises to back away from the enforcement of civil rights, and to rely to a greater extent on student loans and tax credits rather than on federally funded student aid grants, indicated a major policy shift from the Kennedy-Johnson years.[61] Kennedy, it must be remembered, had dispatched the Attorney General's chief deputy, Nicholas Katzenbach to force the desegregation of the University of Alabama. The symbolism of Governor George Wallace removing himself from the doorway at the University was profound; the federal government had pried open the gates of higher education for its black citizens. President Johnson carried that thrust further through his Executive Order 11246 that established affirmative action as a federal policy and through his origination of the Civil Rights Act of 1964. Further, the

Higher Education Act of 1965 sought to make a college education available to millions of Americans whose families might otherwise have been unable to afford the bill.

A Shift in Approach

In March 1970, after a lengthy drafting process, Nixon delivered his suggested higher education policy changes to Congress. They were swiftly criticized by the American Council on Education (ACE) and by most of the higher education lobbying groups. Not only was the increased emphasis on student loans included in the proposal, but the President also sought to give financial aid grants directly to the student rather than to give the money to the colleges and universities to give to their students. Such a change, suggested in the name of consumerism, would mean that students would have much more freedom in making their selection of a college since they would not be as dependent on the decisions of the college's financial aid office, but could rely on a federal grant based on the cost of instruction. This proposal did not come at the best of times since many colleges were beginning to face the hard times that extended through the 1970s to the present.[62] The colleges preferred to retain the control over aid that the existing program permitted.

The ACE attempted to prepare an alternative bill, one that would modify the existing higher education legislation by replacing categorical aid with general institutional aid. However, since they could not generate a consensus within the higher education community regarding how to distribute the funds to the colleges under such an approach, the ACE bill was not able to garner sufficient support, and the Congressional eyes turned toward the Nixon plan.[63]

As finally signed into law, the Education Amendments of 1972 represented a certain amount of compromise. Congress was not willing to move away from broad-based federal student aid grants toward loans as Nixon desired. Instead, it raised the maximum grant award to half of the cost of attending college, up to a maximum of $1,400 per year. This new Basic Educational Opportunity Grant (BEOG) was to go, however, directly to the student as the President had proposed. In order to encourage banks to provide loans to college students, the Student Loan Marketing Association (Sallie Mae) was established. It made possible the replenishment of capital to the banks: by selling government bonds,

Sallie Mae developed the funds necessary to purchase existing student loans from banks so that the banks might have the funds to include more students in the program.

The Education Amendments of 1972 extended many existing federal higher education programs and brought into existence two additional ones that generated some controversy. The act stipulated that each state establish a body (known as the "1202 Commission" since the requirement was Section 1202 of the act) to develop a statewide plan for postsecondary education. Planning grants were made available to these commissions. This provision strengthened the state higher education coordinating boards, much to the chagrin of the institutions.

The other controversial new feature of the legislation was Title IX that prohibited discrimination based on sex. Exceptions were made for undergraduate admissions to traditionally single sex colleges; colleges in transition from single sex to coeducational were to be allowed seven years before the nondiscrimination provisions were made applicable. While colleges were permitted to retain single sex residence halls, they were no longer to be able to exclude persons from programs, academic or otherwise, based on sex. Further, they were to make provision for the equal expenditure of funds for men's and women's athletics. Since such regulations would not have been necessary unless there was widespread inequitable treatment of women (in such areas as the admission to certain programs, the awarding of fellowships, the availability of athletic scholarships, the determination of salaries, and so on), there was resistance from the colleges. In too many instances, women have had to resort to the courts in order to provide meaning to Title IX.

The 1972 Amendments also resulted in the establishment of the Fund for the Improvement of Postsecondary Education (FIPSE). Proposals for the establishment of a federal agency for higher education similar to the National Academy of Sciences had been recently made by a task force chaired by James Hester, president of New York University, and by the Carnegie Commission on Higher Education. In the same light, Daniel Patrick Moynihan, then a member of Nixon's White House staff, proposed a National Foundation for Higher Education to help develop higher education's potential. A modified version of his plan was enacted as FIPSE,[64] which was created to provide funds for the development of new programs that promise to enhance the capacity of higher education to deliver its services. In 1973, FIPSE awarded $9.3 million in grants to eighty-nine institutions, state governments, and others.[65]

The tension between a Republican president and a Democratic Congress did not permit a wholesale redirection of federal higher education policy; neither did it permit a maintenance of the Kennedy-Johnson trend. While not as successful as he would have wished in changing the authorizing legislation, Nixon was more successful at the appropriations stage. While he and Congress wrestled over the funding levels of the authorized programs, the far-reaching national goals that might have been realized under Johnson were not approached. This is particularly so regarding the areas of financial aid and access to higher education.[66] The problem was complicated by rampant inflation brought on by the Vietnam War and the 1973-74 Arab oil embargo. Supporting Nixon's conservative fiscal position was HEW Secretary Caspar W. Weinberger, who stated,

> Both Congress and much of the higher education community resolutely refuse to accept that—for the foreseeable future at the least—all of us must learn to live with the reality that our national wealth is not inexhaustible. Our resources are finite, and we must select priorities.[67]

Needless to say, those more liberal would have selected different priorities.

The Education Amendments of 1972 signalled, according to Conrad and Cosand, a marked shift in federal higher education policy: "a major trend toward 'withdrawal' of direct federal involvement in postsecondary education . . .."[68] The approaches of providing indirect aid to the colleges through portable student financial aid grants and of requiring statewide planning efforts, shifted the locus of power from the institutions to the students and the states, and reduced the role of the federal government without reducing its fiscal commitment to the enterprise.[69] The Education Amendments of 1980 raised authorization levels, but did not tamper much with the overall design. Under this framework, federal outlays for higher education totalled more than $16 billion in Fiscal Year 1980, an eightfold increase over what they had been prior to the Higher Education Act of 1965 and 60 percent over what they had been during Richard Nixon's last year in office.[70]

VOCATIONAL EDUCATION

As was true with higher education, the initial federal support for vocational education, which came in 1874, was aimed at meeting a specific national need, in this case the development of a trained cadre of sailors. To promote this goal, the Navy was authorized to provide fully equipped training ships to six specified nautical schools. By 1911, the effort had been extended to ten such schools, each of which received an annual allotment of no more than $25,000.[71]

Encouraging State Programs in the National Interest

Two years later, Congress established a Commission on National Aid to Vocational Education to recommend a proper federal role. The Commission identified an urgent need for secondary level vocational programs that was so extensive as to warrant federal intervention. Since at that time there was considerable skepticism regarding federal involvement in education, the Commission justified a federal response by pointing to the traditional mobility of the American population. States might not receive a full return on their investment in training programs since the people actually trained, the people taught how to train, and the jobs for which the training was occurring might easily move to another state. Additionally, since vocational education was so expensive, the financial burden on many states would be too great to bear. The Commission reminded the Congress of the Welfare Clause of the Constitution when it called for the establishment for a federal vocational education agency as well as for the infusion of federal funds into the vocational education arena. The Commission's report ultimately resulted in the enactment of Washington's first major voc-ed initiative, the Smith-Hughes Act of 1917.[72]

The sum of $1.76 million was authorized by Smith-Hughes to support secondary level instruction in agriculture, various industrial and trade subjects, and home economics as well as to assist in the preparation of teachers for those subjects.[73] Beyond raising the ire of those traditionally opposed to federal aid to education, the effort ran into heavy criticism for several other reasons. As Mort notes, the funds were to be awarded on a "non-objective basis." The act

set up a federal board with discretionary powers to determine the amounts the states are entitled to receive . . . based on the board's interpretation of the degree to which the states meet the specific objectives set by the board itself.[74]

The objectivity that a formula approach would have allowed was absent. Instead, states were required to submit statewide vocational education plans that needed the approval of the federal board prior to the release of funds. Educators and states had not experienced such an approach before and were disturbed by it. They were also upset by their having to meet minimum standards regarding such matters as how much time had to be spent in a course for it to qualify for funding. Further, the concept of requiring states to match the federal grant with funds of their own (an approach first used six years earlier in the Weeks Act, a measure design to assist with the fire protection of watershed areas)[75] was a part of Smith-Hughes. Poor states and those that preferred to dedicate their money to other things objected. The National Advisory Committee on Education (appointed in 1929 by President Herbert Hoover) was later to complain that while the act had resulted in "constructive advances" in vocational education, it was "a fair question whether these benefits compensated for the inevitable weakening of local responsibility and autonomy . . .," and that this "conflict cannot be settled . . . by taking into account mere educational results."[76]

Congress obviously did not concur. While the concern regarding the possibility of the erosion of local responsibility has always been a factor in Congressional education debate, the nation's legislative branch obviously thought that the results justified the risk. The act was written as it was in order to insure an effort of greater magnitude than would be possible with either state or federal funds alone and as a means of insuring that the manpower training activity was well planned and coordinated.

Smith-Hughes was expanded and updated in 1929 by the George-Reed Act, in 1934 by the George-Ellzey Act, in 1936 by the George-Deen Act and in 1946 by the George-Barden Act.[77] Over the course of those three decades, the Smith-Hughes authorization for vocational education grew over sixteen-fold to $28.85 million annually.[78] (From all federal sources, $90 million was spent in 1943 for precollegiate vocational education,[79] but that was an extraordinary time due to World War II.)

Trained Personnel for New Technologies

Voc-ed was a part of the major education programs of the postwar period. Veterans were able to use the G.I. Bill for vocational training. Further, in 1958, an annual appropriation of $15 million to support vocational programs was authorized by Title VIII of the National Defense Education Act. This resulted in the training of over 30,000 technicians.[80]

Early in his administration, President Kennedy had HEW Secretary Abraham Ribicoff undertake a review of the federal voc-ed effort. The study revealed that there were approximately 21 million grade school children who would not go to college but would seek employment in an era when jobs for unskilled labor were rapidly disappearing. It also indicated that the changing job market required the retraining of millions already in the labor force.[81] Thus, the evidence was available to support an expanded federal role.

Originally presented as part of Kennedy's omnibus National Education Improvement Act (but subsequently made a separate piece of legislation as a result of the adept vision of Congressman Adam Clayton Powell), the Vocational Education Act of 1963 was not passed by Congress until after the president's assassination. The bill authorized the expenditure of $60 million in its first year, nearly twice that amount in the following year, and $225 million for each of the next two years. Among its unique features were (1) the reservation of 10 percent of the funds for research and demonstration projects, (2) a provision for voc-ed boarding schools (five of which were designated to be in inner-city areas), and (3) an effort to reduce school drop-out rates by providing work-study programs.[82] The act resulted in a 30 percent jump in enrollment (to 5.8 million) in the vocational and technical schools by the end of the first year alone. The number of such schools increased dramatically; not only were 125 schools under construction in the summer of 1965, but 209 more were on the drawing boards.[83]

A popular program, the Vocational Education Act was updated in 1968, 1972, and 1976. Each reauthorization sought to insure that a better job was done in tailoring training programs to occupations that promised long-term employment. Each also stated clearly the Congressional intent to provide training opportunities for women, minorities, and the handicapped. The Smith-Bankhead Act of 1920 had established a federal role in vocational rehabilitation. This was reaffirmed in 1943 with the establishment of the Office of Vocational Rehabilitation.[84] Nevertheless, a 1966 study indicated that in the entire country there were only seventy-nine vocational training programs nationally for students with special needs.[85]

Examples of the strength of the subsequent Congressional commitment to the handicapped, women, and minorities are readily apparent in the 1976 reauthorization (P.L. 94-482), which, in a section entitled "National Priority Programs," reserved at least 10 percent of the funds available to the states for use for the vocational education of handicapped persons; a minimum of 20 percent more was reserved for disadvantaged persons and those with limited English-speaking ability.[86] The act's "Declaration of Purpose" indicates that one aim is

> to overcome sex discrimination and sex stereotyping in vocational education programs (including programs of homemaking), and thereby furnish equal educational opportunities in vocational education to persons of both sexes.[87]

A later section, which requires each state to submit five-year plans describing its programs and persons to be served, is more specific. Here is the mention of the priority for "support services for women who enter programs designed to prepare individuals for employment in jobs that have been traditionally limited to men," as well as vocational education for

> persons who had solely been homemakers but who now, because of dissolution of marriage, must seek employment; persons who are single heads of households and who lack adequate job skills; persons who are currently homemakers and part-time workers but who wish to secure a full-time job; and women who are now in jobs which have been traditionally considered jobs for female and who wish to seek employment in job areas which have not been traditionally considered for job areas for females, and men who are now in jobs which have been traditionally considered jobs for males and who wish to seek employment in job areas which have not been traditionally considered job areas for males.[88]

The 1976 amendments authorized $995 million for fiscal year 1978 with annual increments that raised the total to $1.64 billion by fiscal 1982,[89] with allocations made to the states based on population ratios.[90]

ELEMENTARY AND SECONDARY EDUCATION

Due primarily to the same concerns regarding the desirability of maintaining local control and responsibility, federal support for elementary and secondary education developed as slowly and cautiously as it did for higher and vocational education. There have been two continuing controversies that have accompanied the debate regarding elementary and secondary school aid. One has been the extent to which federal monies should be made available to schools run by churches. The Northwest Ordinances permitted the establishment of church schools open to all students regardless of religion. Interestingly, it was a religiously affiliated institution that received the first direct federal aid to a school; in 1810 Thomas Jefferson facilitated the distribution of funds from the Interior and War Departments to help pay the rent of a Detroit Catholic school.[91] Nevertheless, church-state arguments have been a part of most education policy debates.

The other continuing part of the federal education policy controversy has been the matter of race. With the Freedman's Bureau came an 1866 appropriation of $521,000 to support schools for the recently freed slaves. Over the course of the succeeding five years, a total of ten times the original sum came from the federal coffers for that purpose. (Private philanthropy nearly matched the federal contribution.)[92] The nineteenth century concept of federal assistance to blacks provided for the support of schools open exclusively to blacks; a hundred years later this was replaced by a position in support of black access to quality education in an integrated setting.

A Half Century of Inaction

In the third quarter of the nineteenth century, the majority of blacks still lived in the states where slavery had been permitted. Their lack of educational opportunity during the antebellum days had been legally mandated in order to maintain the societal status quo. Needless to say, there was no rush by Southern governments to make major changes on behalf of the education of blacks once their freedom had been secured. Even for the white population, publicly supported universal compulsory education was slow to reach the South. While states like Massachusetts led the way in attempting to develop state-aid formulas to assist poorer communities with the expense of operating schools to serve the masses,[93] the South was laggard. The results were clear: in 1870 fewer than 8 percent of the adults in the North were illiterate (in the Pacific states the proportion was approximately twice as high), but a whopping 42.1 percent of Southern adults could neither read nor write. Although that proportion decreased by 5 percent over the course of the decade, the absolute number of illiterates in the old Confederacy grew by over a half million. It was an exception if the school year in Southern states was as long as four months.

Much of the proposed federal education legislation of the 1870s and 1880s was aimed at improving the Southern conditions.[94] The first of such legislation was introduced in 1870 by Massachusetts Republican George F. Hoar. At that time, only a quarter of Southern children were in school.[95] The bill's purpose, according to Congressman Hoar was

> to compel by national authority the establishment of a thorough and efficient system of public instruction throughout the whole country, . . . not to supersede, but to stimulate, compel and supplement action by the State.[96]

Under the provisions of the bill, if a state failed to provide adequate educational opportunities for its residents, the president would be empowered to appoint a federal superintendent of schools for the state, and the Secretary of the Interior would be empowered to appoint inspectors to oversee offending school districts. The power of eminent domain for the purpose of school construction as well as the authority to produce textbooks was to be provided to the federal government. The price tag would be borne primarily through a tax of fifty cents on each person in the states where intervention was necessary. Opposition to Hoar's bill came from all quarters, including the Catholic Church, which feared secular control of religious education. The bill died without a vote.[97]

The other education legislation of the 1870s was equally unsuccessful. The first, introduced by Republican Congressman Legrand W. Perce of Mississippi, proposed the sale of public lands to support teachers' salaries in states with a school year of at least three months in duration, and to support teacher-training programs. The bill passed in the House by a scant nineteen votes but was not favorably acted upon by the Senate.[98]

On December 7, 1875, President Ulysses S. Grant, seizing upon a national wave of anti-Catholic sentiment, proposed a constitutional amendment to require the states

> to establish and forever maintain free public schools adequate to the education of all children in the rudimentary branches within their respective limits, irrespective of sex, color, birthplace or religion; forbidding the teaching in said schools of religious, atheistic or pagan tenets . . ..[99]

Under the provisions of this proposal, no public funds could be used for religious schools. Maine Republican James G. Blaine formally introduced the measure in the House, where it passed the following August. However, it failed to achieve the required two-thirds majority in the Senate and died. (Since that time, similar legislation has been introduced in Congress some twenty times but has never gone beyond committee stage.)[100]

In all, eleven education-related bills failed in the 1870s.[101] The next decade did not prove to be any more hospitable for proponents of federal school aid, the strongest of whom was Senator Henry W. Blair from New Hampshire. In 1882, Blair proposed a ten-year anti-illiteracy effort that would provide $15 million in the first year and a million less each year thereafter. Funds would not be used to construct schools but would support teacher training, and instruction of reading, writing, and speaking English as well as arithmetic, geography, and American history; the territories would be permitted to use a portion of the funds for vocational education. Money would be distributed based on state or territorial illiteracy rates, and would need to be matched by nonfederal funds.[102]

Supporters of the bill included the Knights of Labor (who saw it as promoting one of its goals, universal compulsory education) and the National Education Association. Based on the Jacksonian principle that democracy would be strengthened by having a literate electorate, they argued that the Welfare Clause of the Constitution required the federal government to involve itself in this effort, particularly as regarded the South generally and its black citizens specifically. Proponents of the bill endorsed the concept of directing the dollars to locations where they were needed most, of mandating the expenditure of funds on the curricular areas that demanded the most attention, and of requiring (through the matching provision) that the effort be supported by local funds as well as federal funds.[103]

Opponents claimed that the bill was not only unconstitutional, but that it lacked broad public support; that rather than being democratic, it was communistic. They disagreed that the bill would promote the equality of blacks, but feared that it would keep the race issue alive in a harmful way. They also pointed to progress being made by the South as an indication that federal intervention was not required. They believed it wrong for funds to be distributed on the basis of the proportion of the population that was illiterate since that approach unfairly redistributed wealth and promoted a lack of effort by the poor states. Further, they argued that federal funds (if they were to come) should be spent, not according to federal guidelines, but by the states as their legislatures saw fit and without a matching requirement that would be difficult for many to make. They feared too much federal control of education would result.[104]

Opponents carried the day in 1882 and again every two years thereafter until 1890. Blair was able to win Senate support in 1884, 1886, and 1888, but was never able to garner sufficient backing in the House. His last effort in 1890 died without passage by either branch of the Congress.[105]

Thirty years elapsed before Congress passed a bill of fiscal benefit to elementary and secondary education. A 1918 study by the Commission on the Emergency in Education focused on the educational levels of those in the armed services during the First World War. They found educational attainment to have been so poor as to warrant their recommendation that $100 million per year be distributed by the federal government to the schools.[106] While this report did not result in the passage of a general aid package, Congress did act in a very limited way shortly thereafter. Under the provisions of the Mineral Lands Act of 1920, 37.5 percent of the receipts from rentals, royalties, and bonuses from mineral development on federally owned land would be dedicated to the development of roads and public education. This legislation did not provide for an award to all states, only to those producing revenue from lands owned by the United States government. The states receiving the money were free to determine the division of funds between roads and schools and were permitted to use the education portion however they saw fit.[107] Thus, this legislation overcame some of the earlier constraints to federal aid: it did not redistribute wealth; it did not require state policy to follow federal policy; it did not raise the fear of federal control. However, it fell short of providing the sort of broad national aid that would have been required to enhance the quality and quantity of education in America.

The New Deal Years

The Great Depression began with great unevenness across the states with regard to educational opportunity and quality. Only 6 percent of Southern high schools enrolled blacks in 1929. Black school children in the South in 1930 received an average per capita public commitment of $15.86 while white children in those states received $42.39. White teachers in the South were paid an average salary that was over 50 percent higher than black teachers. The school year for black schools was shorter than for white schools.[108] While such differences were not as glaring in the rest of the country, they were, nonetheless, present.

Unevenness went beyond race. In 1930, there were nearly 149,000 one-teacher schools,[109] located primarily in rural areas. Conditions in rural schools were so bad that they were found to be at least a generation behind those in urban areas.[110] The National Survey of School Finance (1933) found among the states a lack of uniformity of effort and a disparate ability to pay. The wealthiest states were able to provide $130 per student, the average $60. At that time, all of the schools in Alabama, Florida, and North Carolina spent less than $60 per student; comparatively, in Massachusetts and New Jersey such an expenditure level was found in only 3 percent of the schools. For it to be able to provide $68 per student, the average state would need to dedicate 33 percent of all tax revenues to education: Mississippi, at one end of the continuum, would have to put its entire tax receipts to education to reach this level; while, at the other end, Nevada would need to direct only 17 percent of its tax effort.[111]

Needless to say, the Depression only aggravated the situation. While no general aid-to-education programs were enacted by Congress during that period, many New Deal programs included a focus on education. A 1934 report issued by the Federal Emergency Relief Administration indicated that relief funds were paying the salaries of 40,000 teachers, and that federal relief efforts directed toward education were costing two to three million dollars per month.[112] In 1934-35, the Works Progress Administration (WPA) earmarked $22 million in order to keep schools open for the full academic year. Under other WPA programs, federal money underwrote nursery schools, parent education, correspondence courses, writing programs, adult and worker education, public affairs education, homemaking education, and more. More than 44,000 instructors were hired from relief rolls to teach 1.25 million students.[113] To aid in the battle against hunger, the WPA served more than 600 million school lunches.[114] Further, the $250 million provided by the WPA for school construction[115] resulted in approximately 5,000 new schools and renovations to 30,000 more.[116] An additional $1 billion was provided by the Public Works Administration for school construction.[117] The Civilian Conservation Corps and the National Youth Administration were among the other education-related efforts of the Roosevelt Administration. However, the New Deal programs were intended to be temporary in nature. As the economy improved, the various projects were phased down and discontinued.[118]

Keeping America Strong

In 1938, the Advisory Committee on Education proposed that federal grants be made to the states for specific educational purposes.[119] Broad education aid bills that would have distributed $300 million per year to the schools were proposed by Senator Robert A. Taft on a number of occasions during the 1940s, but were never passed.[120]

Instead, Congress took a more limited approach. In 1941, it passed the Lanham Act that recognized the burden placed on local communities by the presence of federal installations. Communities with military bases and defense plants were obligated to provide education for the children of those stationed or employed there. The federal government provided funds to minimize the financial strain on the local budget in such areas.[121] This effort came to be referred to as "aid to impacted school districts." In the decade of the 1950s, more than 4,500 impacted school districts received $759.3 million for construction and $955 million to assist with operating expenses.[122] By Fiscal Year 1978, the program had grown to an annual expenditure level of $770 million.[123]

In 1946, Congress enacted a measure that was to be enjoyed by millions of parents and complained about by equal millions of children, the National School Lunch Act, a program that provided low-cost lunches for school children. The Agriculture Act of 1954 broadened this endeavor by providing the schools with subsidized milk.[124] Surplus foods served as the basis for the school lunch program in later years. In 1970, broadening legislation permitted the provision of free or reduced price meals to children from families below the poverty level. Beginning in 1974, as surplus foods became more scarce, the Agriculture Department began to reduce its reliance on that approach.[125] Nevertheless, the program is still in existence.

As America entered the 1950s, it still had no general aid-to-education program. As a result, states like California were spending three times as much as states like Mississippi on teacher salaries. The ability of the latter state (as well as its fellow rural states) was limited by its low per capita income. For example, the per capita income per child of New York exceeded Mississippi's by nearly four times during that period.[126] Nevertheless, broad aid was not forthcoming.

Washington continued to rely on the focused approach. One of the most notable education efforts of the early 1950s was the National Science Foundation. At the elementary and secondary levels, the NSF facilitated curricular development and in-service teacher education in chemistry, biology, physics, mathematics, and earth sciences. Such innovations as "Illinois Math," "PSSC Physics," and "BSCS Biology" resulted from NSF grants.[127] Their success was astounding. Within seven years, for example, 30 percent of the biology classrooms were using BSCS materials; the total cost for their development and dissemination turned out to be only fifty cents per student.[128] During the decade of the 1950s, over 58,000 school teachers attended NSF workshops in order to learn the approaches to science teaching that were emanating from the curriculum development projects.[129] Atkin and House have observed that, given the historic exclusion of Washington from the local education enterprise (particularly regarding what was to be taught), it was "startling" that no objections to this new role were voiced. The Cold War and the nuclear threat had raised the nation's consciousness regarding the national defense, and educational efforts such as these were seen as strengthening those defenses.[130]

These efforts also paved the way for the National Defense Education Act of 1958 (discussed earlier), which doubled the federal share of elementary and secondary expenditures to two cents of every lower education dollar.[131] One example of the NDEA's effect can be seen by the fact that the installation of language laboratories increased from forty-six in 1958 to in excess of 7,000 in 1965.[132] Further, during the NDEA's first five years, more than 180,000 public school equipment projects were funded, and more than $102 million was spent on guidance, counseling and testing services.[133]

The year 1965 saw the enactment of legislation that finally provided broad-based federal education aid. It doubled and doubled again the proportion of the lower education dollar coming from the federal government, and by Fiscal Year 1980 rose to an appropriation level of approximately $7 billion.[134]

Passage of the Elementary and Secondary Education Act of 1965 did not come easily, however. It originated at the end of the first month of John F. Kennedy's presidency as the School Assistance Act of 1961. Under that bill, $2.3 billion would have supported teacher salaries, school construction, and aid to school districts in depressed areas.[135] Experimental projects and pilot programs were slated to receive 10 percent of the funds. Since the entire appropriation was to be directed toward the public schools, the bill received strong opposition from the Catholic Church. Further, since it proposed to withhold funds from segregated school districts, the bill was opposed by Southerners. The measure passed the Senate but was killed in the House Rules Committee.[136]

Kennedy tried again in 1962 with a more limited bill that fared no better than his first try.[137] He was back the following year with an omnibus bill that included higher education, vocational education, and elementary-secondary education. As has been previously discussed, the higher education and vocational education portions were enacted into law shortly after Kennedy's assassination. However, the lower education portion did not reach a vote during 1963.[138]

In an effort to move Congress to action, President Johnson called a White House Conference on Education in July 1965. Those assembled recommended a comprehensive federal education effort, and thus paved the way for favorable Congressional action on the Elementary and Secondary Education Act (ESEA) of 1965.[139]

Several other events had also helped push the act forward. First, the Civil Rights Act of 1964 had broken the back of opposition from those who argued in opposition to sanctions against segregated school districts. Title IV of the Civil Rights Act required "the assignment of students to public schools and within such schools without regard to their race, color, religion or national origin" and empowered the Attorney General to seek court action against school districts that were not in compliance with the provision.[140] Title VI precluded discrimination in any program receiving federal funds.[141] The Civil Rights Act of 1964 had a profound effect on education. According to Notre Dame President Theodore M. Hesburgh, the act, with its "built-in sanctions was able to do [in five years] what a decision of the Supreme Court of the United States was unable to do in ten years"—integrate about 70 percent of the offending districts.[142] Others credit it with having created a new climate for black children "who now view their rights to access to facilities and services as being as American as apple pie."[143]

The second factor that eased the way for the ESEA of 1965 was President Johnson's landslide victory in the 1964 elections that swelled the ranks of Northern and Western liberals and provided a mandate for liberal reform. Democrats controlled the Congress by better than a two to one margin in each house.[144]

Finally, always the artful compromiser, President Johnson ingeniously packaged the bill so as to satisfy most critics. Those who feared that states would use the funds to reduce the local tax effort were satisfied that the bill's categorical aid approach would enhance local education rather than merely providing a new means to pay for the status quo. It also allowed conservatives to support the direction of federal funds to specific problem areas while maintaining their historic position of opposition to federal aid to general federal financial assistance to education. Opposition from parochial educators was eased by the provision for aid to all impoverished children regardless of whether they were enrolled in a public or private school. Much credit for the bill's passage was given to Education Commissioner Francis Keppel, who was able to hold together a fragile coalition of lobbying groups formerly at odds with each other.[145]

The legislation was adeptly managed as it moved through Congress. Identical versions were introduced in both houses, and subsequent Senate amendments were immediately added into the House version so as to preclude the possibility that disagreements in final versions could lead to the bill's death. Further, the bill was steamrolled to a vote to foreclose the opportunity of opponents to bottle up the measure.[146] The grand strategy worked: the three Rs that had earlier blocked federal education initiatives—"Race, Religion and Reds" (fear of federal control)—[147]had been side-stepped, and the ESEA of 1965 became law.

Signing the bill in the same one-room school in Texas that gave him his early education, President Johnson declared, "As the son of a tenant farmer, I know that education is the only valid passport from poverty."[148] It is no surprise, then, that Title I of the ESEA authorized $1 billion for compensatory education programs for those whose economic deprivation had led to educational disadvantage. Title II provided $100 million for books and other instructional materials. Another $100 million was authorized by Title III for educational improvement centers intended to provide school districts with mobile libraries and labs, audiovisual materials and television equipment, programmed learning materials, and guidance services. Title IV established a network of university-based educational research and development centers and regional education laboratories charged with disseminating the knowledge gained from successful demonstration projects. (This was an attempt to tie together the usually separate activities of research, program development and dissemination, and, thereby, to reduce the lengthy period—often decades—between the discovery and application of knowledge.)[149] Title V provided $25 million to state departments of education in order to strengthen their coordination and information functions.[150]

The categorical aid approach did bring with it a certain level of complaining since it required that federal rules and regulations be followed, applications to be made for grants, and reports to be filed in order to qualify for more money. Critics argued that Johnson was seeking to wrest control of education from local authorities, a charge vigorously denied by the President, who argued that ESEA provisions enhanced the capacity of the local districts to deliver quality education to all children.[151]

Despite the controversy, Congress stuck with the concept. In 1966, the ESEA was expanded to include a title that sought to strengthen the education provided to handicapped children.[152] The act was broadened again in 1967, but this time House Republicans attempted to convert Titles I, II, III, and V into a general aid block grant. Appearing before the Labor and Education Committee, Commissioner of Education Harold Howe held that categorical efforts such as the Title I compensatory education program sought "to get at a broad national problem." He argued that

> the states have not tended to attack the problem with funds available to them until the time this act was placed in being. In all likelihood the pressures in the States would be very great to use these [block grant] funds for purposes of raising teacher salaries generally . . . and you would not . . . be bringing special services to deprived youngsters.[153]

In a vote split along party lines, the block grant proposal was defeated in committee 19 to 13; however, the Republicans brought the matter to the full House. The coalition that came together to support the ESEA of 1965 made itself felt again. Catholic educators, pointing to the prohibition against the expenditure of public funds for religious schools in thirty-five states, argued that the categorical aid approach would keep federal money in the parochial schools. They were joined by the superintendents of big city school districts who believed that statewide political considerations would divert funds that were currently flowing to them. The AFL-CIO, the NAACP, the National Farmer's Union and such education groups as the National Education Association, the National Congress of Parents and Teachers, the American Council on Education, and the American Association of University Women all lobbied against the proposed change to block grants. The amendment was defeated, but the House did pass several significant changes: one to give the states full authority over the educational improvement centers (Title III); the other to limit the authority of the Office of Education regarding the denial of funds to segregated school districts. The Senate added an amendment of its own: a provision to support a legal test of the constitutionality of federal aid to religious schools (rather than to their students as provided for by the ESEA). When the two versions came to conference committee, the House withdrew its proposal to limit the authority of the USOE over segregated districts, and the Senate withdrew its court-test measure. Both agreed to take a phasing-in approach concerning state control of the educational improvement centers.[154]

Thus, after a major political test, the ESEA emerged in strong fashion. The following year, Congress added a new bilingual education title.[155] Once the 90th Congress had completed its work, the question of the propriety of a broad federal role in education was resolved for some time to come.[156] Lyndon Johnson, who left the White House shortly thereafter as a result of the political firestorm of the Vietnam War, was able to take pride that his wish to be known as the "Education President" had been realized: over 100 categorical programs administered by more than forty federal agencies were disbursing much-needed assistance to American education.[157] During his presidency, Johnson saw annual federal education expenditures increase from $3.1 billion to $9 billion.[158]

The Nixon-Ford Years

Much to the chagrin of education supporters, however, the price tag of what was to be this nation's longest war had begun to strain the federal budget. In August 1969, President Nixon declared that it was no longer fiscally prudent to increase federal education expenditures. He and Congress spent considerable time wrangling over the size of the education budget. Despite their arguments over money, however, basic policy questions were not generally at issue.[159]

While Nixon was not as strong a proponent of education as was his predecessor,[160] his major education initiative, the Education Amendments of 1972, was among the most far reaching. Not only did it transform the federal approach to assisting undergraduate collegiate education and extend vocational education (as have been mentioned earlier in this chapter), but it also extended the existing ESEA and added several major new programs, the Emergency School Aid Act (ESAA) and the National Institute of Education.

Nixon originally proposed ESAA type aid on March 24, 1970, when, acknowledging that (despite his wishes to the contrary) the Supreme Court had given its nod to the acceptability of school desegregation plans ordered by lower federal courts, he proffered that the federal government assist local districts "to meet special problems incident to court-ordered desegregation."[161] The 1972 version had provisions to encourage voluntary desegregation; however, the major share of the $1 billion authorization was reserved for use by districts under a court order to desegregate. Funds were provided to help raise the achievement levels of minority children whose education had suffered as a result of racial isolation. A major feature of the act was its focus on in-service teacher education programs in such areas as race relations training and the development of new language and cultural heritage courses. Community relations programs, new career education programs, and guidance and counseling programs were also supported. The effort to ease tensions in the classroom included the funds for teacher's aides; parents of children from neighborhoods affected by the desegregation plan were to be given preference in the filling of these positions.[162]

The use of ESAA funds to underwrite the cost of busing undertaken to meet a court order was precluded. Congress had never been among the supporters of court-ordered busing to achieve racial balance. The Civil Rights Act of 1964 held that *desegregation* "shall not mean the assignment of students to public schools in order to overcome racial imbalance." It also precluded any federal official or federal court from issuing "any order seeking to achieve a racial balance in any school by requiring the transportation of pupils." While this provision was subsequently ruled unconstitutional, the intention of the Congress was clear.[163] The antibusing provisions of the Education Amendments of 1972 found themselves repeated in the major update that occurred in 1978:

Sec. 616. Nothing in this title shall be construed as requiring any local educational agency which assigns students to schools on the basis of geographic attendance areas drawn on a racially nondiscriminatory basis to adopt any other method of student assignment.[164]

Since most neighborhoods are predominantly uniracial, this section seems to be at odds with the earlier section that sets forth the purpose of the ESAA provisions.

Sec. 602. (a) The Congress finds that the process of eliminating or preventing minority group isolation and improving the quality of education for all children often involves the expenditure of additional funds to which local educational agencies do not have access.

(b) The purpose of this title is to provide financial assistance—

(1) to meet the special needs incident to the elimination of minority group segregation and discrimination among students and faculty in elementary and secondary schools; and

(2) to encourage the voluntary elimination, reduction, or prevention of minority group isolation in elementary and secondary schools with substantial proportions of minority group students.[165]

Given the fact that neighborhood segregation is the underlying cause of much of today's school segregation, it is difficult to understand how the process of eliminating minority group isolation could be accomplished without school reassignments and busing.

For a school district to qualify for funding under the ESAA, it had to satisfy the Office for Civil Rights of the Department of Health, Education and Welfare (HEW) that it was in compliance with HEW civil rights regulations or that it was seeking to redress its past injustices through fulfilling the wishes of the court.[166] Perhaps by definition, school officials under court supervision were not general-ly pleased with having to redesign their pupil assignment policies and educational programs to conform with judicial decrees. They were, however, happy that federal funds were available to assist them through a difficult period.

A few years later, there were many school officials who were not so pleased with a federal response to another problem identified by the courts. Throughout most of American history, physically and emotionally handicapped children, as well as those who were developmentally disabled, received only the most minimal of educational services. In the early 1970s a major case, *Pennsylvania Association of Retarded Citizens v. Commonwealth of Pennsyl-vania,* established the rights of developmentally disabled children to the fullest possible life.[167] Over thirty such suits had either recently been settled or were in progress by 1973. A movement developed to make clear that the federal guarantees for equal educational opportunity applied also to handicapped children. Groups such as the Children's Defense Fund and the Council for Exceptional Children assisted in the development of the Education for All Handicapped Children Act of 1975 sponsored by New Jersey Senator Harrison Williams; curiously missing from this process were the usual educational lobbying groups such as the National Education Association and the American Association of School Administrators. Since advocates of handicapped children had been influential in the drafting of the bill, it was written with the children, and not the school districts, in mind. The legislation mandated the education of handicapped children, regardless of the nature of their disability, and included strict due process requirements intended to protect the rights of these children. School officials were required to consult with parents regarding the classification of their child. Parents had the right to challenge both the classification and the educational program that was developed for the child. Parents were also permitted to bring legal counsel to those meetings.[168]

It did not take long before the child-study teams started arguing with classroom teachers, the parents started challenging the educators, and the educators started complaining about the law. Despite the inconvenience to school officials, however, it would not be the most politically popular move for a politician to advocate that the educational rights of handicapped children be returned to their pre-1975 status.

The Education Amendments of 1978

In 1978, during the presidency of Jimmy Carter, the ESEA was updated once more. Its existing elements were retained and ten new small programs were added. The major substantive change focused a greater share of the Title I (compensatory education) funds in central city and poor rural school districts.[169] The funding authorizations of the Education Amendments of 1978 were expansive. Title I language stated that funds shall be provided "on the basis of entitlements"[170] and that expenditures should include "such sums as may be necessary for fiscal year 1980 and for the three succeeding fiscal years."[171] (Similarly Title II, Basic Skills Improvement, was an entitlement program.)[172] Other titles included dollar limitations for specific purposes. For example under Title III (Special Programs), $20 million per year for five years was provided both for metric education and arts education.[173] The 1978 version of ESAA (Title IV) authorized a total of $422.25 million annually.[174] The Bilingual Education provisions (Title VII) included $200 million for elementary and secondary education for fiscal year 1979; that amount to increase by $50 million per year to a 1983 high of $400 million. (An amount increasing from $12 million in fiscal 1979 to $16 million in 1981 was included for use in bilingual programs in the colleges and universities.)[175]

ESTABLISHMENT OF A CABINET-LEVEL DEPARTMENT OF EDUCATION

Carter's educational legacy was the creation of a federal Department of Education (ED) with a secretary who is a member of the President's Cabinet. In many ways, the organization of the federal government's delivery effort paralleled the growth of the federal education effort itself. As far back as 1800, Thomas Jefferson entertained the proposal by DuPont de Nemours that the president appoint a national education council that would oversee educational affairs and would present an annual report to Congress regarding the condition of education in America.[176] The country was not yet ready for such a council, however, due to the strong popular sentiment that favored local control over education and feared a strong national government.

Creation of a Federal Agency

In 1838, after finding no agency in Washington that possessed reliable information concerning literacy rates in various parts of the country, Connecticut educator Henry Barnard proposed "the establishment at Washington of a permanent statistical bureau charged with the decennial census, which should present an annual report on the educational statistics and progress of the country."[177] While this led to the collection of educational statistics in the 1840 census,[178] the establishment of a permanent education bureau was still more than a quarter century away. The idea gained steam after Barnard's proposal was first endorsed in 1865 by the National Teachers Association and then the following year by the National Association of State and City School Superintendents. The latter group presented Congressman James A. Garfield with a position paper citing the need for such a bureau. Garfield sponsored a bill, passed by Congress in 1867, that created the Department of Education, but that did not confer upon it cabinet status.[179]

The legislation required the Commissioner of Education to report to Congress on the manner in which the federal education land grants were being used, and "such statistics and facts as shall show the condition and progress of education in the several States."[180] Although the bill established the new agency with a primary focus on the collection and reporting of data, opponents feared that it would become much more. Congressman Pike of Maine claimed that

> the school-houses of the country will go under the control of the Federal Government. Churches, I suppose, are to follow next. So, taking the railroads, telegraphs, school-houses and churches, it would seem Congress would leave little to us but our local taxation and our local pauperism.[181]

President Andrew Johnson was reluctant to sign the bill but did so after being satisfied that it neither intended nor required a nationalization of the education enterprise. Garfield assured Johnson and other doubters that "The genius of our Government does not allow us to establish a compulsory system of education, as is done in some countries of Europe . . . .. It is for each state to decide."[182] It was fitting, due to his initiation of the concept of a federal education agency, that Henry Barnard was named by Johnson to serve as the first Commissioner of Education.[183]

Fears about centralization remained, and, desiring to symbolize the primacy of the state role in education, Congress changed the name of the agency to the Office of Education (effective on June 30, 1869), and placed it under the Secretary of the Interior. The next year it was renamed the Bureau of Education, its moniker until 1929 when it was again termed the Office of Education.[184]

Not everyone was satisfied with the role worked out for the Bureau of Education. On the one hand was the fear of federal controls that led many colleges and universities to refuse to participate in data collection efforts;[185] on the other were the concerns of many members of Congress regarding the high levels of illiteracy in many parts of the country. This latter worry led to the World War I era Smith-Towner bill, one facet of which would have been the creation of a Cabinet-level education department.[186] Only one of seventy such bills filed between October 10, 1918, and March 4, 1925, Smith-Towner fell to the arguments that served to block the general aid to education proposals of that period. Southerners, proponents of religious education and other local control advocates joined to defeat all of these efforts.[187]

The National Advisory Committee on Education

In 1929, President Herbert Hoover appointed a National Advisory Committee on Education. Its report, *Federal Relations to Education,* was issued two years later. Comprised of educators, the Committee surveyed the federal education role and drew conclusions that took the high road of decrying federal financial aid at the cost of any loss of local authority over the schools.

They noted that local educational autonomy "grew naturally out of the conditions of pioneer life,"[188] and stated their belief that the trend of "encouraging some special phase of education" through land grants and federal aid bills that required the spending of federal funds in compliance with federal regulations, infringed upon that autonomy. While they pointed to the "constructive advances" in vocational education, for example, that resulted from the 1917 Smith-Hughes Act, they held that it was "a fair question whether these benefits compensate for the inevitable weakening of local responsibility and autonomy. Further, they contended that the cost-benefit conflict "cannot be settled . . . by taking into account mere educational results."[189] As they put it, "A nation built upon a theory of popular sovereignty . . . can ill afford, for the sake of quick results, to weaken itself where it has long been verile."[190]

They saw local educational autonomy as the source of that verility:

> The political domination of education by a remote central government . . . has always led to the evils of bureaucratic unresponsiveness to local and changing needs, to bureaucratic standardization, red tape and delay, and to official insensitiveness to the criticism of far-distant parents and citizens.[191]

Local education was also seen as a block against totalitarianism:

> A class or party may capture a central government by revolution or by some exigency of politics; it cannot as readily capture forty-eight States and more than 145,000 local school communities.[192]

Viewing specific aid programs with requirements that states provide matching funds as instruments that result in federal control and local budget difficulties, the Committee recommended that "no additional laws that grant federal financial aid to the States in support of special types of education" be enacted and that existing programs not be expanded. Further, they called for an end to matching requirements, to the filing of statewide plans and to the application of federal standards to state programs.[193] They did leave open the door for general aid grants with no control.[194] Since it was unlikely that such an approach would be found acceptable to Congress during that period, the Committee was forsaking all federal funds in favor of local autonomy. (With the country in the early days of the Great Depression, one would have to wonder how the local districts would be able to survive without federal assistance.)

The Committee also spoke to the matter of the organization of the federal education effort. Their study indicated that

> If education is taken in its broadest sense as meaning all deliberate attempts to inform people, to change their attitudes, or to perfect their skills, it may be said that there are few administrative units in the ten Executive Departments and the thirty-seven independent establishments of the Federal Government which are not concerned directly or indirectly with education.[195]

They found that "the present scattering of activities is, in many cases, plainly without justification" and that it is impossible "to list accurately or comprehensively all the formal educational activities of the Federal Government."[196]

They worried that

> [T]he Federal Government has no inclusive and consistent public policy as to what it should or should not do in the field of education. Whatever particular policies it seems to be pursuing are often inconsistent with each other, sometimes in conflict. They suggest a haphazard development . . .[197]

Thus, the Committee concluded that

> the time has come to ordain and establish a federal headquarters for education that shall be competent to meet the increasing national responsibility for education in ways that are consistent with the policies and procedures recommended [by the Committee].[198]

It recommended that a Cabinet-level education department be established, since "without an educational officer of equal status with the heads of all other Departments concerned," it would not be possible to guarantee the cooperation necessary "to integrate the educational resources of the Government."[199] Given the Committee's fear of centralized control, this recommendation is curious, since an education department with cabinet status would surely grow in power over time.

It must be noted that the Committee's recommendations were not unanimous. Citing the statistics that indicated that less than half of the 3.3 million school age black children were attending school in 1930, that salaries of black teachers averaged only $524 per year, and that the per capita expenditure for the education of black children was less than one-fifth the national average, the black educators on the Committee dissented from the recommendation regarding the abolition of special purpose federal grant programs.[200] The Catholic members, fearing greater federal controls, demurred from the recommendation to establish a cabinet-level education department.[201]

As often happens when the educational community is divided on proposals for major change in the nature of the federal educational effort, the status quo was retained. There was little sentiment in Congress to move ahead with education reorganization of the sort proposed by the Committee, particularly after the 1932 elections that provided the mandate for federal intervention on a wide-scale basis to resolve the fiscal exigencies of the Great Depression.

HEW and the USOE

In the first year of FDR's administration, his Commission on Economic Recovery found that the "inadequacy of local programs in education is increasing."[202](This led to many of the New Deal education programs that have previously been discussed.) Toward the end of that decade, many of Roosevelt's domestic programs were grouped into a new Federal Security Agency. Among the administrative units transferred to this new agency was the United States Office of Education (USOE).[203]

In 1943, the National Resources Planning Board (NRPB) recommended an expansion of the USOE in order that it might "offer educational leadership to the Nation." It also postulated that "increases in expenditures for education in the postwar period must be financed principally by Federal funds."[204] While there were many Americans who wanted the New Deal approach of government involvement in domestic matters such as education to recede once the economy was on a sound footing, Roosevelt's NRPB was signalling that there would be no return to the days of laissez faire. For the better part of the next four decades, a visible federal role in domestic, social issues transcended partisan politics. While the Democrats clearly wanted a greater federal presence than did the Republicans, there was no broad-based Republican rejection of the New Deal direction until Ronald Reagan's election to the presidency. In fact, it was during the presidency of Dwight D. Eisenhower that the Federal Security Agency became the Cabinet-level Department of Health, Education and Welfare (HEW).[205] The prominance of education in the name of the new department was symbolic of stature as an area for national concern.

As has been discussed earlier, the federal education effort grew by quantum leaps as a result of the NDEA and the subsequent Great Society education programs. With these new programs came a change in the role of the USOE from gathering data and aiding local school officials to one of operating programs.[206] This called for a solid administrative and organizational effort. However, subsequent to the passage of the ESEA of 1965, those around President Lyndon Johnson began to view the USOE as an ineffective, hidebound bureaucracy made up of former state education officials and faculty from collegiate schools of education who followed the policy preferences of the major educational lobbying groups blindly and who had apparently lost their ability to be creative. A task force appointed by Johnson indicated that the state of affairs in the USOE was "unbelievably bad," that "administrative operations had become an end in themselves," and that the Office's direction was being set from without rather than from within. It recommended a reorganization and strengthening of the USOE.[207]

But neither internal revitalization nor the appointment of prestigious educators to the position of Commissioner of Education (and the conferral upon them of the title Assistant Secretary of HEW for Education) alleviated the basic problem, as Nixon appointee, Commissioner James A. Allen, Jr., found out. Of the $11.3 billion spent by the federal government for education, only 58 percent was in the HEW budget and only 39 percent was in the USOE budget. Not only was a small share of the federal effort under the authority of the nation's chief education officer, but Commissioner Allen quickly learned that his power to affect what happened in the other agencies and departments was extremely limited.[208]

Taken in a broader context, the lack of authority and power of the Education Commissioner is even more dramatic. In Fiscal Year 1963, the USOE had a budget of $447 million. Ten years later, that figure had grown to $5.5 billion.[209] By 1976, the total ran $8.1 billion[210] but that did not even represent the majority of the federal education effort. Despite what appears to be a huge amount of money, federal education dollars account for less than 5 percent of the total federal budget. As has been noted by Chester Finn, education, per se, has usually been the secondary focus of the federal education effort. The majority of education programs have been the result of broader policy measures intended to meet national concerns regarding science and technology, defense, and the debt owed to veterans, income maintenance, manpower shortages, and so forth.[211] They have been administered by persons from those primary policy areas.

Creating a New Department

Because state and local governments were hard hit in the mid-1970s by energy-driven inflation, and since taxpayers had begun to voice their concern about passing on to government increasing portions of their earnings, government at both the state and municipal levels began to look for ways to trim their spending. The declining numbers of school-aged children made education budgets a ready target. Consequently, the education lobby turned to the federal government for aid, and found a friend in Presidential candidate Jimmy Carter, with whom they built an alliance. To groups such as the National Education Association, Carter represented that advocate for a focused and strengthened federal education effort that had not been present since LBJ. In the National Education Association, Carter found a major bloc of voters who may well have been responsible for his narrow victory over President Ford.

Within the first several months of his inauguration, Carter appointed a task force to examine the position of education within the federal bureaucracy. In November 1977, the study group presented the President with three possible approaches to the solution of the problems of the lack of coordination and inadequate status of education at the federal level: (1) create a Cabinet-level Department of Education; (2) create a broader Department of Education and Human Development; or (3) raise Education's status within HEW. In fulfillment of his pledge to the NEA, Carter opted for the first proposal, a position that he announced during his January 1978 State of the Union Address.[212]

This provided momentum for the Department of Education Organization Act that had been introduced in March 1977, by Senator Abraham Ribicoff,[213] himself a former Secretary of HEW. Despite the fact that the legislation had the co-sponsorship of fifty-seven senators (thereby guaranteeing passage in the Upper Chamber),[214] the debate, both in Congress and across the nation, was sharp.

Arguments in Favor

Arguing his proposal, Senator Ribicoff noted that nearly thirty percent of all Americans were participating directly in education, either as students or staff; that education accounted for approximately 38 percent of state and local expenditures; but that federal effort was scattered across forty different federal agencies, with two-thirds of the federal programs housed outside of HEW. As he put it, "no serious work is done in developing a coordinated federal role in education. Nor will this role ever be developed as long as the top education officials remain at the level of Commissioner and Assistant Secretary," particularly if the tenure of that person were to remain at its historic average of only one year. Believing that education "is a poor cousin" within HEW, Ribicoff held that the removal of education from that department of government would result in stronger administration in all three fields.[215]

Senate hearings on the proposal occurred between October 1977, and May 1978.[216] Appearing before that body, Democratic Congressman Cecil Heftel of Hawaii told the senators:

> We cannot begin to set our educational house in order until we first put it back together again by consolidating its functions into a single agency and restoring it to the independent stature it deserves.

He contended that the federal educational structure was at present "so vast, so unwieldy and so fragmented that it is inherently incapable of bringing to our educational system the coherence it so desperately requires."[217]

Noted political scientist Stephen K. Bailey put it somewhat more concretely:

> Once matters of policy and budget recommendations go beyond the level of the HEW Assistant Secretary for Education, there lies a rocky path past the Assistant Secretary, Comptroller; Assistant Secretary (Planning and Evaluation); Assistant Secretary (Legislation); Under Secretary; Secretary; OMB and the White House. There is no high-level federal spokesman for education except by accident of special Presidential interest.[218]

In all, at least sixty organizations of educators supported the creation of a new education department.[219] NEA President John Ryor cited the "tremendous lack of accountability, direction and coordination" of the educational effort by HEW. He worried,

> If such a pattern exists under the nose of the Government's top education officials, we are almost afraid to look at what may be and probably is happening where education is only an afterthought in some other agency's responsibilities.[220]

Ryor's testimony before the Senate Committee on Governmental Affairs was supported by other representatives of the educational community, including Dr. Donald L. Robinson of the American Association of University Professors[221] and Dr. Helena Howe, President of the Mesa Community College in Phoenix, Arizona. Representing the American Association of Community and Junior Colleges, Dr. Howe told the Committee that "the time has come to stop the scare headlines about American education and to do something about improving American education and reaffirming our commitment to provide for the national welfare."[222]

Other proponents argued that such a financial commitment as called for by Howe would not be possible as long as education remained a part of HEW. They noted that education is a controllable expenditure within a department where programs such as Social Security, medical care and welfare, by their nature, are characterized by uncontrollable increases. Every time the proportionate increases in those programs exceed the proportion of HEW's budgetary increase, education is the loser. Breaking it loose from HEW would give it a better chance for fiscal equity.[223]

Further, claimed proponents, the mere fact of a change to Cabinet-level status would drive up the public's awareness of education issues and would, therefore, result in increased funding. To support their case, they cited the increase in national stature that accompanied the transformation of the Federal Security Agency (without modification of function) into the Department of Health, Education and Welfare: not only did press coverage of its activities immediately increase ten fold, but the new Secretary became a more potent presidential assistant.[224] Since Ribicoff's bill would not only create a new Cabinet-level department but also would consolidate in that department education programs and functions of departments outside of HEW, there would be an even greater increase in status than accompanied by the creation of HEW.

That did not mean that Ribicoff or the Carter Administration sought to nationalize education. Indeed, James T. McIntyre, Jr., Director of Carter's Office of Management and Budget, assured the Senate Committee that it was the intention of the proposal "to strengthen our pluralistic, locally controlled system of education."[225]

Senate Action

Reorganization efforts always bring forth opposition arguments from persons who do not want their unit moved into the proposed entity; they are joined in their appeal by organizations satisfied with the services provided under the existing structures. Such was the case in this instance.[226] As a result of intense pressure, the Senate Governmental Affair's Committee agreed to leave Head Start in HEW's successor, the Department of Health and Human Services. When the bill came before the full Senate on September 18,1978 school lunch and other nutrition programs were deleted from its provisions (remaining in Agriculture) and the various Indian education programs were retained within the Department of Interior. The Senate voted down attempts to stop the transfer of the National Science Foundation and the education programs operated by the Defense Department for military dependents. After three days of debate, the Senate passed this modified version of the Department of Education Organization Act.[227]

Arguments in Opposition

The strategy employed by the Johnson Administration as the ESEA was pushed through Congress in 1965 was not used by Carter in this instance. The large number of proposed amendments to the reorganization act indicated that passage would not be swift. Thus, the bill did not reach the House floor in 1978. Since the House calendar was crammed with legislation that the leadership believed demanded attention before the Congress broke for the midterm elections, it was felt that a debate on this issue might preclude the passage of that session's "must legislation." Thus, there was no press to have the bill pushed forward at that time.[228]

In 1965, ESEA opponents did not have enough time to mobilize their forces. However, here the delay occasioned by the elections provided those in opposition the breathing room they needed to mount a more convincing effort against the creation of a new Education Department. One of the foremost opponents to the notion was Albert Shanker, President of the American Federation of Teachers. At first, he stood nearly alone, but as time passed, he was joined by groups on both sides of the political spectrum.[229]

While Shanker acknowledged that greater status would be enjoyed by education if it were to be separated from HEW, he felt that it was unwise to "trade off prestige for real power and influence." Not only would a new department be small, but its secretary would have less influence than did the secretary of HEW.

Further, Shanker feared the dissolution of the broad-based coalition that had served to promote education's interest in Congress. He recalled that the Nixon and Ford Administrations had proposed reductions in education appropriations, but that Congress balked, even to the point of overturning presidential vetoes. He believed that Congress had responded "because the people who were interested in health issues were not isolated from those who were interested in issues of education." Further, he argued that a new department would reduce, rather than enhance, the sort of coordination that is necessary to overcome major problems. For example, he pointed to welfare reform that, in order to be successful, would require education, job training, and child care, as well as income maintenance; in such an instance three rather than two Cabinet departments would need to cooperate if education were removed from HEW.[230] He worried that by leaving Head Start, school lunches, Indian education, manpower training, and other programs out of the new department, it would not even be able to insure effective coordination in the education area. Finally, he wondered why one concern of the American people—education—should be given the status of a Cabinet department, while other such as consumer protection, environmental protection, and safety did not have such status.[231]

This latter concern was also voiced by Congressman Benjamin Rosenthal of New York who felt that "Cabinet-level departments should be established only where there is a major national policy to carry out. There is no such major national policy with respect to Federal education efforts." National policy was at issue, he contended, when the Departments of Housing and Urban Development, Transportation, and Energy were established.[232] For example, the Energy Department was created when it became apparent that strong federal leadership was required to manage scarce nonrenewable energy resources and to develop new ones. Such an approach in education would seem to be contrary to an accepted tradition, particularly when education is doing fairly well within the current organizational scheme.[233]

Congresswoman Shirley Chisholm was particularly concerned about the dissolution of the old labor, education, civil rights, health, and welfare coalition:

> [T]he American labor movement has long demonstrated a commitment

to the quality of public education. This vigorous support for equal educational opportunity and social justice was a driving moral and political force behind passage of much of the civil rights legislation designed to prohibit discrimination by recipients of Federal financial assistance . . .. Now, to thoughtlessly destroy these coalitions and distract attention from more critical education problems . . . in order to achieve the dubious goal of a separate department appears foolhardy.[234]

Once the old coalition had been torn apart, it might be possible for its opponents to move on to other fronts. Organized labor feared that the Department of Labor, a small department, might find itself dismembered, its programs parcelled out to other agencies in the name of coordination, thus leaving the working population without a focal point for its concerns.[235]

Chisholm was also concerned that educational reorganization was being proposed for political rather than educational reasons. As she put it, "I find it extremely difficult to dissociate formation of this department from its onerous political origins." Here she was, of course, referring to the strong support that the NEA had provided President Carter in the 1976 election.[236] There was great fear that the new department would become the captive of the NEA.[237] NEA affiliates are the collective bargaining agents for most elementary and secondary districts as well as for a large share of higher education. Their domination of a Cabinet department, it was feared, would jar the whole education system.

Certainly, Illinois Congressman John N. Erlenborn saw it that way. He called the proposal "a political payoff in every sense of the word. It is the cargo preference legislation of the education community." Further, he worried that the new department "will either be a colossal bureaucratic blunder wasting tens of millions of dollars, or if successful it will result in the domination of education by the Federal Government." He raised that traditional fear that with the creation of a new department,

more educational decision-making as to course content, textbook content, and curriculum will be made in Washington at the expense of local diversity . . . . The Department of Education will end up being the nation's super schoolboard. That is something we can all do without.[238]

Erlenborn was joined by the Secretary of Education of the United States Catholic Conference, Monsignor Wilfred Paradis, who told the House Committee on Government Operations that

there is good reason to fear that a new Department of Education will further increase Federal interference in both public and private education in areas that rightfully belong to parents and the local community . . . [something] counter to the Nation's traditional acceptance of and respect for pluralism in education.[239]

Without question, the debate concerning the Department of Education Reorganization Act was the "hottest education issue in Washington"[240] and was surely one of the hottest political issues on Capitol Hill. Several of the nation's most influential newspapers lined up with opponents in an effort to defeat the proposal. The New York *Times* claimed that

a separate department of education would provide merely the illusion of reform. Unless all education-related items were to be plucked from their present jurisdictions and lumped together to create the Big E, the new department would have less clout than education does [within HEW] . . . . But why, for example, would uprooting a program like manpower-training from its functional niche in the Labor Department enhance its effectiveness?[241]

The Chicago *Sun-Times* wondered "how creating a new bureaucracy is the answer to real school problems such as teaching Chicago youngsters how to read." It called upon Congress to "flunk the idea."[242]

The Washington *Post* worried that a new department might, indeed concern itself with the specific problems of teaching urban children how to read. It was skeptical that it

would work pretty much as a harmless conduit of federal funds and coordinator of federal programs, all the while respecting the primacy of the states and localities in school affairs, and that it would do all this much more efficiently than is done under the present slovenly dispensation. Consulting ancient and modern bureaucratic precedent and looking around us at the evidence of our senses, we discover no reason at all to believe this is how things will turn out. They never do.[243]

All three papers feared the NEA connection to the proposal.

The New Department

The pressure was mounting against the proposal, and when it finally came to a vote in the House, it passed by a scant four-vote margin, 210-206. According to David Savage, what was shocking was not that it passed, but that it had lost so much support since it was first proposed. Savage contends that the bill's decline paralleled that of President Carter. It began with high goals, but was vague on how those goals would be accomplished. The more scrutiny it got, the less Congress liked it. Midway through the process, the Carter Administration stopped promoting the high goal of enhancing education and began focusing on such issues as reducing the number of bureaucrats and saving money. That tactic probably got the bill the votes it needed to secure passage in the House, but by the time of passage, it was clear to all that high purpose had been replaced by special interest[244] (a fact that was not forgotten by the NEA in 1980 when it provided Carter with strong backing in the presidential primaries and November election.)

On October 17, 1979, President Carter created the Department of Education [245] by signing PL 96-88, which states,

> The Congress declares that the establishment of a Department of Education is in the public interest, will promote the general welfare of the United States, will help ensure that education receives proper treatment at the Federal level, and will enable the Federal Government to coordinate its education activities more effectively.[246]

It gave the new Department 152 programs that had been a part of six different Cabinet departments, 17,349 personnel (of which nearly 11,000 were employed in Overseas Dependents Schools formerly run by the Department of Defense), and a budget in excess of $14 billion.[247] It also made it clear, however, that state and local authorities were to maintain their primacy over education.

> It is the intention of the Congress . . . to protect the rights of State and local governments and public and private educational institutions in the areas of educational policies and administration of programs and to strengthen and improve the control of such governments and institutions over their own educational programs and policies. The establishment of the Department of Education shall not increase the authority of the Federal Government over education which is reserved to the States and the local school systems and other instrumentalities of the States.[248]

President Carter appointed Shirley Hufstedler, a federal judge from California, to serve as the first Secretary of ED. Utah Education Commissioner Terrel H. Bell (himself a former Commissioner of the USOE) looked forward to an active department:

> I hope the new secretary will be lean and hungry and mean as hell. We in education have been strangled and muffled down in the bowels of the HEW bureaucracy for so many years that we need a new voice that is loud, clear and cuttingly direct. In short, a fresh new breeze needs to blow through the federal education structure.[249]

Secretary Hufstedler barely had time to move into her new office when President Carter lost the 1980 election to Ronald Reagan. The new president, who had vowed to do away with ED, appointed Terrel Bell to be its secretary, and, presumably, to oversee its demise.

REFERENCES

1. Washington *Post* Editorial reprinted in *American Teacher, 63(7):* 9, 1978.
2. Williams, M.F., American Education and Federalism. In Williams, M.F. (Ed.): *Government in the Classroom, Dollars and Power in Education.* New York, Praeger, 1979, p. 2.
3. Hales, D.: *Federal Control of Public Education, A Critical Appraisal.* New York, Columbia University, 1954, p. 38.
4. Tiedt, S.: *The Role of the Federal Government in Education.* New York, Oxford University Press, 1966, p. 14.
5. Mort, P.: *Federal Support for Public Education.* New York, Columbia University, 1936, p. 44.
6. Hales (1954), *Federal Control of Public Education,* pp. 35-36.
7. National Center for Educational Statistics. *The Condition of Education, 1978 Edition.* Washington, U.S. Government Printing Office, 1978, p. 66.
8. Tiedt (1966), *The Role of the Federal Government,* p. 36.
9. Tiedt (1966), *The Role of the Federal Government,* p. 16.
10. Lee, G.C.: *The Struggle for Federal Aid, First Phase, A History of the Attempts to Obtain Federal Aid for the Common Schools 1870-1890.* New York, Columbia University, 1949, p. 7.
11. Lee (1949), *The Struggle for Federal Aid,* p. 11.
12. Hales (1954), *Federal Control of Public Education,* p. 55.
13. Lee (1949), *The Struggle for Federal Aid,* p. 12.
14. Pierce, T.: *Federal, State and Local Government in Education.* Washington, Center for Applied Research in Education, 1964, p. 25.
15. Lee (1949), *The Struggle for Federal Aid,* p. 13.
16. Lapati, A.: *Education and the Federal Government, A Historical Record.* New York, Mason/Charter, 1975, p. 15-16.
17. Mort (1936), *Federal Support for Public Education,* pp. 45-46.
18. Lee (1949), *The Struggle for Federal Aid,* p. 7.
19. Lee (1949), *The Struggle for Federal Aid,* pp. 7-8.
20. Lapati (1975), *Education and the Federal Government,* p. 52.
21. Lapati (1975), *Education and the Federal Government,* p. 53.
22. Lee (1949), *The Struggle for Federal Aid,* p. 9.
23. Lee (1949), *The Struggle for Federal Aid,* p. 14.
24. Lee (1949), *The Struggle for Federal Aid,* p. 17.
25. Mayville, W.: *Federal Influence on Higher Education Curricula.* Washington, American Association for Higher Education, 1980, p. 9.
26. Mayville (1980), *Federal Influence on Higher Education,* p. 9.
27. Conrad, C. and Cosand, J., *The Implications of Federal Education Policy.* Washington, American Association for Higher Education, 1976, p. 5-6.

28. Lee (1949), *The Struggle for Federal Aid*, p. 18.
29. Mort (1936), *Federal Support for Public Education*, p. 49.
30. Mort (1936), *Federal Support for Public Education*, p. 2.
31. Cheit, E.: The Benefits and Burdens of Federal Financial Assistance to Higher Education, *American Economic Review, 67(1):* 90, 1977.
32. Mort (1936), *Federal Support for Public Education*, pp. 50–51.
33. Hales (1954), *Federal Control of Public Education*, p. 55.
34. Lapati (1975), *Education and the Federal Government*, p. 60.
35. Lapati (1975), *Education and the Federal Government*, p. 61.
36. Lee (1949), *The Struggle for Federal Aid*, p. 58–59, 85.
37. Lapati (1975), *Education and the Federal Government*, p. 61.
38. Evolution of the Present Federal Role in Education, *Congressional Digest, 57(11):* 260, 1978.
39. Lapati (1975), *Education and the Federal Government*, p. 62.
40. Lapati (1975), *Education and the Federal Government*, p. 62.
41. Hales (1954), *Federal Control of Public Education*, p. 56.
42. Hales (1954), *Federal Control of Public Education*, p. 57.
43. Tiedt (1966), *The Role of the Federal Government*, p. 22.
44. Evolution of the Present Role (1978), p. 261.
45. Hales (1954), *Federal Control of Public Education*, p. 62.
46. Hales (1954), *Federal Control of Public Education*, p. 63.
47. Lapati (1975), *Education and the Federal Government*, p. 65.
48. Conrad and Cosand (1976), *The Implications of Federal Education*, p. 7.
49. Tiedt (1966), *The Role of the Federal Government*, p. 25.
50. Pierce (1964), *Federal, State and Local Government, p. 32.*
51. *Evolution of . . . (1978), p. 262.*
52. *Green, E.: The Federal Role in Education, In (no Ed): Education and the Public Good.* Cambridge, MA, Harvard University Press, 1964, p. 3.
53. Wilson, J.: *Higher Education and the Washington Scene: 1982.* Chicago, University of Chicago, 1982, p. 1.
54. Pierce (1964), *Federal, State and Local Governments*, p. 38.
55. Tiedt (1966), *The Role of the Federal Government*, p. 30.
56. Wilson (1982), *Higher Education*, pp. 1–2.
57. Lapati (1975), *Education and the Government*, pp. 76–79.
58. Lapati (1975),*Education and the Government*, p. 80.
59. Thomas, N.: *Education in National Politics.* New York, David McKay Company, 1975, p. 52.
60. Thomas (1975), *Education in National Politics*, pp. 96–98.
61. Finn, C., *Education and the Presidency.* Lexington, MA, Lexington Books, 1977, p. 13.
62. Finn (1977), *Education and the Presidency*, pp. 78–79.
63. Wilson (1982), *Higher Education*, p. 5.
64. Finn (1977), *Education and the Presidency*, pp. 67, 84.
65. Weinberger, C.: The Federal Stimulus in Postsecondary Education, In Hughes, J. (Ed): *Education and the State.* Washington, American Council on Education, 1975, p. 87–88.

66. Mayville (1980), *Federal Influence on Higher Education,* p. 40.
67. Cosand, J.: Setting National Goals and Objectives: Postsecondary Education, In Hughes, J. (Ed): *Education and the State.* Washington, American Council on Education, 1977, p. 34.
68. Weinberger (1975), *The Federal Stimulus,* p. 87.
69. *Conrad and Cosand (1976), The Implications of Federal Education,* p. 10.
70. Cleary, R.: Federal Higher Education Policy: A View from the Campus, *Policy Studies Journal, 10(1):* 86, 1981.
71. Hales (1954), *Federal Control of Public Education,* p. 58.
72. Lapati (1975), *Education and the Federal Government,* pp. 97-98.
73. Tiedt (1966), *The Role of the Federal Government,* p. 23.
74. Mort (1936), *Federal Support for Public Education,* p. 3.
75. Mort (1936), *Federal Support for Public Education,* pp. 2-3.
76. National Advisory Committee on Education. *Federal Relations to Education, Part I.* Washington, National Capital Press, 1931, p. 12-13.
77. Lapati (1975), *Education and the Federal Government,* p. 99.
78. Hales (1954), *Federal Control of Public Education,* p. 58.
79. Hales (1954), *Federal Control of Public Education,* p. 63.
80. Tiedt (1966), *The Role of the Federal Government,* p. 31.
81. Lapati (1975), *Education and the Federal Government,* pp. 105–106.
82. Tiedt (1966), *The Role of the Federal Government,* pp. 153–154.
83. Lapati (1975), *Education and the Federal Government,* p. 107.
84. Hales (1954), *Federal Control of Public Education,* p. 59.
85. Lapati (1975), *Education and the Federal Government,* p. 114.
86. P.L. 94-482, Title I, Section 110.
87. P.L. 94-482, Title I, Section 101.
88. P.L. 94-482, Title I, Section 120.
89. P.L. 94-482, Title I, Section 102.
90. P.L. 94-482, Title I, Section 103.
91. Vitullo-Martin, T., Federal Policies and Private Schools, in Williams, M.F. (Ed): *Government in the Classroom, Dollars and Power in Education.* New York, Praeger, 1979, p. 124–125.
92. Lee (1949), *The Struggle for Federal Aid,* pp. 20–21.
93. Mort (1936), *Federal Support for Public Education,* p. 63.
94. Lee (1949), *The Struggle for Federal Aid,* pp. 29–33.
95. Tiedt (1966), *The Role of the Federal Government,* p. 19.
96. Lee (1949), *The Struggle for Federal Aid,* p. 42.
97. Lee (1949), *The Struggle for Federal Aid,* pp. 43–44, 47, 53.
98. Lee (1949), *The Struggle for Federal Aid,* pp. 57-58.
99. Lapati (1975), *Education and the Government,* p. 18.
100. Lapati (1975), *Education and the Government,* pp. 18–20.
101. Lee (1949), *The Struggle for Federal Aid,* p. 57.
102. Lee (1949), *The Struggle for Federal Aid,* pp. 89–93.
103. Lee (1949), *The Struggle for Federal Aid,* pp. 149–155. Tiedt (1966), *The Role of the Federal Government,* pp. 20–21.
104. Lee (1949), *The Struggle for Federal Aid,* pp. 149-155. Tiedt (1966), *The Role of the Federal Government,* pp. 20–21.

105. Lee (1949), *The Struggle for Federal Aid,* pp. 88–89.
106. Mort (1936), *Federal Support for Public Education,* p. 5.
107. Evolution of . . . (1978), p. 261.
108. Marcus, L. and Stickney, B.: *Race and Education: The Unending Controversy.* Springfield, IL, Charles C Thomas, 1981, p. 35.
109. Mort (1936), *Federal Support for Public Education,* p. 268.
110. Mort (1936), *Federal Support for Public Education,* p. 13.
111. Mort (1936), *Federal Support for Public Education,* pp. 7-9, 24.
112. Tiedt (1966), *The Role of the Federal Government,* p. 24.
113. Hales (1954), *Federal Control of Public Education,* pp. 61-62.
114. Evolution of . . . (1978), p. 261.
115. Hales (1954), *Federal Control of Public Education,* p. 62.
116. Evolution of . . . (1978), p. 261.
117. Hales (1954), *Federal Control of Public Education,* p. 62.
118. Evolution of . . . (1978), p. 261.
119. Hales (1954), *Federal Control of Public Education,* p. 67.
120. Tiedt (1966), *The Role of the Federal Government,* p. 26.
121. Evolution of . . . (1978), p. 261.
122. Pierce (1964), *Federal, State and Local Government,* pp. 31-32.
123. Major Federal Programs Now in Force, *Congressional Digest, 57(11):* 265, 1978.
124. Pierce (1964), *Federal, State and Local Government,* p. 35.
125. Lapati (1975), *Education and the Government,* p. 23.
126. Hales (1954), *Federal Control of Public Education,* p. 51.
127. Atkin, J.M. and House, E., The Federal Role in Curriculum Development, 1950-1980, *Educational Evaluation and Policy Analysis, 3(5):* 7, 12, 1981.
128. Atkin and House (1981), The Federal Role in Curriculum, p. 13.
129. Pierce (1964), *Federal, State and Local Government,* p. 38.
130. Atkin and House (1981), *The Federal Role in Curriculum,* p. 9.
131. Guthrie, J.: The Future of Federal Education Policy, *Education and Urban Society, 14(4):* 512, 1982.
132. Lapati (1975), *Education and the Government,* p. 26.
133. Tiedt (1966), *The Role of the Federal Government,* p. 30.
134. Guthrie (1982), The Future of Federal Education Policy, p. 512.
135. Tiedt (1966), *The Role of The Federal Government,* p. 145.
136. Lapati (1975), *Education and the Government,* pp. 33-34.
137. Tiedt (1966), *The Role of the Federal Government,* pp. 147-148.
138. Lapati (1975), *Education and the Government,* p. 35.
139. Lapati (1975), *Education and the Government,* p. 35.
140. Lapati (1975), *Education and the Government,* p. 29.
141. Thomas (1975), *Education in National Politics,* p. 27.
142. Hesburgh, T.: Legislating Attitudes, In Hughes, J. (Ed): *Education and the State,* Washington, American Council on Education, 1975, p. 248.

143. Martin, R.: The Social Influence of Legislative Acts, In Hughes, J. (Ed): *Education and the State,* Washington, American Council on Education, 1975, p. 260.
144. Thomas (1975), *Education in National Politics,* pp. 27, 30.
145. Thomas (1975), *Education in National Politics,* pp. 28-29, 38.
146. Guthrie (1982), The Future of Federal Education Policy, p. 515.
147. Thomas (1975), *Education in National Politics,* p. 3.
148. Tiedt (1966), *The Role of the Federal Government,* p. 192.
149. Dollar, B.: Federal Attempts to Change the Schools, In Williams, M.F. (Ed): *Government in the Classroom, Dollars and Power in Education,* New York, Praeger, 1979, p. 116.
150. Lapati (1975), *Education and the Government,* pp. 35-36.
151. Thomas (1975), *Education in National Politics,* pp. 38-39.
152. Lapati (1975), *Education and the Government,* p. 37.
153. Thomas (1975), *Education in National Politics,* pp. 74-75.
154. Thomas (1975), *Education in National Politics,* pp. 78-90.
155. Lapati (1975), *Education and the Government,* p. 37.
156. Thomas (1975), *Education in National Politics,* p. 34.
157. Bailey, S., *Education Interest Groups in the Nation's Capital.* Washington, American Council on Education, 1975, p. 36.
158. Finn (1977), *Education and the Presidency,* p. 11.
159. Finn (1977), *Education and the Presidency,* p. 12.
160. Thomas (1975), *Education in National Politics,* p. 234.
161. Finn (1977), *Education and the Presidency,* pp. 42-43.
162. Lapati (1975), *Education and the Government,* pp. 41-43.
163. Lapati (1975), *Education and the Government,* pp. 29-30.
164. P.L. 95-561, Title VI, Section 616.
165. P.L. 95-561, Title VI, Section 602.
166. Radin, B: Equal Educational Opportunity and Federalism, In Williams, M.F. (Ed): *Government in the Classroom, Dollars and Power in Education,* New York, Praeger, 1979, p. 81-82.
167. 834 F. Supp. 1257 (1971) and 343 F. Supp. 279 (1972).
168. Guthrie (1982), The Future of Federal Education Policy, pp. 517-519.
169. Berke, J. and Demarest, E., Alternatives for Future Federal Programs, In Williams, M.F. (Ed): *Government in the Classroom, Dollars and Power in Education,* New York, Praeger, 1979, p. 58.
170. P.L. 95-561, Title I, Section 102.
171. P.L. 95-561, Title I, Section 116.
172. P.L. 95-561, Title II, Section 241.
173. P.L. 95-561, Title III, Sections 314 and 323.
174. P.L. 95-561, Title VI, Section 604.
175. P.L. 95-561, Title VII, Section 702.
176. Growth and Present Role of the U.S. Office of Education, *Congressional Digest,* 57 (11): 263, 1978.
177. Lapati (1975), *Education and the Government,* p. 7.

178. Growth and Present Role . . . (1978), p. 263.
179. Lapati (1975), *Education and the Government*, pp. 7-8.
180. Growth and Present Role . . . (1978), p. 264.
181. Lee (1949), *The Struggle for Federal Aid*, p. 25.
182. Lee (1949), *The Struggle for Federal Aid*, pp. 25-26.
183. Lapati (1975), *Education and the Government*, p. 8.
184. Lapati (1975), *Education and the Government*, p. 8.
185. Morgan, P.: Academia and the Federal Government, *Policy Studies Journal*, 10 (1): 7, 1981.
186. Tiedt (1966), *The Role of the Federal Government*, p. 23.
187. Lapati (1975), *Education and the Government*, p. 8.
188. National Advisory Committee on Education (1931), *Federal Relations*, p. 11.
189. National Advisory Committee on Education (1931), *Federal Relations*, pp. 12-13.
190. National Advisory Committee on Education (1931), *Federal Relations*, p. 24.
191. National Advisory Committee on Education (1931), *Federal Relations*, p. 29.
192. National Advisory Committee on Education (1931), *Federal Relations*, p. 29.
193. National Advisory Committee on Education (1931), *Federal Relations*, p. 37.
194. National Advisory Committee on Education (1931), *Federal Relations*, p. 31.
195. National Advisory Committee on Education (1931), *Federal Relations*, p. 5.
196. National Advisory Committee on Education (1931), *Federal Relations*, pp. 5, 7.
197. National Advisory Committee on Education (1931), *Federal Relations*, p. 8.
198. National Advisory Committee on Education (1931), *Federal Relations*, p. 93.
199. National Advisory Committee on Education (1931), *Federal Relations*, p. 94-95.
200. National Advisory Committee on Education (1931), *Federal Relations*, pp. 106-107.
201. National Advisory Committee on Education (1931), *Federal Relations*, p. 103.
202. Green (1964), The Federal Role in Education, p. 6.
203. Lapati (1975), *Education and the Government*, p. 8.
204. Green (1964), The Federal Role in Education, p. 7.
205. Lapati (1975), *Education and the Government*, p. 8.
206. Thomas (1975), *Education in National Politics*, p. 122.
207. Thomas (1975), *Education in National Politics*, pp. 32-33.

208. Finn (1977), *Education and the Presidency,* p. 15.
209. Dollar (1979), Federal Attempts, p. 109.
210. Kirst, M: The Carter Administration: What News for Education? *Compact* 11 (2): 2, 1977.
211. Finn (1977), *Education and the Presidency,* p. 104.
212. Action in the 95th Congress, *Congressional Digest, 57 (11):*268, 1978.
213. Action in the 95th Congress, (1978), p. 268.
214. Education Roundup, *Compact, 12 (2):* 2, 1978.
215. Ribicoff, A.: A Separate Department of Education: Why Not the Best? *Change, 10 (2):* 27, 63, 1978.
216. Action in the 95th Congress (1978), p. 268.
217. Should Congress Establish a Separate Cabinet-Level U.S. Department of Education? *Congressional Digest, 57 (11):* 270, 1978.
218. Bailey (1975), *Education Interest Groups,* p. 54.
219. Report No. 96-143, United States House of Representatives, May 14, 1979, p. 4–5.
220. Should Congress Establish . . . (1978), *Congressional Digest,* p. 276, 280.
221. Should Congress Establish . . . (1978), *Congressional Digest,* p. 282.
222. Should Congress Establish . . . (1978), *Congressional Digest,* p. 284.
223. Kirst (1977), The Carter Administration, p. 4.
224. Miles, R.: A Cabinet Department of Education: An Unwise Campaign Promise or a Sound Idea? *Public Administration Review, 39 (2):* 104, 1979.
225. Should Congress Establish . . . (1978), *Congressional Digest,* p. 272.
226. The Question of a U.S. Department of Education, *Congressional Digest, 57 (11):* 259, 1978.
227. Action in the 95th Congress (1978), *Congressional Digest,* p. 268.
228. Action in the 95th Congress (1978), *Congressional Digest,* p. 269.
229. Neill, G., Washington Report: Department of Education Nears Showdown in House, *Phi Delta Kappan, 60 (10):* 701, 1979a.
230. Should Congress Establish . . . (1978), *Congressional Digest,* p. 285, 287.
231. Shanker, A.: Speaking Out Against a Separate Department of Education, *American Teacher, 63 (7):* 8, 1979.
232. Should Congress Establish . . . (1978), *Congressional Digest,* p. 271.
233. Miles (1979), A Cabinet Department, p. 105.
234. Should Congress Establish . . . (1978), *Congressional Digest,* p. 279.
235. Kirst (1977), The Carter Administration, p. 4.
236. Should Congress Establish . . . (1978), *Congressional Digest,* p. 277.
237. Miles (1979), A Cabinet Department, p. 105.
238. Should Congress Establish . . . (1978), *Congressional Digest,* p. 273, 275.
239. Should Congress Establish . . . (1978), *Congressional Digest,* p. 283.
240. Neill (1979a), Department of Education, *Phi Delta Kappan,* p. 701.
241. Editorial, New York *Times* (reprinted in *American Teacher, 63 (7):* 9, 1979).

242. Editorial, Chicago *Sun Times* (reprinted in *American Teacher, 63 (7):* 8, 1979.
243. Washington *Post* (1979), reprinted in *American Teacher,* p. 9.
244. Savage, D., With Education in Washington, *Education Digest, 45 (1):* 63, 1979.
245. Wilson (1982), *Higher Education,* p. 8.
246. P.L. 96-88, Title I, Section 102.
247. Neill, G.: Washington Report: Observers See Danger, Challenge in Building Education Department, *Phi Delta Kappan, 61 (4):* 236–237, 1979b.
248. P.L. 96-88, Title I, Section 103.
249. Neill (1979b), Observers See Danger, p. 236.

Chapter 2

THE WINDS OF CHANGE

Despite Carter's success in giving education departmental status, it is important to remember that candidate Carter had campaigned in 1976 *against* Washington. Like Nixon's "dual federalism," Carter's "creative federalism" suggested a changing partnership between national and state government that would reduce Washington's power. The success of the Carter campaign strategy has been viewed by many as a political accident, for it deviated significantly from the Democratic Party's canon of creating a stronger federal government. However, it is also likely that Carter was tapping a conservative trend that, by 1976, had influenced a significant segment of the Democratic Party. Declaring war on government waste, red tape, and bureaucratic inefficiency has always been an expendient stand for any presidential candidate, but the fact that the Democratic Party's standard bearer in 1976 gained such political advantage from his anti-Washington rhetoric was another indication of public dissatisfaction with the current state of federalism.

The body politic also appeared to have become more discontent with public education. Since 1974, the Gallup Poll has sampled the population's grade rating of the local schools and has reported a steady decline in the overall number of A's and B's given by the populous to its schools between 1974 and 1979.[1] Discontent with government in general and the schools in particular was symbolized by the passage of the tax-limiting Proposition 13 in California in 1978 and Proposition 2½ in Massachusetts in 1980, and by the voters in towns across Ohio whose unwillingness to raise necessary local revenues forced their school's closing for several months. Somewhat less dramatic has been the reluctance of voters to approve school bond issues that would support the construction of new schools. Voter reluctance to support the adequate financing of public schools may be affected by the declining percentage of adults with school-age children. Jack Jennings, Counsel and Staff Director of the House Subcommittee on Elementary, Secondary, and Vocational Education, contended that the significant drop in the percentage of the adult population with children in public schools between 1970 and 1980 (a decrease from 44 to 25 percent) contributed to a *decline in education's political magic.*"[2]

In March 1980, eight months before Ronald Reagan's election to the presidency, Jennings predicted a holding of the line on federal spending on education during the decade of the 1980s no matter who was occupying the White House. According to Jennings, political pressure to curtail federal spending had already led to a 26 percent constant dollar decline in vocational education funding between 1972 and 1977.[3] In addition, although the Carter Administration had successfully sponsored a broadening of financial assistance for college students through the 1978 passage of the Middle Income Student Assistance Act, it is Jennings's contention that mounting political pressure was reflected in the Carter Administration's growing opposition in 1979 and 1980 to Congressional bills extending college student assistance and its attack on student lunch subsidies in the federally financed school lunch programs.[4] Jennings also sensed the absence of a broad base of support from both the general population and the community of educators for narrowly focused federal programs for the disadvantaged and handicapped, for the "uncomfortable changes" caused institutions in their compliance with regulations affecting age, sex, race, and handicapping condition. Indeed, it is Jenning's contention that the many requirements and additional paperwork associated with serving populations that localities were reluctant to serve in the first place has often caused "resentment" against federal educational involvement.[5]

Size and Regulation

The size and regulatory power of the federal government had increased dramatically throughout the 1960s and 1970s. According to the Advisory Commission on Intergovernmental Relations in forty-seven of the forty-eight major cities (excluding New York) the federal government's contribution to each dollar raised locally increased from twenty-six cents in 1957 to nearly fifty cents in 1978. By 1980, largely because of general revenue sharing and the swelling of block and categorical grant programs, the federal government had taken over the funding of many services long controlled by the states and localities and was making its presence felt in nearly every state house and city hall in America. Indeed, in 1977, the Advisory Commission on Intergovernmental Relationship stated that it had difficulty finding "a single major state and local function in which the federal government was not involved."[6]

By the end of the 1970s, the primary means of providing federal assistance was through categorical grants that constituted approximately 75 percent of all federal grant outlays. Typically targeted for specific populations to meet rather narrowly defined needs, the categorical grants available to states and localities increased some 300 percent between 1962 and 1978. In January 1978, state and local governments could apply for no fewer than 429 Washington-based categoricals. Between 1950 and 1980, federal grant outlays increased from 10.4 percent to 25.3 percent of state and local expenditures.[7]

In higher education, the costs and burdens associated with the increased regulatory power of the federal government raised the ire of many individuals long sympathetic with federal initiatives in promoting equality of educational opportunity. In 1976, Derek Bok, President of Harvard University, contended that Harvard's "compliance with federal regulations consumed over 60,000 hours of faculty time and costs almost $8.3 million in 1974–75 alone." Bok later lamented that "regular meetings of university presidents are devoted almost entirely to issues of government relations rather than questions of education and research," and that "government forms and reports . . . devour thousands of faculty hours each year, hours that are taken in large part from research, class preparation, and counseling with students."[8] There is no argument, Bok continues, with government intervention in cases of discrimination or the National Science Foundation determining whether its allocation should be used on basic or applied research.[9] When universities and colleges are burdened by the excessive regulatory measures that accompany what may be just intervention ("For example, who could have anticipated the 10,000 words of regulatory prose that emerged from just 45 words of legislation requiring adequate opportunities for the handicapped?"), the cost value of compliance becomes questionable.[10]

A 1978 study that interviewed some 200 higher education administrators and department chairpersons at eighteen institutions described Ohio State University's president, Harold Enarson, as complaining "that his 'compliance bill' includes $50,000 a year to meet EPA (Environmental Protection Agency) requirements, $25,000 for staff time and computer charges to satisfy the Buckley requirements, and $885,000 over two years in anticipation of OSHA (Occupational Safety and Health Act) requirements."[11] The study also described Columbia's president, William McGill, as contending "That the *Federal Register,* where agencies publish their regulations, grew from 3,450 pages in 1937 to 60,221 pages in 1975 and that during the past year alone [1977] 7,496 new federal regulations were instituted, all of which Columbia must deal with at great cost."[12] According to the study's author, Cornell's Robert Scott, "These presidential protests represent only the tip of the iceberg. At colleges across the country, an enormous block of resistance is building to the huge expense of social legislation."[13]

Calling universities "nationalized" and "wards of the state," Daniel Patrick Moynihan, former Harvard professor and currently the senior Senator from New York, contends that "in the main, the university community was most supportive of the government activism that is now affecting it." Recalling his work in preparing Executive Order 11246 on equal employment opportunity as an assistant secretary of labor in the Johnson Administration, Moynihan points out that this equalitarian order "was directed against a specific evil and accomplished much good" as the basis for the federal government's affirmative-action programs. He goes on to ponder,

> But who in the executive branch fifteen years ago would have dreamed the day would come when the federal courts would require a census in which all employees and judicial officers be classified by "race/national origin groups" including the subgroups "Arabic" and "Hebrew?" This was just the sort of thing we assumed we were working against.[14]

Moynihan contends that as universities became more and more dependent on federal support, they sacrificed their institutional distinctiveness; that the "activist, multifaceted state" places little value on institutional autonomy or academic freedom. Thus, despite "bitter academic opposition," the Office of Management and Budget (OMB) was able to impose complex accounting rules governing federally sponsored research imposed in 1979. According to Moynihan, "dependence is the key issue" and such subservience permitted the implementation of OMB's "most onerous" regulation that "established procedures by which universities must keep track of the time and effort of their professors to ensure that the government pays only for those activities integral to federally sponsored research projects." It was estimated that this regulation would increase the federal reports submitted by Stanford University alone from 3,010 to 80,000 annually.[15]

By 1980, at least eight federal agencies, which had the responsibility of directly enforcing the various executive orders and legislation, had a major role in the governance of America's colleges and universities. In addition, the requirements of numerous federal grants had involved several other agencies, and the private suits brought under federal statues had increased the influence of the federal courts. According to the Sloan Commission, "this bewildering array of regulations" could be placed into two major areas, one zeroing in on faculty concerns such as hiring, retention, and tenured proportion, and the other targeted toward equalizing student opportunities in gaining admission, and after entry, securing a quality experience.[16] Responsibility for enforcing faculty concerns has been shared by the Departments of Justice and Labor as well as the Equal Employment Opportunity Commission and the Office of Federal Contract Compliance Programs. Student interests have been protected primarily by the Office of Civil Rights and Department of Justice. It is the contention of the Sloan Commission that a good deal of the antagonism between higher education and the federal government has resulted from numerous agencies and government personnel overseeing compliance with myriad regulations.[17]

By the end of the 1970s, concern with the excessiveness and complexity of regulations had even provoked the anger of House Education and Labor Committee Chairman Carl Perkins, long one of Congress's most respected and influential advocates of nationally funded programs to enhance the opportunities of disadvantaged

Americans. Addressing the subcommittee on Elementary, Secondary, and Vocational Education in October 1979, Congressman Perkins recommended that the "regulations be written in such a way that they are clear, logical and consistent with the law." Because "regulations are considered as having the same effect of law, . . . [the] regulations should clearly set forth what the true intent of the program is and not go beyond the law."[18] Reflecting on regulations of an earlier age, Perkins continued:

> The old WPA regulations were not overly complex, or the old NRA regulations. I was a county official at that time in the early part of the 1940s . . . The laws were very simple. The language was very simple, and I know that we can do that same thing in connection with Title I regulations, if we try.[19]

Perkins warned that regulations that are excessively restrictive erode political support for federal education programs:

> What we are doing is causing animosity on the part of the people at the local school board levels. They feel that they are trying to do the best possible job in carrying out the intent of the law, only to find out that the General Accounting Office has said they have violated the law because they overstepped the regulations . . . this situation makes it more difficult to obtain funding in the U.S. Congress, and let me tell you that is one thing that has happened to us now.

> You are unable to get the best supporters of education to come forward and talk to Congressmen because they are miffed about regulations . . . . We on the political scene run into that every day.[20]

Perkins chastised the "timid souls within the Department of Education that still feel that they have got more know-how than the Congress . . ." He hoped "that somewhere somebody could kindly press them down just a little by throwing some of those regulations in the wastepaper basket until those timid souls have more knowledge about the public in this country . . ." The Chairman concluded that education "programs are greatly underfunded . . . [but] before we are going to get the funding that we need, we are going to have to do a much better job in the U.S. Congress, and we are hampered presently because of the regulations."[21]

Program Ineffectiveness

Overencumbering regulations and unchecked bureaucratic elitism were not the only sources of concern in the public mind regarding federal education issues. Throughout the 1970s, there were increasing reservations about the success of the programs themselves, particularly those that had been legislated to remediate the learning problems associated with children of low economic status. The growing negativism associated with schooling in general and federal education programs in particular was predicated in part by the pessimistic findings of educational research when James Coleman and his colleagues released their massive investigation of educational inequities in 1965. Appropriately entitled *Equality of Educational Opportunity Survey,* the so-called "Coleman Report" was designed to assess "the lack of availability of equal opportunities for individuals by reason of race, color, religion or national origin in public institutions at all levels in the United States." The survey included the testing of some 570,000 pupils, the questioning of some 60,000 teachers and the description of over 4,000 schools. To Coleman and his staff, educational equality meant not only resources and per pupil expenditures, but pupil achievement on standardized tests. Traditionally, poor test performance was associated with the conditions of poverty and discrimination and part of the Coleman Report's design was to tell us what the schools should be doing to compensate for environmental inadequacies. The report's conclusion on this issue was shocking. School facilities (per pupil expenditure, class size, books in library) and school curriculum had very little to do with pupil achievement. According to Coleman, "differences in school facilities and curriculum, which are the major variables by which attempts are made to improve schools, are so little related to differences in achievement levels of students that, with very few exceptions, their effects fail to appear in a survey of this magnitude." Certain "teacher characteristics" and "student body characteristics" (the percentage of whites modestly affected black achievement) were associated with pupil learning, but even the variables racial integration and teacher verbal facility were dwarfed by the influence of environmental background. Factors such as family size and structure, family income, and availability of reading materials at home were much more strongly correlated with achievement than any of the few school factors that appeared to make a difference. Indeed, it was Coleman's contention that "schools bring little influence to bear on a child's achievement that is independent of his background and general social context." Equalizing educational opportunity "must imply a strong effect of schools that is independent of the child's immediate social environment and that strong independent effect is not present in American schools."[22]

By the time the Coleman Report was released, Congress had legislated Head Start and Title I, which were designed to provide a strong independent effect. As a preschool program for children from low-income families, one of Project Head Start's primary goals, when initiated in 1964, was to prepare children for the academics of schooling by raising their I.Q. Five years after Head Start's inception, a national longitudinal study of the program by Ohio University and the Westinghouse Learning Corporation found that the program was associated with significant I.Q. gains but that these increases in measured cognition were not sustained.[23] By the end of the second grade, the I.Q.'s of most Head Start children were not significantly higher than their disadvantaged counterparts who had never experienced the program.[24] Indeed it was the longitudinal research on experimental preschool programs similar to Head Start that yielded similar results apparently responsible primarily for Arthur Jensen's contention that genetic endowment may be responsible for compensatory education's "apparent failure."[25]

At the elementary and secondary level, equally discouraging research results had prompted Roger Freeman's comments on the ineffectiveness of Title I of the Elementary and Secondary Education Act (ESEA) of 1965. Primarily a remedial reading and math program for underachieving children, Title I's effect on achievement was assessed in 1968 and 1969 by testing national samples of elementary Title I school children. In neither study could an overall positive effect on achievement be demonstrated. As early as 1970, the Hoover Institute's Roger Freeman, an education aide to President Nixon (and later Reagan), summarized Title I evaluations by stating that although "we now spend more than $1 billion a year for educational programs under Title I of the Elementary and Secondary Education Act . . . most [of which] have stressed the teaching of reading, . . . before and after tests suggest that only 19 percent of the children in each program improve their reading significantly, 13 percent appear to fall behind and two-thirds remain unaffected—that is they continue to fall behind."[26] A year earlier, Berkeley's distinguished educational psychologist, Arthur Jensen, ignited an impassioned renewal of the nature-nurture controversy by his suggestion that compensatory education's "apparent failure" was due more to genetic endowment than inadequacies of the home environment or public schooling.[27]

In the early 1970s, the educational research on inequality was being cited by such persons as New York *Times* news analyst Max Frankel, in whose discussion of various egalitarian strategies it was stated "that raising expenditures for facilities and teachers in largely segregated schools of poor communities is the least promising approach."[28] In its 1974 "Annual Education Review," the *New York Times* cited research questioning the ability of schooling to reduce poverty as "striking a very raw nerve" among many educators. "With the annual cost of schooling more than doubled since 1960, many have had cause to wonder if it was worth it."[29] The following year, the *American School Board Journal* found "the research pretty much saying that no matter what we do in operating our schools it has virtually no affect on the way children turn out." The Journal continued by quoting a research review concluding that Head Start and Title I "resources involved have not made much of a difference in the progress of children from disadvantaged environments."[30] Discouraging as well was a national evaluation of Title VII of ESEA or the so-called Bilingual Education Act legislated by Congress in 1968. During the 1975-76 school year, the American Institutes for Research (AIR) compared students enrolled in Title VII Spanish/English projects with similar children who had not participated in those bilingual programs. AIR found Title VII children achieving slightly lower in reading than nonparticipants and about the same in math as the children without bilingual education.[31]

Research such as this has perhaps contributed to criticism of bilingual education found in academic journals, literary magazines, and the daily press. For example, the *Modern Language Journal*, a publication geared to teachers of language, has contained articles by scholars from the field of psychology, linguistics, and English that have questioned the pedagogical merit of bilingual education, and Tom Bethell, the Washington editor of *Harpers* magazine, has delivered a scathing attack on bilingualism, labeling the government who spends millions annually on such bilingual education as having a "death wish" to turn the United States of America into little more than ethnic enclaves.[32] The *Washington Post* has feared that bilingual education will weaken the "common American glue" and *Time* magazine has reported the "swamping" of English by Hispanics in southern Florida.[33] Even the *New York Times*, traditionally associated with liberalism, assailed "expensive bilingual education programs" that "every known pedological theory" tells us will never work.[34] In another editorial, the editors found most bilingual education "unacceptable politically as well as educationally" since it appears to be championed largely by "people who believe that non-English-speaking separatism is indispensable to their own political influence."[35]

U.C.L.A. Graduate School of Education Dean John Goodlad wrote in 1975 that "it is exceedingly doubtful that schools, *as now generally conceived and conducted*, can make much of a difference. Noting the brevity of the school experience ("less than seven percent of all learning hours by the age of thirteen; a little more than eight percent by the age of seventeen"), Goodlad contended that "profound changes" in education must occur for schooling to significantly reduce existing achievement inequalities stemming from home environment inequalities.[36]

During the middle to late 1970s, the research on preschool education and Title I began yielding more promising results, and by 1980 there was also some impressive evidence that the process of schooling *did* make a difference.[37] Nevertheless, the disappointing research findings of the 1960s and early to mid-1970s may have contributed to a national mood of dissatisfaction with education in general and federal programs in particular that prevailed throughout the late 1970s and early 1980s.

Resistance to Busing

The negativism associated with federally sponsored initiatives in the field of compensatory education was mild in comparison with the outcry over busing, another egalitarian strategy that received most of its impetus from the federal level. Following a period of snail's-paced compliance with the 1954 and 1955 Supreme Court decisions that declared "separate educational facilities . . . inherently unequal" and ordered school segregation to be eliminated "with all-deliberate speed," it was not until the Kennedy-Johnson civil rights initiative was finally signed into law as the Civil Rights Act of 1964 that there was any federal bite behind the desegregation bark. Accordingly, by the spring of 1965, Frances Keppel, United States Education Commissioner, had threatened the unavailability of federal funding for any school district that had not completely desegregated its schools by September 1967.[38]

While most Americans may have opposed school segregation, they were sickened by the antics of racists in Little Rock, Arkansas, Oxford, Mississippi, and Montgomery, Alabama, or by the necessity to use armed troops to guarantee safe passage for James Meredith at the University of Mississippi; it became increasingly evident throughout the late 1960s and 1970s that the body politic did not favor the use of the schoolbus as a desegregation tool.

Reflecting up on a decade of polling public attitude toward education, George Gallup stated that between 1969 and 1978 "the problems associated with integration have been named often enough to place integration/segregation second only to discipline as the major problem facing the local schools. However . . . it is not integration itself that is the main source of the trouble but the means for bringing it about: namely busing."[39] Gallup polls in April 1970, and September of 1971, for example, show respectively 86 percent and 76 percent of the sample opposing busing, suggesting a ground swell of antipathy that appeared to affect both executive and legislative Washington. By March 1972, President Nixon had asked for a "moratorium" on all new court-ordered busing; three years later, a reported twenty-three antibusing proposals were pending in Congress![40] Reflecting upon George Wallace's victory in the Florida primary in 1972, the *New York Times* made these comments:

> The score sheets of the Florida primary indicates that a majority of the voters were united on just one issue—opposition to school busing . . . [However] responsible candidates ought not overlook that other Florida referendum, overwhelmingly endorsed by the voters, which urged quality education for all children and rejected a return to a dual, segregated school system.[41]

In his book entitled *Busing*, social psychologist Thomas Cottle suggested that opposition on the part of many to busing goes well beyond simple bigotry: "Anyone who listens to the people whose lives are directly affected by busing, or indeed people who feel implicated in busing decisions," contends Cottle, "knows well that what he or she is hearing is not the expression of a simple attitude or opinion. One hears powerful recitations that evoke theological and sociological imagery, historical accounts and personal episodes, experiences that have resounded so intensely in the lives of these people, their bodies respond in the telling of their stories."[42]

By the midseventies, the bleeding that was Boston served as an ugly symbol of the often violent opposition to busing that may have become particularly virulent because it threatened the security of working class whites with a strong sense of identity and neighborhood in predominately ethnically Irish South Boston. Contending that desegregation policies unfairly inflict greater pain on the working class than on the poor, Harvard psychologist Robert Cole quotes a white mother living in South Boston.

> I'm not against any individual child. I am not a racist, no matter what those high-and-mighty suburban liberals with their picket signs say. I just won't have my children bused to some God-awful slum school, and I don't want children from God knows where coming over here. We put our last cent into this home. We both work to keep up with the mortgage and all the expenses . . . We just want to live peacefully out here. We want our children to grow up in a quiet, decent neighborhood . . . We want to see them off to school, and not sit for the rest of the day wondering, are they safe, and will there be a fight, and are they afraid even to walk home if they miss the bus?[43]

Cole's argument has been forwarded by Lillian Rubin of the Wright Institute, who concludes a study of attitudes toward busing in Richmond, California, by stating that "from Boston and from Richmond the response is the same—a cry of outrage and pain . . . [by] the people who have worked hard all their lives and have little to show for it." According to Rubin, working and lower middle class opposition to busing is greater than among the middle class and stems in part because they feel "less secure about their children's fare under the plan to integrate, and less sure that they would be able to influence that plan or their children's destiny."[44]

Part of reason why the white middle class was less opposed to busing than their working class counterpart may have involved their departure from desegregated situations. At the height of Boston's racial disorders, sociologist James Coleman and his colleagues received considerable public attention for their research in major urban school districts that concluded that middle class whites were indeed influencing their children's destiny by fleeing school districts because of concerns over forced busing. A decade earlier, Coleman's *Equality of Educational Opportunity Survey* had ignited a national debate over the effects of schooling. Interestingly, Coleman's 1966 report found "composition of the student body" (percentage of whites) as one of the few school variables that had a consistent, positive relationship with pupil achievement; blacks appeared to benefit modestly from desegregated schooling. Coleman's data had been used repeatedly in support of constructing busing policies. This time, however, Coleman argued that forcing the issue was counterproductive: "Ironically, desegregation may be increasing segregation . . . eliminating Central City segregation does not help if it increases greatly the segregation between districts caused by white loss."[45] In Coleman's mind, busing was the major culprit in promoting the "white flight" he observed in twenty of the nation's largest school districts.[46] Publicly espousing his views during 1975 in racially troubled Boston and before the Senate Judiciary Committee, Coleman's testimonies at this time provided scholarly ammunition for opponents of desegregation through busing. As a well-known early proponent of desegregation, Coleman's apparent about-face received extensive media coverage, while the numerous scholarly rebuttals in the professional questioning of the scientific validity of his conclusions went virtually unnoticed.[47]

Urban Population Change

For whatever reason, the 1960s and 1970s saw an increasing displacement of whites by minorities in urban centers throughout the nation. By 1977, every major American city (with the exception of Jacksonville, Columbus, Ohio, Indianapolis, Nashville, Milwaukee, Pittsburgh, San Diego, and Seattle) had a minority of white pupils in its public schools. Diane Ravitz summarizes this phenomenon by pointing out that "between 1968 and the last school year [1976-77] Atlanta lost 78.3 percent of its white enrollment; Detroit 61.6 percent, San Antonio, 53.3 percent; St. Louis, 45 percent; Denver 42.4 percent and Los Angeles, 37.5 percent."[48] The fact that most large American urban districts are predominately composed of minority is not unusual in itself, for it is little different from the existing situation around the turn of the century when children from large immigrant enclaves populated many of the nation's urban schools. What is different today, contends Ravitz, is that we now have policies that call for significant integration of the minority and majority populations that become increasingly difficult (if not impossible) as the minority becomes increasingly numerically superior. As Ravitz states it, another "important point is that a very large proportion of these children come from low-income families, in many instances from female-headed, welfare-dependent families and that this is the most difficult and most expensive pupil population to educate." Ravitz continues that "the cost of educating a poor population—providing the necessary special education, remedial instruction, medical and social services, as well as security guards and vandalism repairs is clearly greater than that of educating a middle class population," particularly when one includes urban teacher salaries, and such things as the greater energy and supply costs.[49]

Accordingly, the major dilemma facing most schools in recent years appears to be particularly acute in urban areas. Concurrent with the growth of the "objective needs" of urban education has been a diminishing revenue base to pay for services. How to do better with less becomes even more difficult when the urban tax base is eroded, when population decline and voter registration decline reduces political clout of the major cities in the legislature, and when urban schools must compete more vigorously with other crucial services such as police and fire protection and health care. According to Ravitz

> When the big cities turn to the state government for aid, they tend to get an unsympathetic response from legislatures dominated by a suburban and rural majority with little interest in paying more taxes to subsidize city schools . . . . The fact that the schools are perceived as nonwhite enclaves that are inefficient, ineffective and poorly disciplined and infinitely capable of consuming tax money without producing tangible results merely confirms the present position of state legislators not to provide additional subsidies.[50]

Even if the urban systems were to receive the same sympathetic ears from suburbia that occurred in the 1960s, it is unlikely they would receive adequate funding due to the diminished financial support for schooling in general. Throughout most of the period spanning the last four decades, there had been a substantial increase in per pupil expenditures, having risen from $100 per annum in 1940 to nearly $2,000 a year in 1980. Even when controlling for inflation, school expenditures increased more than 500 percent during that forty-year period. During the late 1970s, however, the tide had begun to turn and spending for education in most states was no longer keeping pace with inflation.[51]

The New Right

Contributing further to the erosion of support for public education during the late 1970s was the politics of the "New Right." Represented by such "well-heeled" conservative organizations as the Pro-Family Movement, the Moral Majority, the National Conservative Political Action Committee (NCPAC), and the Conservative Caucus, much of the rhetoric of the "New Right" is directed toward a reaffirmation and reimposition of what has been termed "traditional" American values, including an emphasis on a public role for religion. Viewing the world as embattled by the polarized and irreconcilable forces of good and evil, activists such as Paul Weyrich, leader of the self-proclaimed "Pro-Family Movement," speak of the "age-old conflict . . . between the forces of God and the forces against God," the latter of which is attempting "to prevent souls from reaching eternal salvation." Accordingly, the supposed pro-family movement "feels not just a political commitment to battle these forces."[52] Education political analyst J. Charles Park describes Weyrich and other New Right leaders as a part of a "Star Wars conflict . . . between the forces of political and religious truth and those of evil and godliness" and that ". . . public education, with its commitment to pluralism and religious neutrality, is cast in the role of arch-enemy Darth Vader."[53] Such persons believe that the public schools are permeated by the godless religion of "secular humanism," which does not teach right and expose wrong, and does not view family or American values with the necessary respect.[54] Principal targets within the educational arena have been the bans on school prayer, the use of improper books, and the teaching of evolution as scientific truth.

It would, of course, be unfair and unwise for educators to think of the New Right as largely conspiratorial, and representing only the lunatic fringe, for the zealousness and growth of the movement is, in part, responsive to the mood of a sizable share of the public. While the granting of equal time to the teaching of "creationist science" may have little public support, there is little question that the New Right's positions on such issues as the legitimacy of school prayer and more careful textbook selection for private schools were supported by a significant percentage of American body politic at the end of the seventies. A Gallup Poll in 1980 found 55 percent of the sample in favor of permitting prayer in the public schools.[55] Regarding the textbooks issue, the Office of Intellectual Freedom of the American Library Association reported more than 910 censorship cases during the decade between 1966 and 1975 (62 percent of which were directed at K-12 schools and the remainder at the public libraries and higher education), reflecting an increase of 3,707 in the number of censored items.[56] Although there was a leveling off of censored items in the early 1970s, the American Library Association has reported an upsurge of censorship cases during the late 1970s. During the 1980 school year an American Library Association Survey found more than 30 percent of American libraries and 20 percent of the nation's school districts reporting censorship problems.[57]

Responding to J. Charles Park's comments, Connaught Marshner, Chairman of the National Pro-Family Coalition, points out that millions of Americans in 1980 "adhere to the great tenet of Judeo-Christian civilization: that truth exists and that we can know it" and that rather than restrict pluralism, the Pro-Family movement actually enhances it by supporting ". . . the rights of private schools to exist" and the broadening of the curriculum to include such topics as creationism as well as evolution.[58] Continues Marshner:

> Some parents will want their children taught progressive education. We say fine, that is their right to choose. But some other parents will want their children taught traditional education. Why cannot Park grant that that is our right to choose? Why cannot public education be responsive to all parents' wishes?[59]

Writing in 1980, Marshner felt that "it is the education establishment which is so paranoid to view the very existence of private education as a threat to them. Why is it so terrified by competition from the private sector? Because somehow or other, their publicly funded, lavishly ideologized product, public education, is having trouble competing."[60]

The 1980 Campaign

During 1980, much of the moralistic rhetoric associated with the right wing extremism of the few* became the recommended policy of the many. Contending that public education was indeed in trouble and infested by "manipulative and sometimes amoral indoctrination," the 1980 Republican Party platform "support[ed]... initiatives in Congress to restore the right of individuals to participate in voluntary, nondenominational prayer in schools . . . [and] a system of educational assistance based on tax credits that will in part compensate parents for their financial sacrifices in paying tuition at the elementary, secondary, and post-secondary level." In addition, the platform addressed the broader issues of local control and deregulation by stating that "because federal assistance should help local school districts, not tie them up in red tape, we will strive to replace the crazy quilt of wasteful programs with a system of block grants that will restore decision making to local officials responsible to voters and parents." Furthermore,

> We understand and sympathize with the plight of America's public school teachers, who so frequently find their time and attention diverted from their teaching responsibilities to the task of complying with federal reporting requirements. America has a great stake in maintaining standards of high quality in public education. The Republican Party recognizes that the achievement of these standards is possible only to the extent that teachers are allowed the time and freedom to teach. *To that end, the Republican Party supports deregulation by the Federal Government of public education, and* encourages elimination of the Federal Department of Education.

It was precisely Ronald Reagan's endorsement of the Department of Education's demise that provoked the ire of the largest and most influential body of teachers, the National Education Association (NEA), 1.678 million members strong. As noted in the previous chapter, NEA efforts to elect Carter in 1976 helped pave the way for

---

*According to Paul Weyrich, the Congressional component of the so-called "pro-family" movement included Garn (R-UT), Jesse Helms (R-NC), Gordon Humphry (R-NH), Paul Laxalt (R-NV), John Ashbrook (R-OH), Bob Bauman (R-MD), Phil Crane (R-IL), Jim Jefries (R-KS), Larry McDonald (D-GA), Bob Dorman (R-CA), Henry Hyde (R-IL), and B. Walker (R-PA).

the ED's creation, an occurrence that symbolized for many Washington's commitment to education. Accordingly, in 1980, the NEA strongly opposed the Reagan candidacy. In a preelection editorial in *Today's Education, the Journal of the National Education Association,* NEA President Willard McGuire chastised Reagan's opposition to "the continued existence of the Department of Education" and "even the moderate level of federal support for education that exists today." McGuire contended that since January 1977, "the President and teachers . . . with Congressional friends . . . have dramatically increased federal support for education [and have] brought about a separate Department of Education (ED) [that] . . . increases the visibility of education and enhances its position among the nation's highest priorities."[62]

The NEA's position that the reelection candidacy of Carter and Mondale offered proponents of strong public education "a clear-cut choice" and was based, not only on the opposing views of the Democratic and Republican parties concerning the existence of ED and general federal support for education, but on their differing stance on such issues as tuition tax credits, sex equity and block grants. The NEA contended that "this year's presidential election will have a tremendous impact on our country throughout the rest of the century."[63] The nation's largest teachers' union lauded the Democratic education platform that hailed the 73 percent increase in federal education aid under Carter, excluded any endorsement of tuition tax credits, renewed "its commitment to eliminating discrimination in education because of sex [by demanding] full and expeditious enforcement of Title IX," reiterated its pledge to support "concentrated spending" on such groups as "the disadvantaged, the handicapped, those with limited language skills," as well as the American Indian, and the racially segregated.[64]

The NEA's position on an array of educational and social issues such as censorship ("The Association urges its affiliates to seek the removal of laws and regulations which restrict the selection of a diversity of instructional materials or which limit educators in the selection of such materials"),[65] unionization, sexual equality and national health insurance ("the President and teachers will continue to work toward—establishment of collective bargaining rights for teachers and other public employees, ratification of the Equal

Rights Amendment, establishment of a system of health insurance that would . . . guarantee . . . the availability of basic medical services"); taxation and resource distribution ("The Kemp-Roth 30 percent tax-cuts proposal . . . would be far more beneficial to wealthy citizens [and] would drastically reduce funds . . . for human needs"), and national defense ("a 30 percent reduction in taxes"), plus Reagan's plans for "a massive increase in military spending [that] . . . would obviously cripple the funding of remaining programs," may have made its more activist members* a microcosm of liberal America in 1980.[66]

Given its loyalty to President Carter, its general association with liberalism, and its distaste for the Republican alternative, the National Education Association played an influential role in the political events leading up to the November 1980 presidential election. In 1979, the NEA Political Action Committee recommended that Carter be supported in the Presidential primaries, a policy that was later endorsed by the Association's Board of Directors by the overwhelming margin of 118-4. Forty-nine of the fifty NEA's state-level affiliates concurred with the national body's recommendation and the Association's energies were pumped into supporting Carter's early successes in the Florida and Iowa primaries. Following a Carter address to the NEA Representative Assembly in Los Angeles in early July, the 7,500 delegates voted by a margin of more than 3-1 to support the President's candidacy for reelection. At the August Democratic National Convention in New York, teachers were represented as delegates or alternates in unprecedented numbers, and 414 of the 464 were Carter backers. NEA representatives also occupied important positions at the convention as state delegation chairs and as members of key committees, for example, the Chair of Human Needs Section of the Platform Committee, the component that addresses educational and social issues, was an NEA member.[67]

---

*The fact that NEA leadership has played an important role in Democratic Presidential politics does not necessarily mean that the organization's representatives mirror its members' political views. In 1980, 40 percent of NEA members were Democrats, 24 percent were Republican and 35 percent claimed no party affiliation. (Source: *Today's Education: The Journal of the National Education Association*, 69(4): p. 20GE, November-December 1980.)

Reagan Takes Office

Political analysts have offered a myriad of reasons for the failure of Jimmy Carter to gain the voters' approval in November of 1980. Among the more frequently cited explanations are the failure of the hostage rescue mission in Iran, spiraling inflation, the President's image as an ineffective leader, and the reluctance of many influential Democrats to endorse the Carter candidacy until late in the game. (Indeed, if Carter had received the same degree of support from the Democratic party organization that he received from the National Education Association, such unanimity in itself might have been enough to reelect him. Beyond Carter's own performance, voter discomfort with the traditional liberalism associated with dominant forces within the Democratic Party since the days of Franklin Roosevelt was another contributory factor to the election of the conservative alternative, Ronald Reagan. In 1980, the citizenry seemed to be tired of Washington-generated social programs that were often viewed as costly and ineffective. The liberal approach of spending more money and concentrating greater power in Washington in order to tackle the problems associated with such conditions as poverty and discrimination appeared to have run its course in many voters' minds. Tired of the burgeoning growth and regulatory powers of the federal government, many state and local officials welcomed, or at least were receptive to, the Republican call for greater decentralization and deregulation. Capitalizing on a conservative trend that saw the public increasingly concerned about a stagnating economy enabled champions of antiabortion legislation, school prayer, and fundamentalist values to call themselves the "moral majority." Ronald Reagan found the climate ripe for proposing fundamental changes in the tax structure, for dramatically reducing social spending, for reiterating Republican distaste to forced busing, and for standing in opposition to the Equal Rights Amendment. Ironically, a political current that had popularized Carter's candidacy in 1976 may have been partly responsible for his 1980 demise. As a God-fearing, grass roots politician from Georgia, Carter's quiet simplicity and anti-Washington rhetoric had captured the attention of many in the midseventies who had become increasingly antagonistic toward the federal government. In 1980, however, Carter the Outsider had become Carter the

Washington Establishment, associated with the governmental ills of bureaucratic growth, regulation, and deficits.

In his July 17 Republican nomination acceptance speech, Ronald Reagan's public message was that "our Federal Government is overgrown and overweight . . . [and] should go on a diet." Calling for a "freeze on Federal hiring" and a "detailed review of every department, bureau and agency that live by Federal appropriation," candidate Reagan promised to "put an end to the notion that the American taxpayer exists to fund the Federal Government. The Federal Government exists to serve the American and to be accountable to the American people. On January 20, we are going to reestablish that truth."[68]

And as he might put it himself, Reagan hit the ground running. Addressing a nation that had given him a landslide electoral victory, his inauguration speech reiterated his pledge "to curb the size and influence of the Federal establishment and to demand recognition of the distinction between powers granted to the Federal Government and those reserved to the states or to the people."[69] Nearly a month later, in his State of the Union Address, the new President recommended that the traditional American governmental reliance on decentralization be reestablished in part by "convert[ing] a number of categorical programs into block grants to reduce wasteful administrative overhead and to give local government entities and states more flexibility and control." Responding to those who feared "reduction of aid to schools'," Reagan "point[ed] out that Federal aid to education amounts to only 8 percent of total educational funding [and] for this the Federal Government has insisted on a tremendously disproportionate share of control over our schools. Whatever reductions we've proposed in the eight percent will amount to very little of the total cost of education [but] . . . will, however restore more authority to states and local school districts."[70]

Proposal to Dismantle the Department of Education

Within the first few weeks of his swearing-in, President Reagan focused on proposals for federal spending cuts, consolidation of programs and administrative agencies, as well as "search[ing] out areas of waste, extravagance and costly administrative overhead which could yield additional and substantial reductions."[71] Plans to abolish the Department of Education (ED) were first outlined in the Reagan budget, released on February 6, 1981. The President proposed replacing ED with a "Foundation for Educational Assistance," with a substantially reduced budget of $8.8 billion. Several programs with a $1.2 billion dollar price tag, including the enforcement of civil rights, would be transferred elsewhere. For Fiscal Year 1981 (the 1980-81 school year), it was recommended that education spending total $10.3 ($4.4 billion for elementary, secondary, and vocational education; $4.8 for colleges and universities; and $1.1 billion for research and miscellaneous programs), a figure significantly under the $13 billion figure proposed by Jimmy Carter for FY 1982 (1981-82 school year). Included in Reagan's FY'83 budget were substantial cuts in Title I of the Elementary and Secondary Education Act (the largest federal education program aiding underachieving children), sharp reductions in programs assisting college students such as Pell grants, work study, the basing of student loans on a financial needs test, and the elimination of loans for graduate students, as well as the elimination of scores of categorical programs such as consumer education and ethnic heritage by their incorporation into block grants. The new administration also proposed rescinding more than $1 billion from FY'82 (school year 1981-82) educational appropriations.[72]

The dramatic success of the Reagan Administration in securing many of the recommended cuts and program consolidations or eliminations will be addressed in the forthcoming chapter. However, Reagan's efforts to abolish the Department of Education have not moved with equal speed. While the President believes that "the creation of the Department of Education symbolized the progressive intrusion of the Federal Government into an educational system that has drawn its strength from diversity, adaptability, and local control," he and his Congressional supporters have been more concerned with reducing spending and legislating programmatic changes than in attacking symbols, particularly given what appears to be Congress's lukewarm feelings about tampering with the new Education Department.

The foundation concept suggested by the President has disappointed ED opponents nearly as much as its supporters. Writing for the *Congressional Quarterly Weekly Report*, Andy Plattner and

Harrison Donnelly stated that "Reagan's foundation proposal, outlined in the budget, was an uneasy compromise between his promise to get rid of ED as a cabinet agency and (Education Secretary) Bell's reluctance to allow education once again to be submerged in some other, larger department."[73] Part of Bell's opposition to reconstituting a Department of Health, Education and Welfare (HEW) stems from the frustrations he apparently felt as United States Commissioner of Education during the Ford Administration, when education was often viewed with little value within HEW.

Proponents of a separate Education Department will not roll over easily. For example, Senator Dan Quayle of Indiana and Representative John Erlenborn of Illinois believe that education programs should not be centralized in any form. Erlenborn, a leader of the opposition to ED's creation, still contends that, as a part of HEW, the Office of Education "was interfering too much with local education agencies even then," and thus he desires the dispersal of education programs among several departments.[75] The new Department of Education had received opposition from such groups as the Taxpayers' Education Lobby and the Public Service Research Council that had engineered Congressional letter-writing campaigns soliciting opposition to ED. The foundation concept took "the steam out of the drive." *The Congressional Quarterly Weekly* analysts believe that "for while the proposal would demote the department from cabinet status, it would still retain a federal education entity, which is what the conservative groups object to."[76] It appears that most of the education lobby groups based in Washington still support the departmental concept and have assembled a broad coalition prepared to defend ED if and when the administration launches its legislative assault.

At this writing (summer of 1983), President Reagan appears to have temporarily abandoned any plans to abolish the Department of Education. With only 23 percent of the sampled public endorsing ED's abolition,[77] the Reagan team is probably ill suited to fight a legislative battle that, at best, would result in a victory more symbolic than substantive. More important to the Administration has become the Congressional budget battle over domestic spending and education funds and the political implications of a report by the National Commission on Excellence in Education (NCEE), in which the American education system was chastised for its mediocrity in academic standards and teacher preparation. Calling for such reforms as school requiring more English, math and science, and teacher merit pay, the public appears to have embraced some of the report's recommendations.

The degree of public endorsement of the NCEE's essentially conservative recommendation is indicative of some stability to a political wind that has preservered until the early 1970s. In the minds of many, the Washington-based educational order contributed a good deal to the public dissatisfaction by busing children to schools far from home, pushing in what has been termed "reverse discrimination masquerading as affirmative action," imposing on school administrators and school boards onerous, costly regulations; appearing to sacrifice discipline and safety in pursuit of egalitarian principles; consistently opposing any form of prayer in the classroom; and by overwhelming the educational institutions with a hodge podge of categorical programs that seemingly promoted everything (consumerism, ethnic growth, metric growth, sex equity) but academic excellence.

Thus the mood of the body politic in general and state officium in particular was receptive to changes in the political order, and, once changed, became even more responsive to the persuasiveness and political acumen of the newest occupant of the executive mansion.

REFERENCES

1. Elam, S.M.: *A Decade of Gallup Polls of Attitudes Toward Education, 1969-1978.* Bloomington, Indiana, Phi Delta Kappa, Inc., 1979.
2. Jennings, J.F.: The Federal Role In Paying For Education In The 80's. In Miller, R. (ed.): *The Federal Role in Education: New Directions For The Eighties.* Washington, D.C., Institute For Educational Leadership, 1981, p. 5–13.
3. Jennings, The Federal Role, p. 11.
4. Jennings, The Federal Role, p.
5. Jennings, The Federal Role, p. 10.
6. See Stanfield, R.: Federal Aid To Cities: Is It A Mixed Blessing?, *National Journal Reports,* 65 (22): 868–72, 1978.
7. For analyses of the changing federal role see Schuster, J.: Out of the Frying Pan: The Politics of Education in a New Era. *Phi Delta Kappan,* 63(9): p. 583-91, May 1982, Berke, J. and Moore, M.: A Developmental View of the Current Federal Government Role in Elementary & Secondary Education, *Phi Delta*

Kappan, 63(5):333–37, Jan. 1982; Edwards, H.: *Higher Education and The Unholy Crusade Against Government Regulation.* Cambridge, Mass.; Harvard University Institute for Educational Management, 1980.

8. Quoted in Scott, R.: The Hidden Court of Government Regulations, *Change.* 10(4): 16–23, April 1978.

9. Scott, R., The Hidden Court of Governmental Regulations, pp. 16–23.

10. Scott, R., The Hidden Court of Governmental Regulations, p. 86.

11. Scott, The Hidden Court of Governmental Regulations, p. 16.

12. Scott, The Hidden Court of Governmental Regulations, p. 16.

13. Scott, The Hidden Court of Governmental Regulations, p. 16.

14. Moynihan, D.P.: State vs. Academe, *Harpers*, 261: 31–40, December, 1980.

15. Moynihan, State vs. Academe, p. 32.

16. *A Program For Renewal Partnership. The Report of the Sloan Commission on Government and Higher Education. An Overview*, Cambridge, Massachusetts, Sloan Commission on Government and Higher Education, ERIC Document Reproduction Service, ED 184 497, 1980.

17. *A Program For Renewal Partnership*, ED 184 497, 1980.

18. United States, House Committee on Education and Labor, Subcommittee on Elementary, Secondary and Vocational Education, Hearing on Title I, Elementary and Secondary Education ACT Regulations, 96th Congress, First Session, October 16, 1979, p. 4.

19. United States, House Committee on Education and Labor, p. 4.

20. United States, House Committee on Education and Labor, pp. 4–5.

21. United States, House Committee on Education and Labor, p. 5.

22. Coleman, J., et al.: *Equality of Educational Opportunity*, Washington, D.C., U.S. Department of Health, Education and Welfare, U.S. Government Printing Office, 1966, p. iii, 274, 300, 324.

23. *The Impact of Head Start: An Evaluation of the Effects of Head Start on Children's Cognitive and Affective Development.* Arlington, Virginia, ERIC Document Reproduction Service, ED 036 321, 1969.

24. *The Impact of Head Start*, 1969.

25. Jensen, A.: How Much Can We Boost IQ and Scholastic Achievement. *Harvard Education Review*, 39 (1): 1969.

26. Beckler, J.: Congress and the Administration Scrutinize the Results of Title I. *School Management*, 14 (9): 6, 1970.

27. Jensen, How Much Can We Boost IQ, 1969.

28. Franzel, M.: A Subtle But Sweeping Reversal, *New York Times*, March 8, 1972, p. 66.

29. Reinhold, R.: School Role in Poverty Context, *New York Times*, January 8, 1973, p. 55el.

30. Arnold, B.: Summarized Nicely Is What Educational Research Is Mumbling, *The American School Board Journal*, 160 (2): 6–7, February 1973.

31. Danoff, M.: *Evaluation of the Impact of ESEA Title VIII Spanish/English Bilingual Education Program*, Palo Alto, California, American Institutes for Research, 1978.

32. See Ricardo Otheguy, R. and Otto, R. in The Myth of Static Maintenance in

Bilingual Education, *The Modern Language Journal,* 64 (3): 350-56, Autumn 1980; Edwards, J.: Critics and Criticisms of Bilingual Education, *The Modern Language Journal,* 64(4): 409-15, Winter 1980; Bethell, T.: Against Bilingual Education, *Harper's Magazine,* February 1979. Reprinted in *The Modern Language Journal,* 63 (5-6): 276-80, September-October 1979.

33. Edwards, Critics and Criticism, p. 412.

34. Quoted in Otheguy, R.: Thinking About Bilingual Education, *Harvard Education Review,* 52(3): 301-14, August 1982.

35. Many Voices But One Language, *New York Times* Editorial, August 12, 1979, p. 20e.

36. Goodland, J.: Schools Can Make A Difference, *Educational Leadership,* 33 (2): 108-17, November 1975.

37. See Marcus, L. and Stickney, B., *Race and Education: The Unending Controversy.* Springfield, Illinois, Charles C Thomas, 1981, p. 194-218.

38. Buncher, J. (ed.): *The School Busing Controversy: 1970-75.* New York, New York, Facts on File, Inc., 1975, p. 9.

39. Elam, *A Decade of Gallup Polls,* p. 2.

40. Buncher, *The School Busing Controversy: 1970-75,* p. 10.

41. Buncher, *The School Busing Controversy: 1970-75,* p. 239.

42. Cottle, T.: *Busing.* Boston, Massachusetts, Beacon Press, 1976, p. xiii.

43. Coles, R.: *The Buses Roll.* New York, New York, W. W. Norton & Co., 1974, p. 27, quoted in Buncher, *The School Busing Controversy: 1970-75,* p. 1.

44. Rubin, L.: White Against White: School Desegregation and the Revolt Of Middle America, In Levinsohn, F. and Wright, B. (eds.): *School Desegregation: Shadow and Substance,* Chicago, Illinois, University of Chicago Press, 1976, p. 67-83.

45. Coleman, J.: Racial Segregation In The Schools: New Research With Policy Implications. *Phi Delta Kappan,* October, 57 (2): 75-78, 1975. Quoted in Ribin, S. and Bosco, J.: Coleman's Desegregation Research and Policy Recommendations. *School Review,* 84 (3): 354, 1976.

46. See also, Coleman, J., Kelly, S., and Moore, J.: *Recent Trends in School Integration.* Paper presented at the annual meeting of the American Educational Research Association, Washington, D.C., April 2, 1975.

47. See, for example, Pettigrew, T. and Green, R.: School Desegregation In Large Cities: A Critique of the Coleman 'White Flight' Thesis. *Harvard Education Review,* 46 (1): 1-53, 1976.

48. Ravitch, D.: A Bifurcated Vision of Urban Education. In Newitt, J. (ed.): *Future Trends In Education Policy,* Lexington, Massachusetts, Lexington Books, 1979, p. 75.

49. Ravitch, A Bifurcated Vision, p. 76.

50. Ravitch, A Bifurcated Vision, pp. 76-77.

51. Timar, T. and Guthrie, J.: Public Values and Public School Policy In The 1980's. *Educational Leadership,* 38 (2): 112-15, November 1980.

52. Quoted in Park, J.C.: The New Right: Threat To Democracy In Education. *Educational Leadership,* 38 (2), 146-49, November 1980.

53. Park, The New Right, p. 146.

54. Park, The New Right, p. 146.
55. Gallup, G.H.: Key Educational Issues. *The Gallup Poll.* Wilmington, Del., SR Scholarly Resources, Inc., 1981, p. 250–51.
56. Woods, L.B., Is Academic Freedom Dead in Schools? *Phi Delta Kappan* 61 (2): 104–106, October, 1979.
57. *See* Parker, B.: Target: Public Schools, *Graduate Woman. 75(5):* p. 10–13, September-October 1981.
58. Marshner, C. The Pro-Family Movement, A Response to Charles Parks *Educational Leadership,* 38(2): 152 & 153, November 1980.
59. Marshner, The Pro-Family Movement, p. 152-153.
60. Marshner, The Pro-Family Movement, pp. 152-153.
61. 1980 Political Platforms: The Republican Education Platform. In Miller, R. (ed.): *Federal Role in Education: New Direction for the Eighties.* Washington, D.C., Institute for Educational Leadership, 1981, p. 101–103.
62. McGuire, W. Carter-Mondale: A Clean Cut Choice. Todays Education: *The Journal of the National Education Association* 69(4): 16–18 GE, November-December 1980.
63. McGuire, Carter-Mondale, p. 17 GE.
64. McGuire, Carter-Mondale, p. 17–18 GE; 1980 Political Platforms: The Democratic Education Platform, *Federal Role in Education.* pp. 103-109.
65. Selection of Materials and Teaching Techniques, *NEA Reporter,* Sept., 1980, Reprinted in English, R. Politics of Textbook Adoption, *Phi Delta Kappan* 62(4): 277, December 1980.
66. McGuire, Carter-Mondale, p. 17–18 GE.
67. Teacher Unite to Re-elect Carter Mondale, *Today's Education: The Journal of the National Education Association.* 69(4): 19-71 GE. November-December 1980.
68. Reagan, R.: Republican National Convention Presidential Nomination Acceptance Address, July 17, 1980, Reprinted in *Vital Speeches of the Day,* 46. (21): 642–46, August 15, 1980.
69. Reagan, R.: Inaugural Address, January 20th, 1981. Reprinted in *Congressional Quarterly Almanac,* 1981, Washington, D.C.
70. Reagan, R.: State of the Union Message, February 18, 1981. Reprinted in Ibid., p. 15–18E.
71. *See* Reagan, R.: A Program for Economic Recovery-Address by the President of the United States. Delivered before a joint session of Congress Feb. 18, 1981, *Congressional Record,* 127 (25): H 510-14, Feb. 18, 1981. Reagan, R.: The State of the Nation's Economy. Delivered to the American People from the White House, Feb. 5, 1981, reprinted in *Vital Speeches of the Day,* 47(9): 290-93, February 15, 1981.
72. Ohara, P.: Fiscal 1983 Budget: Cut Education Funds, Abolish Department, Reagan urges, *Congressional Quarterly Weekly Report,* 40(7): 265–66, February 13, 1982.
73. Plattner, A. & Donnelly, H.: No Action Expected This Year on Reagan Plan To Dismantle Two Cabinet Departments, *Congressional Quarterly Weekly Report* 40(15): 783–86, April 10, 1982.

74. Plattner & Donnelly, No Action Expected, pp. 783–786.
75. Stanfield, R.L.: Breaking Up the Education Department—School Aid May Be The Real Target, *National Journal*, 13(43): 1907–1910, October 24, 1981.
76. Plattner & Donnelly, Breaking Up the Education Department, p. 786.
77. The Politics of Education: What the Public Thinks, (A Gallup Organization Education Poll for *Newsweek*). *Newsweek*, June 27, 1983, p. 61.
78. For a similar, more detailed analysis of this conservative trend, *see* Finn, C.E.: Toward a new Consensus, *Change*, 13(6): p. 16–21+, September, 1981.

Chapter 3

CUTS, CONSOLIDATION, AND COMPROMISE

The Reagan "Redirection": Mandate for Change?

If public dissatisfaction with liberalism contributed to the Republican landslide victory in 1980, it is Ronald Reagan, the president, who nurtured the nation's mood to gain general approval of his radical recommendations for altering the federal role in education. Many analysts contend that the huge margin of Reagan's electoral victory and the significant Republican gains in the Senate (12) and the House of Representatives (33) had much more to do with the public's verdict on Carter's competence than a philosophic mandate for conservative government. The fact that many distinguished Democratic senators such as George McGovern and Frank Church were among the legislative victims of the Republican sweep may have had less to do with political learnings than with public rejection of what was perceived as an inept president and his associated status quo. It is unlikely that the average voter in 1980 embraced supply-side economics, was strongly in favor of massive cuts in domestic programs, or had given much thought to substantial deregulation and consolidation at the federal program level. Nevertheless, it took but a few short weeks for Reagan's persuasiveness and political acumen to have seemingly cultivated a new perspective of the federal government's social and educational role. By June of 1981 a *Time* magazine poll reported that 70 percent of those sampled in agreement with the statement "Government has become far too involved in areas of people's lives" and a Gallup Poll found that 58 percent of the queried public supported the new President's recommended cuts in federal spending, including education.[1]

Indeed, by the end of the Reagan Administration's first year in office, it became rather hard to believe that the Democratic platform of 1980 pointed with pride to the 73 percent increase in federal education funding under President Carter and included a referent listing of categorical services covering such groups as "Native Hawaiians" and "limited English-proficiency people" and such programs as "teacher centers" and "Follow Through."[2]

If Reagan's attempted revolution has done nothing else it has prompted a national debate among educators over the appropriate role of the federal government in education. Since the 1980 election, advocates of federal involvement have been forced to examine what it is about what they do that is most worthy and critically examine the effectiveness of their most valued programs. Had Carter been reelected it is likely that educators would have lethargically accepted an expanding federal role with little serious questioning of what that role should be. Therefore, let us, in this chapter, review the process that brought about the recent changes in federal education policy and address the appropriate role issue more fully in the final chapter.

Early Initiatives

Immediately following Reagan's inauguration, he launched a three-pronged attack on existing domestic programs by proposing substantial spending cuts, program consolidation, and federal deregulation. Indeed, during his first day in office, he gestured symbolically toward a redefinement of the federal role by ordering a freeze on federal hiring, suspending 199 government regulations, and eliminating the council on wage and price stability. On February 18, he took his "Program for Economic Recovery," in which he began outlining a recommended $41.4 billion dollar cut in federal spending to Congress. Included in this Congressional submission were plans for converting roughly 550 categorical grant programs into the major block grant arena of health and social services and education. The document also included "a far reaching program of regulatory relief." In the educational arena, the president's economic recovery program recommended a "collapse" of "over 45 narrow categorical programs . . . support[ing] a wide variety of educational objectives" into two block grant programs—one to the states and another to the localities. The block grant system would "shift control over education policy away from the Federal Government to State and local authorities" . . . and prevent "endless byzantine squabbles over myriad accounting regulations that aid bureaucrats, not children."[3]

Aided and abetted by the economic acumen of Office Management and Budget Director David Stockman, skillful Republican Congressional leadership, and so-called "Boll Weevil" Southern Democrats in the House, Reagan was remarkably successful in gaining legislative support for his program. By the opening of school in the fall of 1981, the 97th Congress had approved $35.2 billion in budget cuts for FY'82, had legislated a personal and business tax reduction totaling $729 billion, and had repealed the Elementary and Secondary Education Act of 1965, which for sixteen years had been the major legislative strategy providing federal education aid to the population in general and disadvantaged Americans in particular.[4] In addition, Congress took a step toward eliminating impact aid, a program that assisted school districts with children of federally connected parents, by approving a three-year phase out of payments to districts whose parents either worked or lived on federal property, and made major cuts in college student aid by substantially trimming the Guaranteed Student Loan (GSL) program.[5]

Legislative Strategy

The President's success in winning Congressional approval of major components of his program was predicated in part by his unique use of a Congressional budget reduction tactic termed "reconciliation" and by the weakened authority of Congressional authorizing committees and subcommittees, including those that have supported greater federal funding of education. The reconciliation tool permitted the House and Senate budget committees to combine recommended cuts on individual items into a single bill, which was either endorsed or rejected by each chamber. Billed as a vote on the publicly mandated Reagan program (a Washington Post—ABC News poll of February 19 and 20 found the public endorsing "Reaganomics" by a better than 2-1 margin); the reconciliation strategy was successful.[6] Public support apparently assisted House Minority Leader Robert H. Michel in his bid to gather a solid phalanx of Republican votes for the tax and budget reductions. "Boll Weevil" support was seemingly augmented by the White House's strategy of concentrating power on potential Democratic defectors in Texas, a state that Reagan had won by greater than 600,000 votes despite the fact that Democrats carried sixteen of nineteen Congressional districts. Skillfully incorporating some of the recommendations of Texas-led conservative Democratic Forum into the proposed budget and indeed christening Texas Democrats Phil Gramm and Kent Hance as authors of the budget and tax bills respectively, the President was able to label both initiatives "bipartisan bills" in his televised messages appealing for public backing.[7]

Reagan employed his powers of the presidency perhaps most effectively as a Congressional lobbyist. In his book *Reagan*, Washington *Post* writer Lou Cannon summarized the President's legislative initiatives of his first months in office by noting his "incessant" contact with House members, "prompting some of them to say that they had seen more of Reagan in four months than they had seen of Carter in four years." During the first 100 days of his presidency, no fewer than 467 legislators attended sixty-nine meetings with Reagan. Using his "enormous powers of friendly persuasion," he made personal calls to wavering Congressmen, generously circulated social invitations, photographs, and presidential cufflinks, and even established good rapport with Democratic House Speaker Tip O'Neill while trying to weaken his leadership. Exuding confidence, optimism, and sincerity, Reagan could seduce doubters by his assurance and believability. He envisioned an envigorated, stronger America, had a plan for redirecting the country toward this goal, and acted as if he believed every word of it. Observed Cannon, "Reagan was not believable because he was the Great Communicator; he was the Great Communicator because he was believable."[8]

Although Reagan uttered pieties that would be labeled "corny" if used by other politicians, he came across as believing that America really did have a devine destiny or that lighted candles in darkened windows would somehow help the Poles. Speaking in everyday language and blending self-assurance with an almost boyish humility, Reagan would make resolution of the great issues sound so simple. This was in stark contrast to Carter's tendency to weigh the many positions on issues that appeared, at times, to paralyze the presidency. Reagan, however, simply knew it was right to cut taxes, build defenses, slash social programs, and eliminate the Department of Education; that somehow this agenda would produce fewer deficits and even balance the budget. According to Presidential Aide Mike Deaver, "He's the only person I've ever met who doesn't have to weigh things—his ideas seem to come from the depth of the man. He's resolved something, his being or what he is, a long time ago. He doesn't have to say, on the one hand, or the other. He seems to know what is right."[9]

Reagan's down-to-earth conveyance of his vision came through frequently on television. Few appearances were more artistic than his address to the nation on September 24, 1981. Attempting to rally public support for further cuts in social spending, Reagan drew an analogy between the boxing ring and federal deficits by recalling Joe Lewis's words before he fought Billy Conn. "There had been some speculation," stated Reagan "that Billy might be able to avoid Joe's lethal right hand. Joe said, 'Well, he can run but he can't hide.'" The President followed by quoting Senator Peter Domenici of New Mexico, Chairman of the Senate Budget Committee: "'That's just what we're facing on runaway Federal spending. We can try to run from it but we can't hide. We have to face up to it.'" Continued Reagan, "He's right, of course." The President proceeded by explaining his remedy for deficits that included asking Congress for spending cuts of 12 percent for domestic programs, shrinking the nondefense federal payroll, dismantling the Departments of Energy and Education, and cutting welfare entitlement programs. According to Reagan, the "costly reforms" associated with domestic spending were "well intentional" but they "didn't eliminate poverty or raise welfare recipients from dependence to self-sufficiency, independence and dignity." Accordingly, Americans should join his "crusade" to reduce domestic spending and turn to volunteerism as an appropriate substitute for reduced revenues. Reagan based his optimistic vision on the spirit of the American tourist visiting volcanic Mt. Etna who contended that "We got a volunteer fire department at home [that will] . . . put that thing out in fifteen minutes." This "old boy," stated Reagan ". . . was typical of those Americans who helped build a neighbor's bar [and who] . . . built the best without an area development plan and cities across the land without federal planners." Having "already set the wheels of such a volunteer effort in motion," a new world can begin. Reagan's closing line: "What are we waiting for?"[10]

What Congress appeared to be waiting for in the fall of 1981 was an agenda on reality. While it had agreed with the basic tenets of Reagan's legislative program, Congress was in no mood to hasten the creation of his new world by endorsing further cuts in social programs that had already been slashed by as much as 25 percent. To supplant federal initiatives, to nurture the hungry, to protect the handicapped, and to educate the disadvantaged with volunteerism had little appeal to millions of Americans who saw benefits from these government services. Indeed, in their minds, it was the inadequacies of volunteerism and often the antipathy of the states and localities toward needy populations that had necessitated a large federal role in the first place. Lobbyists representing the handicapped and the disadvantaged had already enjoyed some success in preserving the categorical nature of education of the handicapped and Title I, the two largest federal education programs with respective service to these populations.

With unemployment on the rise and federal deficits becoming even larger, the nation had begun to develop reservations about Reaganomics, particularly in certain areas of federal domestic spending. Accordingly, as the President approached his second year in office, increasing numbers of Americans were calling for course corrections that led to more trouble for Reagan's legislative proposals in the spring of 1982, and to the loss of twenty-five Republican members of the House the following fall.

Thus, Reagan was stopped short of creating a revolution in economics or in education. However, his initiatives during the first year of his tenure have probably generated the greatest domestic change in so short a period of time since the days of FDR. His relative success in cutting spending, curbing and consolidating services, and deregulating programs is likely to affect the federal role in education for years to come.

A Closer Look at Budget Cuts

Ignoring the election results that gave Reagan an electoral landslide victory in 1980, Jimmy Carter still clung tenaciously in his final days in office to the belief that his final budget should include increased taxation and a continuation of most social problems at current funding levels. Reiterating his "deep commitment to programs that help our citizens develop their full potential," President Carter, five days before leaving office, sent Congress a FY'82 budget of $739 billion in outlays, which included some $258 billion for social programs, health and human services and $17 billion for education.[11] Because Carter was leaving office, his budget document represented little more than symbolic support for a holding of the line of spending for education programs (and, perhaps, a hollow reward to those education groups that had provided him with such strong support in the campaign). Throughout the first year of the Reagan presidency, educators would compare again and again the Carter and Reagan figures as a solemn reminder of what would have been if the Democrats had kept control of the White House. For example, under Carter, Title I would have received $3.8 billion, considerably higher than the 2.474 billion dollars eventually requested by Reagan.[12]

Upon taking office, Reagan set, as an immediate goal, top to bottom revisions in the Carter budget. On Inauguration Day, he launched this initiative by asking for a comprehensive audit of the country's economic situation, the results of which he reported to the nation the evening of February 5. Avoiding what he labeled the audit's "jumble of charts, figures and economic jargon," the President proceeded to review a few "attention getters," such as runaway deficits, double digit inflation, increasing unemployment, and so on. Reagan then informed the public that he would shortly present to the Congress the details of his economic package of budget reductions and tax reform. The presidential ax would spare the truly destitute but would fall on "those who are really not qualified by reason of need." The President's rationale: "Since 1966 our government has spent $5.1 trillion; our debt has grown by $648 billion. Prices have exploded by 178 percent. How much better off are we for all that? We all know, we are very much worse off."[13]

The means of making things better were communicated to the legislature and the people February 18th. In a television address to a joint session of Congress, Reagan proposed a four-point program, the details of which was provided to the press and each Congressman under the title "America's New Beginning: A Program for

Economic Recovery." Assaulting government spending, taxation, unproductive regulations, and an inconsistant monetary policy, the president contended that, if fully enacted, his program would curb deficits, control inflation, and create jobs. Zeroing in on spending cuts, Reagan proposed a $695.5 billion ceiling for FY'82 that represented a $41.4 billion reduction from FY'81, a $44 billion decrease from what Carter had proposed ($739 billion) for FY'82. The White House pointed to the escalating rate of increase in federal spending from 1955 to 1964: 6.3 percent; from 1976 to 1981: 11.9 percent; from 1979 to 1981: 15.9 percent) that has taken the federal debt to nearly the $3 trillion mark. Only spending for the nation's defense and social safety net (income security measures begun in the 1930s to protect such groups as the elderly, the unemployed, and truly poor) would be maintained but beyond these priorities, all other federal programs would be subjected to thorough scrutiny and widespread reduction.[14]

On March 10, the results of such scrutiny were submitted in the form of a fully revised FY'82 budget that slashed funding for the category entitled "Education, Training, Employment and Social Services" by $8.4 billion from Carter's recommended outlay of $34.5 billion to the Reagan revision of $25.8 billion. The education component in this category was to suffer a $1.1 billion loss.[15]

Reconciliation, Rescissions, Resolutions

Within 100 days following his inauguration, Reagan's televised appeals and legislative maneuvering began paying robust dividends. Employing the reconciliation tool, the Republican-controlled Senate Budget Committee gave virtual rubber-stamp approval to the administration's budget-cutting recommendations by announcing instructions on March 23, 1981, that fourteen Senate committees must modify their domestic programs to accommodate a $36.4 billion reduction in FY'82 outlays. On April 2, the reconciliation instructions resulted in Senate action. With every Republican, save Lowell Weicker of Connecticut, in conformity with the President's plan, the Senate passed by the resounding vote of 88–10, Concurrent Resolution 9, which ordered an even greater cut (36.9 billion) than the reconciliation instructions.[16]

The fact that thirty-seven Democrats voted for the resolution did not mean that they all favored the legislation. Indeed, Democratic liberals introduced more than twenty amendments designed to restore funds for such categories as school lunches, urban development, and community health centers. Time after time these amendments went down to defeat. Typical of the margins was Daniel P. Moynihan's 33–65 loss of his proposed restoration of $435 million for elementary and secondary education. Consequently, with no chance of winning, many Democrats reluctantly recorded their vote in favor of the savings measure.[17]

Senate Republicans had opted for giving the reconciliation instructions separate legislative stature as a means of pressuring the House to respond quickly to the President's fund-cutting proposals. In the Democratically controlled House of Representatives, however, considerable resistance was building to thwart the reconciliation plan. On April 16, the House Budget Committee reported the first budget resolution for 1982, which contained reconciliation instructions calling for $15.8 billion in cuts. However, the Reagan budget and reconciliation instructions were given powerful support by the House as a whole on May 7 when sixty-three Boll Weevil Democrats joined Republican unanimity by approving the so-called "Gramm-Latta" substitute budget resolution by the impressive tally of 253–176. In both chambers, the various committees had until June 12 to report their spending cuts to their budget committees. While Republican leadership was generally satisfied with the drafted spending saving measures of thirteen of the fourteen Senate committees, the GOP brass in the House decided in mid-June that several committees had failed to cut deeply enough into entitlement programs. "Either we come to grips with the question of entitlement programs now," stated Minority Leader Robert Michel on June 19, "or we will have broken our compact with the American people." Accordingly House Republicans, in alliance with conservative Democrats, drafted "Gramm-Latta II," which offered a token of funding restoration for a few programs such as impact aid, but generally cut heavily into domestic spending by proposing an additional $5.1 billion budget reduction for FY'82.[18]

The Gramm-Latta substitutes symbolized the bipartisan support in the House for the administration's domestic program. Philip Gramm was a conservative Democrat from Texas and Delbert Latta a veteran Republican Congressman from Ohio. Both served on the House Budget Committee, a panel controlled by more liberal representatives. Both were dismayed when proposals for deep cuts were defeated by the committee. Consequently, Gramm and Latta made successful appeals to the entire House to adopt the President's plan. Addressing his Congressional colleagues, Gramm pointed out the $20.7 billion difference between "the President's budget [$36.6 billion of reductions] with bipartisan revisions" and $15.8 billion reconciliation package mandated by the House Budget Committee.[19]

According to Latta, America could no longer afford the substantial increase each year in federal spending that involved taking care of almost every interest group wanting a slice of the pie. Since F.D.R., contended Latta, government had operated on the political adage that taking care of every group's interest would somehow strengthen America as a whole.

> And they went all around taking care of every interest but me, and that was the welfare of the nation. What is good for America? that is what this President is saying he is going to do. He is going to forget the special interest groups for a change and do something that is right for America...[20]

It was Latta's contention that government tampering with what were originally legitimate programs had disregarded the national interest. Using the Guaranteed Student Loan program as an example, Mr. Latta told his Congressional colleagues that "This program was designed to assist students from low-income families get through college . . . [but] just as night follows day in this House, it was not too long before these taxpayer-subsidized loans were made available to all college students, whether they needed them or not." Accordingly, "Between 1979 and 1981 the amount borrowed increased from $2 billion annually to $6.5 billion, and the taxpayers' cost increased from $400 million to $2.5 billion.[21]

But it was not cuts in federal spending geared to the middle class that disturbed Congressman Henry Reuss of Wisconsin about the implication of the Gramm-Latta substitute. Because the proposed $36.6 billion cut would "demolish the modest protections of health, education, housing and legal and economic rights which our poorer citizens now enjoy . . ., inequalities will worsen, hard-won rights and opportunities will be lost." Indeed, California's Augustus Hawkins pointed out to his colleagues that "What the . . . President's budget amounts to is a total dismantling of programs *without regard for evaluation reports mandated by Congress—often in opposition to highly positive performance records* and with irretrievable loser in funds already invested."[22]

Just before the Congressional vote on Gramm-Latta II, Latta addressed the "weeping and wailing" in the House by "proponents of the uncontrolled entitlement spending." Latta reiterated his position that it is "simply not true" that controlling entitlements is just too hard, that too much pain will be visited on the poor and downtrodden. The types of entitlement reforms proposed in this amendment," Latta continued, "will still leave in place a common sense system of generous support to those who are truly in need of assistance . . ." But to Rhode Island Congressman Fernand St. Germain, it is a "fairy-tale" to think that those "who live in assisted housing are lazy, able bodied people who would work if only we forced them to." According to St. Germain, the Reagan cuts ignore the fact that 44 percent of federally assisted tenants are elderly. And, to Kentucky's Carl Perkins, cuts in the school lunch and higher education student assistance will indeed hurt the needy by forcing them to pay nearly eighty cents more a day for lunch and by preventing them from attending college.[23]

Following two days of what has been termed "often acrimonious debate" and considerable lobbying by Reagan, the House on June 26 narrowly endorsed the Gramm-Latta amendment by a vote of 217-211. Despite the similarities between the House Gramm-Latta II and the Senate package (calling for respective cuts of $37.3 and $38.1 billion), there were numerous details to worked out by the House and Senate conferees. Described as the "largest and most complex Senate-House conference in history" (every legislative committee was represented), the Congressional conferees devoted laborious energy to reconciling their differences. By the end of July, the conferees issued their report to both chambers, and on July 31, both the House and Senate voted to accept it (80-14). Termed the Omnibus Reconciliation Act of 1981, the legislation was designed to decrease FY'82 spending by some $35.2 billion and to reduce outlays by $130.6 billion in the three-year period FY'82-'84. On August 13, President Reagan gave his signature to the bill, a measure that provided the greatest budgetary slashing in American history.[24]

One of the knotty issues afflicting the Senate-House conference was what programs were really worth preserving because they were effectively providing services to a genuinely needy population. After long deliberation, the conferees negotiated several compromises on domestic programs that included eventually lumping only twenty-nine education programs (rather than the Reagan recommended forty-four) into the block grant nonrestrictive chunk and allowing college students from families with incomes under $30,000 to borrow up to $2,500 annually in federally supported loans without any test of need, and those with incomes above that level, upon demonstration of need. Preserved by this process were vocational education, aid to the handicapped, and Title I for the educationally disadvantaged. Indeed, Title I not only maintained its categorical status but retained adequate funding, receiving $3.48 billion for FY'82 compared to $3.1 billion for FY'81.[25]

Tax Cuts, Further Spending Cuts

Only four days following Congressional approval of the $35.2 billion budget slashing, the nation's lawmakers enacted legislation that provided a $37.7 billion tax cut for FY'82. In his televised speech to Congress the preceeding February 18, President Reagan had asked for a whopping $53.9 billion cut for FY'82; it involved a 10 percent across-the-board income tax reduction for individuals and business depreciation reforms beginning July 1, 1981, and a similar 10 percent reduction on July 1 of 1982 and 1983. Reagan had to settle, however, for only a 5 percent cut for FY'82 (effective October 1) but did get Congressional approval of his recommended 10 percent tax cut decrease for the following two years. Convinced that such legislation would spur economic growth force and reduced government spending, the President steadfastly endorsed the plan, despite early warnings by various quarters (including some members of his staff) that it would lead to soaring budget deficits.[26] In the twenty-day period between February 18 and March 10, 1981, for example, Budget Director Stockman increased the projected deficit from $30 billion to $44 billion for FY'84.[27]

Reduced revenues of this magnitude alone could not loom well for the future of social programs. However, in combination with record-breaking deficits and a reluctance to tamper with defense expenditures, the tax cut made the continuation of domestic belt-tightening almost inevitable.

Increasingly pessimistic deficit projections also prompted the administration to seek further cuts from Congress following the August 1981 recess. Instead of buoying the financial markets the massive spending cuts and tax reductions fueled a near panic on Wall Street because of fears that huge deficits would promote high interest rates and inflation.[28] Thus, in September, Reagan asked Congress to approve another budget reduction package that involved not only $13 billion in spending cuts but a $3 billion tax increase. Calling for a further 12 percent reduction in nondefense programs, the President was urged to seek further cuts by David Stockman who projected that the unspecified savings needed to balance the budget in FY'84 had jumped from $74 billion to $100 billion. In his September 24 televised address to the nation, Reagan emphasized that "The important thing now is to hold to a firm, steady course," and that additional spending cuts would lower interest rates, inflation and steer the nation toward a balanced budget and economic recovery.[29]

This time, however, Congress had no stomach for further cuts of such magnitude. Even Republican members of the Senate Appropriations Committee contended that they could not exceed an additional $5 billion in budget cutting as the eventful year of 1981 drew to a close. Reservation over legislating additional Reaganomics was augmented by the recognition that America had fallen into a serious recession of possibly long duration. In early December, the Senate and the House narrowly adopted a second budget resolution that merely affirmed the spending figures adopted in the first resolution last May.[30]

In December the Office of Management and Budget had projected a $423 billion deficit for FY'82-83, which represented a $242 billion increase from estimates in September. According to Reagan, balancing the budget by 1984 was now only an economic objective, not a necessity. Administration spokespersons were claiming that there was no impending danger from such huge deficits.[31] Thus, what had become political reality and the economic status quo for preceeding Presidents had come to be acknowledged by Ronald Reagan: despite massive reductions in revenues and substantial increases in defense spending, millions of Americans continued to look to the federal government for protection, support, and security. Before the end of his first year in office, Reagan had to back off from his plans to cut the growth of entitlement programs such as food stamps and medicare. As Reagan was seeking deeper second round cuts, the House Appropriations Committee was recommending increases of nearly $200 million for vocational education. The burgeoning federal deficit spurred by the tax cut made spending for entitlements and education more difficult to justify but legislators were unwilling to terminate appropriate funding for social problems long viewed as providing a safety net congruent with the public good. With "Supply Siders" balking at raising taxes in a recession, and with mounting Congressional opposition to further domestic cuts, Reagan was forced to put off any further budget savings proposals until 1982.

As the Reagan Administration began outlining its FY'83 budget, its war with Congressional liberals centered more and more around "recessions" or cancellations of funds previously appropriated. Most education programs are "forward funded," which means dollar amounts set do not become available until the next year. Because Congress could not come to terms with dollar figures for FY'83, the national legislature passed a so-called "continuing resolutions," a legislative device designed to keep programs going until appropriations are enacted. (Consequently, the continuing resolution figures will be used to compare advance funding amounts with the Reagan recommended rescissions.)

The September and December 1981 continuing resolutions for FY'83 (the 1982-83 school year) generally reflected some Congressional belt tightening. For example, Title I and Indian Education went from FY'81 appropriations of $3.1 billion and $81 million to a continuing resolution figure of $2.9 billion and $78 million respectively. (An exception to this downward trend was education for the handicapped, which modestly increased under the continuing resolution by less than 2 percent to $1,042 billion.) But the Reagan budget for FY'83 and the projections for FY'84 appeared to many educators to be more butchering than belt tightening. Immediately following passage of the December 11 continuing resolution, the Department of Education recommended to OMB massive cuts in education for FY'83 and '84.[32] The Office of Governmental Relations of the American Association of School Administrators

(AASA) subsequently issued an advisory memorandum entitled "Fiscal 1983 Budget is Worst News Yet!!" Claiming that OME deliberately leaked its figures so people will feel "relieved" if only half the cuts are Congressionally approved, AASA predicted differences of about 50 percent between FY'81 and FY'83 budgets.[33] In actuality, the budget Reagan presented to Congress on February 8, 1982 requested only about a 33 percent drop from FY'81 (for elementary and secondary education, $6.713 billion to $4.417 billion; for higher education, $6.913 billion to $4.789 billion) with rescissions accounting for more than $1 billion of the proposed budget cuts.[34]

The spending rescissions of 1981, however, were not to be duplicated by Congress during its 1982 term. In June a rather conservative budget that continued the trend of increases in military spending and reductions in social programs was adopted. Congress refused to rescind money it had already appropriated for education programs and wound up funding most programs just over the levels established by the continuing resolutions. For example, rather than accept Reagan's wish for a $412 million cut in Title I (Compensatory Education), the Congress provided $2.958 billion, $72 million above the $2.886 continuing resolution level.

Saving Title I

While categorical programs such as consumer education and metric education could easily be incorporated by Congress into a block grant, and funding for bilingual education could be cut with little public disdain, it was not politically expedient to tamper much with Title I, by far the largest and perhaps the most successful federal education program. In 1981, Title I provided basic skills services to over 5 million children, and its $3.1 billion appropriation represented 46 percent of all federal money spent on elementary and secondary education. In the fall of 1981, facing threats by the Reagan Administration to curb the program by as much as $1.6 billion by 1984, a coalition representing well-established organizations such as the National P.T.A., the Urban League, the American Association of School Administrators, and the National Education Association was formed to save Title I. Initiating national letter-writing campaigns and the circulation of "dear colleague" letters from members of Congress requesting the endorsement of full funding for the program, the Coalition To Save Title I was a viable political force for the interests of federal education during the 1981-82 school year.[35]

One of the coalition's most compelling questions was how the Department of Education could recommend severe cuts in a program that its secretary "knew" was working. Testifying before Congress in May of 1981, Bell contended that the "The rationale for budget cuts was not based upon any failure of Title I. I know I can testify to this committee, that our Title I programs are successful."[36] Bell explained to Congress later that fall, however, that when he was Commissioner of Education under President Ford, Title I was associated with only a "minuscule difference" in pupil achievement. But now as Secretary, "After being away from here four years and coming back, I can tell you that American education has learned how to educate disadvantaged children."[37] It is somewhat ironic that the program received substantial revenues throughout a period with little encouraging research results yet was recommended for such a slashing shortly after much more positive findings were finally demonstrated.

During the 1981–82 school year, the more recent research on basic skills education in general and Title I programs in particular was formally submitted to Congress at hearings conducted by the subcommittee on Elementary, Secondary and Vocational Education of the House Committee on Education and Labor.[38] On May 7, 1981, Roy Forbes, Director of the National Assessment of Educational Progress, (NAEP) reported significant improvement between 1970 and 1980 in the reading performance of disadvantaged nine-year-olds, with the greatest gains occurring among blacks who out gained their more advantaged white counterparts by roughly 3.5 to almost 10 percent. Although NAEP did not zero in on Title I program effectiveness per se, Forbes found that "Two things are clear from our data: first, funds are being targeted on those most in need of help, the lower performers, and, second, there is a trend toward the closing of the performance gap between students attending Title I eligible and noneligible schools." Forbes reported that "across the board, the data show that the greatest gains were found for the lower performers, those Title I were designed to serve." In summary, "Something very positive is happening to younger students who need help in improving their academic skills,

those for whom compensatory education programs were designed, students attending schools where compensatory services are
provided, the historically lower performing students, those students
are the students gaining, they are closing the performance gap."[39]

Accordingly, it was Forbes's contention that "for our younger
students compensatory education programs are paying off." NAEP
found some increases among disadvantaged 13-year-olds while
higher performers registered declines. Among seventeen-year-olds,
no improvement was recorded for either the advantaged or
disadvantaged populations, but Forbes pointed out that this is the
age where Title I funds are least targeted.[40]

Positive data on younger Title I children was also presented at an
Elementary, Secondary and Vocational Education Subcommittee
hearing on March 24, 1982.[41] Launor Carter, manager of the 1980
Systems Development Corporation's (SDC) "Sustaining Effects
Study" of compensatory education reported that although "There
have been a number of past studies which failed to show gains from
Title I participation . . ., our results show that Title I students benefit
from Title I services in math in all grades and for reading in the first
three grades." According to Carter, previous "Studies have
suffered from inadequate data and from analysis problems [but
that] the sustaining effects study has the most comprehensive data
and the most thorough analysis of any study yet reported." Earlier
studies of Title I examined growth over a single school year,
collected data on smaller samples, and restricted their investigation
to only reading or zeroed in on identifying exemplary programs with
no control groups. However, the Sustaining Effects Study collected
data on roughly 120,000 elementary students (grades 1-6) in reading
and math over a three-year period (1976–1979) and included control
groups who were eligible for but not receiving Title I services.[42]

Carter had reported to the House Subcommittee that better-
than-expected achievement gains for all six elementary math
grades investigated and for grades one through three in reading
were found. But Congressman Augustus Hawkins of California
queried, "You left the conclusion standing that beyond that
apparently students do not receive benefits. Is that correct?" Carter
replied in the affirmative. As one of the coauthors of Title I "Dear
Colleague" letter requesting full funding for the program, Hawkins

appeared to be very concerned about establishing positive compensatory education research data for the public record.[43]

Testifying with Carter, Benjamin D. Stickney pointed out to the subcommittee that although it was entitled "The Sustaining Effects Study," Carter's data came from only the first year of the study (1976-77), beyond which there was little published information. Consequently, the data was five years old and more current data (school year 1979-80) was obtained by recent NAEP findings. Morever, "if you take a look at the long term impact of the program . . . as collected by the National Assessment for Educational Progress over a ten-year period, the evidence is fairly strong that Title I is associated with better than expected pupil gains in reading and math." The fact that black nine-year olds have gained almost ten percentage points in ten years' reading while whites gained only 3 points during that period ". . . gives us some indication of the sustaining effects of compensatory education."[44]

Responding to a subsequent request to augment the written record on the sustaining effects data, Stickney informed the subcommittee that given the fact that

> most educational research has found [that] little or no effective . . . schooling has been targeted at the middle and upper middle income populations [and] if national surveys of such variables as educational television, experiential learning and individualized instruction fail to identify any positive effects for average or gifted children, why should we expect large scale studies of compensatory education to show robust effects of its treatment on low income children? It was suggested that the benefits of schooling may be distorted by what may be called a canceling effect . . . [because] in national studies of schooling researchers are sampling a large heterogeneous population exposed to an infinite variety of teachers employing a myriad of methods[,] . . . it is usually difficult for researchers to identify positive effects of school variables, because effective practices for some are cancelled by inappropriate activities for others. Given the canceling effect and its possible contamination of previous national studies (including the 1968 and 1969 studies of Title I), the fact that the Sustaining Effects Study is reporting greater than expected gains in nine out of twelve grade subjects tested, a relatively positive finding.[45]

Although the research fell short of providing unequivocable support for Title I effectiveness, its lobbyists (in and out of Congress) and segments of the general public have expressed the position that it is a "proven" program. In their "Dear Colleague" letter, Perkins and Hawkins appealed for support from their fellow members of the House by stating, "We cannot understand the rationale for severely cutting a program which, according to all recent evaluations, has been extremely effective in improving the basic skills of educationally-deprived children." The coauthors pointed out that "Even the administration has attested to the success of Title I, through the solid, verifiable research findings summarized in the Secretary of Education's 1981 annual evaluation report and in the testimony of the secretary before our committee."[46]

Such research was not lost in the national media. In the January 22 edition of the CBS Evening News, Dan Rather reported that a Department of Education "major new study shows achievement gains by Title One Students . . . suggest that a fifteen year decline in educational achievement is beginning to be reversed, particularly among low achieving groups."[47]

The Coalition to Save Title I established the goal of funding Title I at $3.48 billion level, the amount Congress authorized *could be spent* for FY'82.[48] Noting that Reagan had already rescinded $412 million from FY'82 and was proposing a severe slashing to 1.9 billion for FY'83, the coalition urged that its members "stress the success of Title I programs."[49] Perhaps the coalition's most impressive activity was its organization of a "Title I Day," a lobbying effort that attracted as many as 1,500 people to Washington on March 16, 1982, to demonstrate support for the program. Visiting some 175 House members and 45 Senators, the supporters left behind information on Title I effectiveness and how the budget cuts would affect the program. Representatives were given a walking tour of an "exemplary Title I program."[50]

In the Senate, Colorado's Gary Hart made a last-minute attempt to ensure more adequate funding for Title I and handicapped education by introducing an amendment that would have raised Title I to $3.1 billion ($200 million above the continuing resolution figure of $2.89 billion), and would have modestly increased handicapped education expenditures. in his Senate address, Hart referred to "Experts [who] almost uniformly agreed that this program has worked and worked very well," quoted Secretary Bell's

Congressional testimony regarding Title I success. And the amendment failed by one vote, however, and Congress voted to hold the line on spending for Title I and handicapped education for FY'83.[51]

Conciliation and Compromise

Congressional ambivalence about cutting aid to the disadvantaged and handicapped in the summer of 1982 appeared congruent with increased national reserve over Reaganomics. With unemployment exceeding 10 percent and the economy maintaining its state of recession, voter anxiety over Republican policy was apparently reflected in the significant gains afforded the Democrats in the midterm elections that November. Although the Republicans retained their margin of control in the Senate, the Democrats picked up twenty-five seats in the House (roughly twice as many as typically predicted), and increased their share of governorships by seven. Consequently, Reagan adopted a more conciliatory tone when he delivered that State of the Union Address. His emphasis was on "what we can do together not as Republicans and Democrats, but as Americans." He hoped that Americans "of every political shade," inspired by a bipartisan spirit, would endorse both his idealistic and realistic plans for economic recovery. While noting his belief that for years it had been government that had precipitated the problem, Reagan announced that "We who are in government must take the lead in restoring the economy." To that remark, many Democrats signaled their alleged shock and delight by giving the President a standing ovation.[53]

Beyond recommending a special job-training program for the long-term unemployed, cuts in previously recommended increases in defense spending and a foreseeable income tax surcharge and tax on oil, the President's 1983 State of the Union Message provided little deviation from his philosophic canons. Federal deficits came still "from the uncontrolled growth of the budget for domestic spending (rather than rooted in the tax cuts) and a federal spending freeze was mandatory. Regarding education, Reagan reiterated his goals of a constitutional amendment permitting voluntary school prayer ("God should never have been expelled from America's classrooms in the first place"), and of passing legislation allowing tuition tax credits for parents of private school children. Reagan also proposed the establishment of tax-exempt educational savings accounts to provide lower and middle families with savings incentives for their children's higher education as an alternative to a reliance on federal aid.[54]

The implications of the federal freeze awaited the submission of the FY'84 budget to Congress on January 31, 1983. In reviewing the figures for education, one is struck by the relatively small cuts proposed by the President in his third budget. In FY'83, the Administration had requested only $10.3 billion for education programs and proposed even greater reductions in future years. But these recommendations were rejected by a Congress that eventually approved $15 billion for education for FY'83.* With the addition of twenty-five Democrats and the perserverance of many members who sought full funding for disadvantaged and handicapped education, Reagan's plans to substantially reduce the federal role in education were at least temporarily thwarted. The FY'84 budget request included $13.2 billion in budget authority for education ($5.7 billion for elementary and secondary; $5.8 billion for higher education; $1.6 billion for research and miscellaneous programs), with only modest proposed reductions in the forms of rescissions in Title I (which is now Chapter 1 of Education in Solidation and Improvement Act of 1981), and handicapped education. The President recommended no rescissions in funds for vocational education and adult education. The rather staple proposals for education compare quite favorably with his recommended reductions in social programs such as food stamps and child nutrition, which would experience reductions from FY'83 to FY'84 of $12 billion to $10.9 billion and $638 million to $535 million respectively.[55]

Included in the new budget, however, was a radical restructuring of federal financial aid for college students. Under this "self-help" plan, students would have to pay 40 percent of the cost of college before becoming eligible for a federal higher education grant. The eligibility criteria would change as well, focusing on the neediest persons in the population. The new "self-help" program would replace the Pell Grants that provided, as basic entitlement, grants to low and moderate income college students.[56]

---

*An increase of $300 million over the FY'82 figure and $5.1 billion greater than the Administration's budget request for FY'83.

Congressional reaction to the President's FY'84 education programs was generally critical. As expected, Senator Clairborne Pell of Rhode Island, "father" of the grants-in-aid student programs and ranking Democrat on the Senate Labor and Human Resources Committee, found the "self-help" proposal seriously lacking and "particularly discouraging."[57] Calling the President's proposal for $50 million to enhance science and math education in this period of technological change "a drop in the bucket," Carl Perkins managed to win the resounding approval (27–3) of the House Education and Labor Committee for a substitute bill that would provide $250 million to the states and localities for math and science programs.[58] Additional problems for the President came from both Democrats and Republicans alarmed at the record-breaking deficit forecasts ($207.7 billion for FY'83, as opposed to a $91.5 billion forecast in February '82; $188.8 billion for FY'84 and $194.2 for FY'85),[59] as well as from those opposed to a spending freeze on domestic programs.

Program Consolidation and Block Grants

As opposed to categorical grants, which are typically funds targeted for a narrowly defined need and governed by relatively extensive regulations, block grants are revenues intended to address national goals by supporting broad programs, largely at the discretion of the participants.

Proposals for education block grants preceed the Reagan Administration. As discussed in the previous chapter, there has long been much sentiment for general rather than categorical aid in education. Block grants, per se, were originally the "brain child" of the Hoover Commission in 1949, which proposed them for a restructuring of parts of the federal system. Beginning in 1953, numerous block grant bills were introduced in Congress, and by 1980, five block grant bills had been adopted by the national legislature: the Partnership for Health Act of 1966; the Omnibus Crime Control and Safe Streets Act of 1968; the Comprehensive Employment and Training Act of 1973; the Housing and Community Development Act of 1974; and the 1975 Title XX Amendments of the Social Security Act of 1935.[60] In 1967, Congressional Republicans labored unsuccessfully to consolidate ESEA programs into blocks.[61] During the seventies, both Nixon and Ford urged Congress to support block grants for education, but they failed to win legislative approval. Submitted to Congress in 1976, the Ford proposal involved consolidating twenty-four elementary and secondary programs into one block grant to be spent at the discretion of the states. Similar to a revenue-sharing plan proposed earlier by Nixon, the Ford proposal would have made it mandatory for the states to spend 75 percent of their education funds on handicapped and disadvantaged children.[62]

While program consolidations is typically associated with block grants, block grants do not require consolidation and consolidation can occur without block grants. Sandra Osbourn of the Library of Congress Congressional Research Service offers example of both from the Omnibus Reconciliation Act of 1981. According to Osbourn, Sections 541-546 consolidate "several existing authorities for refugee education into a single authority. However, the administrative relationships were not changed so in essence this becomes a larger categorical grant, and not a block grant." Included in block grants not involving consolidation are the "Primary Care Block Grant that includes only the Community Health Centers Program [and] . . . the Puerto Rico Food Stamp Block Grant [that] applies to only one program in one jurisdiction." Generally speaking, however, block grants have been a principle means of consolidating programs, which has become a key component of Reagan's budget-cutting and "new federalism" strategy.[63] According to Osbourn's analysis, "The various forms of Federal aid can be placed on a continuum of diminishing Federal authority, with categorical grants characterized by the strongest Federal role, and special or general revenue sharing the weakest." Because Reagan wished to augment considerably state and local authority, his administration's block grant proposals were closer to special revenue sharing than to block grants that were currently in operation.

Originally Reagan proposed a relatively comprehensive block grant system that called for a merger of eighty-five categorical grants into seven blocks. However, under the Omnibus Reconciliation Act, Congress chose to consolidate only fifty-seven categorical programs into the following nine block grants:

1. Alcohol, Drug Abuse and Mental Health (3 programs consolidated)

2. Community Services (1)
3. Community Development (1)
4. Elementary & Secondary Education (33)
5. Maternal & Child Health Services (6)
6. Low Income Energy Assistance (1)
7. Primary Care (1)
8. Preventive Health & Health Services (9)
9. Social Services (2)

In numerical terms, the hardest hit consolidation area was the field of education, which saw a merger of twenty-nine programs into the block grant Elementary and Secondary Education. Subtitled the "Education Consolidation and Improvement Act of 1981" (ECIA), the education block included (in Chapter II) most programs authorized by the Elementary and Secondary Education Act of 1965, part of the Higher Education Act of 1965, a section of the National Science Foundation Act of 1950, the Alcohol and Drug Abuse Education Act, the Career Education Incentive Act, and, on a phased basis, the Follow Through Act.[64] However, in opposition to the administration, Congress chose to maintain the categorical integrity of ESEA's largest program, Title I, which continued to provide remedial services for "disadvantaged children" as ECIA's Chapter I.[65] Other major programs escaping consolidation included the Education for all Handicapped Children Act (P.L. 94-142), Head Start, the Women's Educational Equity Act, the Vocational Education Program, and ESEA's Title VII Bilingual Education Program.[66]

Educational block grants (or Chapter 2 funds) are divided between the U.S. Department of Education, the territories, and the states, with 1 percent allocated for the trust territories of the Pacific and Northern Mariana Islands, Guam, American Samoa, the Virgin Islands, and 93 percent reserved for distribution at the state capitals.* Currently, 6 percent of the revenues are retained by the Secretary of Education as discretionary funds for identified national programs. The percentage of Chapter 2 funds received by a state is based on the percentage that its school-age population (ages 5 to

---

*Including the District of Columbia and Puerto Rico.

17) bears to the school-age population of the nation. Each state is permitted to keep up to 20 percent of the block grant before distributing a minimum of 80 percent of funds to the school districts. The distribution to the localities is based principally on pupil enrollment in public and private schools, with some adjustment for "high cost" children such as those from low-income families, from economically depressed areas or from sparsely populated areas.[67]

Although the states assume the basic responsibility for Chapter 2 funds administration, the law requires "that this responsibility be carried out with a minimum of paperwork and that the responsibility for the design and implementation of programs ... shall be mainly .. . school superintendents, principals, and classroom teachers and supporting personnel, because they have the most direct contact with students and are most directly responsible to parents." In addition, the Omnibus Reconciliation Act requires each to establish a gubernatorially appointed advisory committee to provide input on the distribution and usage of funds. The advisory committee should be "broadly representative of public and private school teachers, parents, school board members, school administrators, higher education and the state legislature. The block grant advisory committee is intended to advise the state on what proportion (up to 20 percent) of the grant the state should retain, the formula for its distribution (how much should be based on low income, population sparsity, etc.) and on the planning, implementation and evaluation of state funded programs."[68]

In consolidating the twenty-nine ESEA programs, Congress lumped these categoricals into the three broad areas (or subchapters) of "Basic Skills Development," "Educational Improvement and Support Services" and "Special Projects." "Basic Skills" includes the former ESEA categorical Title II. "Educational Improvement and Support" includes such programs as ESEA Title IV (innovative programs and identification and diffusion of exemplary programs) and Section 532 of Title V of the Higher Education Act of 1965 relating to the Teacher Corps and Teacher Centers. "Special Projects" may involve such former ESEA categoricals as ethnic heritage, career education, community schools, and metric education.[69]

Adopting the dictum of deregulation and decentralization, most states have chosen to impose few restrictions on the flow of funds to the localities and have weighed pupil enrollment much more heavily than is often found in federal programs' funding formula. For example, Colorado's seventeen-member block grant advisory committee, appointed by Governor Richard Lamm in the fall of 1981, recommended not to continue any programs or categories established by previous federal education acts, advised that local school district accountability committees be used to identify statewide priorities, and proposed that at least 80 percent of the funding distribution be based on pupil enrollment. Accepting the recommendations of the advisory committee, the Colorado Board of Education finally adopted a distribution formula based on enrollment—83 percent, low income—16 percent, and population sparcity—1 percent.[70] In New York somewhat greater concern for the disadvantaged may be evident in its state-wide block grant plan that states that "aid increases as a district's wealth per pupil decreases, because pupils with special educational needs . . ., limited English proficiency . . ., handicapping conditions and sparsity have the effect of lowering a district's relative ability to pay . . .." The complex distribution formula adopted by that state permits the poorest districts to receive a significantly greater percentage of block grant funds than more economically advantaged districts of similar size.[71]

Although the primacy of poverty is commonly associated with funding for such programs as Title I, Head Start, and Bilingual education, it would be a mistake to view block grants as necessarily showing less sensitivity to the conditions of the less fortunate than do former categorical programs. It is likely that a majority of block grant advisory committee members in the various states represent rather conventional interests (in Colorado, school administrators and representatives of school boards and private schools comprise nine of seventeen slots on the committee; the remaining members include public school teachers, students, state legislatures, and parent representatives, of which only one person representing parents is commonly associated with the rights of the states' minority or disadvantaged population)[72] and those reluctant to plan heavy emphasis on the plight of the impoverished or disadvantaged. Yet, it is important to note that the former categorical programs included not only desegregation plans funded by the Emergency School Aid Act and multicultural curriculum models supported by Ethnic Heritage Programs, but involved other areas of national interest such as environmental, consumers, and gifted and talented education—projects typically serving the more affluent population. Moreover, because revenues to fund categorical programs were typically contingent upon involvement in a highly competitive, time-consuming, grants-writing process, wealthier, more urban districts would appear to have been at an advantage. While this process would likely benefit disadvantaged students in the cities, it probably provided a paucity of assistance to low-income students in sparsely populated areas. Typically, small districts in rural America could not afford to hire a grant writer, much less be aware of the funding schedules and regulations associated with numerous categorical programs. Only if a district subscribed to the *Federal Register* or asked specifically to be on a program mailing list, would it receive any information on a competitive categorical that would often include a deadline application notice of only a few weeks. Because the accompanying regulations appeared mind-boggling to many district personnel and because, in some cases, the cost of writing the grant was undoubtedly viewed as exceeding the prize, it is probable that only a small percentage of the districts even aware of funding availability bothered to submit an application. Consequently, institutions of higher education and more affluent districts were more often awarded the money supporting most categorical programs.

Although many categorical programs may have provided funding for projects clearly congruent with national needs, many apparently fell by the wayside because they had little or no data to endorse their effectiveness. Commenting on why federal discretionary programs lost to consolidation, Gerald Elbers, a twenty-five year project manager veteran at the Office and Department of Education, has contended that "while most successful applicants [for categorical money] are good at conceptualizing their ideas and presenting them in the form of proposals, few have experience in evaluation." Because "they see their projects primarily as a means of achieving support for what they feel to be (and what often is) an excellent idea..., the evaluation plans of most proposals are sketchy and often are not carefully related to declared objectives." Categorical funding was intended primarily for funding demonstration projects for the purposes of "providing" what was effective and disseminating the results for replication. Unfortunately, it is Elbers' observation that "The proposal writers do not cast their proposals in the form of a national demonstration but in the form of a request for assistance." Consequently, when the final reports are written, they "are chronicles of what occurred, with considerable emphasis given to the process, to what happened, and not to proven results or outcomes."[73]

Elbers' conclusion on the importance of demonstrated effectiveness gains support from Arvin Bloom, an accomplished Washington observer as Chairman of Federal Liaison Representatives of the Council of Chief State School Officers. "Having sat in a number of hearings on categorical programs," recalls Bloom, "there was simply not sufficient hard data for the money expended." This included IV-B and IV-C ESEA, which were, respectively, library grants and district-initiated innovative projects. These were programs "the schools liked but never had strong Congressional support," in part because of the paucity of hard data presented to Congress.[74]

Although it was Congress that originally initiated most categorical legislation, Congressional support for many categorical programs was apparently not very strong because it had been principally reactive, rather than proactive, reflecting a bending to this or that pressure group. In addition, unlike the supporters of education for the handicapped and disadvantaged, the groups supporting many categorical programs had become rather fragmented by the time Reagan's block grant legislation was proposed.[75] Concludes Elbers, "the resulting list of [categorical] programs is not a bad one, and a rationale can be formed to justify each one, but one can seriously question whether it represents a *meaningful* agenda for this decade, or even for the past one."[76]

The late Ohio Congressman John Ashbrook, author of the educational block grant law, contended that it should be the decision of states and localities regarding what to do with federal money. Ashbrook saw consolidation as promoting deregulation and spoke with pride about his authorship of the block grant program which includes "a provision stating outright that the regulations which are issued shall not have the standing of a federal statute. This brings to a screeching halt the practice of executive branch bureaucrats making laws through regulation."[77]

Deregulation

Perhaps the most noteworthy feature of the education block grant is its simplicity. Occupying a scant twelve pages in the *Federal Register* (November 19, 1982), its regulations are little more than a reiteration of the law. Thus, in combining most of the ESEA programs, Chapter 2 of ECIA actually has fewer regulations governing twenty-nine programs than was typically associated with a single categorical. For example, spanning the years 1976-80, the rules or proposed rules for the programs Basic Skills Improvement, Gifted and Talented, Emergency School Aid, and Community Education respectively occupied six, fourteen, twenty, and twenty-six *Federal Register* pages.[78] Applications for most categorical money would be circulated in an "Application for Grants" booklet, which often contained 60-100 pages. Usually included in the booklet would be information on the law, the regulations, application forms of a descriptive and financial nature and assurances forms to prevent discrimination based on race, sex, and handicapping condition. Community advisory councils had to be formed, data on ethnicity collected, and letters of endorsement provided.[79] (At one time, the approximately 150 pages of application information for funds under the Emergency School Aid Act included twenty-one pages of forms and instructions on civil rights compliance alone.)[80] In addition, a proposal usually involved submitting a lengthy narrative, an abstract, a detailed budget, and resumes of key personnel.

In striking contrast to the categorical legislation and accompanying rules are the block grant requirements that do little more than define the block grant concept, discuss regulatory flexibility, and define private school participation. Auditing procedures "supplement, not supplant" (*add to*, not *take the place of*) instructions and maintenance of effort information (one can easily get a waiver), and are also included in the regulations but are rarely translated to the forms the states construct for LEA application for block grant funds. For example, Colorado's nine-page block grant application includes only space for signatures, objectives (a single objective written in any form is acceptable), the briefest narrative, private school participation, and a standard budget form. One may use block grant funds for any or all of the typical areas of the former categoricals, which in reality means that the revenues can support nearly any school activity from basic skills development to community recreation.[81]

Although the Reagan Administration has enjoyed success in revising regulations associated with such areas as higher education and research and improvement (currently 107 sets of regulations of the more than 200 on the books have been reviewed and deregulated), it has been relatively ineffective in tampering with programs that escaped block grants and maintained their categorical status. At this writing the inter-intrastate migrant program has been deregulated, but there has been no changes in the regulations governing such programs as Indian education, sex equity, Vocational Education, and Project Follow Through. Nor has it been able to make any alterations in the regulations accompanying education of the handicap (Education for all Handicapped Children Act, usually refered to as P.L. 94-142). Legislated in 1975, P.L. 94-142 is the second highest revenued education program, providing grants-in-aid to the states of roughly $1 billion annually for the provision of free and appropriate education for handicapped children. States have a choice of whether to accept P.L. 94-142 funds, but once accepted, a recipient must comply with substantial procedural regulations.[82]

Maintaining Education of the Handicapped

Most advocates apparently believe that comprehensive requirements are needed to ensure that handicapped children are properly educated. As recently as 1974, it was reported that forty-eight states and the District of Columbia had exemptions by law from compulsory attendance for children who were handicapped mentally, emotionally, or physically.[83] Today forty-nine of the fifty states (only New Mexico does not participate) have established policies and plans congruent with P.L. 94-142 requirements, and, thanks to the enactment of the 1975 law, handicapped children's right to quality education has been firmly established.[84] Bette Hamilton and Daniel Yohalem of the Children's Defense League typify the voice of advocates in a recent article in Education and Urban Society.

> There can be no serious doubts that all parties would be significantly better off if P.L. 94-142 and strong regulations remain intact... Children, of course, would lose the most... in many states if the law were to be

repealed, Individualized Education Programs (IEPs) would be lost, special education placements would become more segregated from nonhandicapped children [and children] ages 3 to 5 and 18 to 21 would no longer receive a special education in most cases.[85]

In assuring that the status provide what the advocates believe are quality educational services for handicapped children, P.L. 94-142 requires that (1) all children with handicaps must receive, at *no* expense to parents, appropriate educational instruction and "related services," such as speech pathology and audiology, occupational and physical therapy, and psychological services, (2) parents be involved in the planning of their children's special education, (3) so-called Individualized Educational Programs (IEPs), created equally by parents and professionals, constitute the educational prescription (specifying goals and services) and legal binding for each child's schooling needs, (4) impartial due process opportunities before an independent hearing officers for parents dissatisfied with the school district's prescription for their child, (5) handicapped children be educated in the least restrictive environment, meaning typically an integrated setting (involving both academic and nonacademic services) with nonhandicapped children.[86] Complying with such requirements can be very expensive to local districts since the federal contribution usually represents only a fraction of the cost of a handicapped child's education. In 1979, the average annual per-pupil cost for handicapped children was $3,638, yet the federal government's contribution was only $200. With budget cuts combining with inflation, the federal share dropped to $135 for academic year 1981–82 and would have declined to an estimated $67 if Congress had accepted Reagan's recommendations for 1981–82.[87]

Economics aside, the comprehensive, detailed procedural regulation and accompanying P.L. 94-142 have stood as a tempting target to an administration committed "to reduce the burden and cost of existing and future regulations."[88] Having failed to gain Congressional approval of consolidating handicapped education into the education block grant, the Reagan Administration has tried to amend the All Handicapped Children Act and significantly modify the regulations. In March 1982, the Administration sent the Congress draft legislation intending to simplify P.L. 94–142. Entitled "Education of the Handicapped Amendments of 1982," the proposed new law would maintain "essential" federal protection but give districts a good deal more flexibility in educating handicapped children.[89] Although the Administration had difficulty finding any Congressional sponsors willing to introduce the legislation,[90] it pushed ahead proposed regulatory reform.

In early August 1982, the Department of Education unveiled its proposal for new handicapped regulations designed "to provide more administrative flexibility for state and local education agencies ... reduce unnecessary Federal regulation,... eliminate burdensome and unnecessary paperwork,... effect cost savings through reduced administrative requirements... and make the regulations clearer and easier to understand."[91]

The administration insisted that another goal and purpose of the proposed rules was "to continue to ensure that the rights of handicapped children are fully protected."[92] Indeed, at a news conference announcing the proposed changes, Education Secretary Terrel Bell emphasized that "Educating all children and meeting their needs is a responsibility we should shoulder willingly, not a burden."[93] In shouldering the responsibility, the new regulation would permit a reduction of related services (for example, by not requiring school districts to foot the bill for such items as eyeglasses, hearing aids, surgical procedures), an easing of the Individualized Education Program requirement, a softening of procedural safeguards for parents, and greater flexibility in determining the least restrictive environment.[94] In addition, the new regulations would significantly reduce paperwork by such changes as the simplification of the state plan, local application, the IEP, and multidisciplinary evaluation.[95]

Anticipating considerable controversy over the proposed regulation, ED scheduled a longer than usual public comment period of ninety days (rather than sixty days) for participation in the regulatory review process.[96] During September 1982, hearings were held in eleven cities throughout the country.[97] Fierce opposition had been building for some time, however, and it came as no surprise to administrative officials that the public hearings produced widespread condemnations of the proposed regulations. In early 1982, the press carried accounts of a working paper prepared by the Education Department's Special Education Program (SEP) staff that reportedly "proposed relief for 'fiscal, paperwork, compliance and other burdens,'" while "liberating public educational agencies from unnecessary federal direction and control."[98] To handicapped advocates, such descriptive calls for regulatory relief were really a guise for insensitive policies aimed at undoing the many educational guarantees for handicapped children. Viewing administration communiques sending as "an intensified message of despair, pain and anger," Jo Thomason, President of the Council on Exceptional Children, handicapped children's major national advocacy group, felt that "these policies will undo much of what we have worked so long and so hard to accomplish." Outlining these thoughts in a June 2 letter to Secretary Bell, she expressed the council's "total dissatisfaction with the current direction of the administration."[99]

By late summer of 1982, it had become apparent that the only enthusiasm for the proposed change in P.L. 94–142 by a major politically oriented group came from the National School Boards Association that "applauded" the proposed regulations as a policy to "free state and local officials from excessive paperwork, regulatory detail, and costs."[100] On the other side, the Children's Defense Fund made much of the proposed deletion of health services for handicapped children. Indeed, the volume of requests from organizations and individuals seeking time to comment on the rules in the September public hearings prompted ED to add Kansas City and Philadelphia to its original nine-city roster for meeting sites.[101]

Such public discontent was not lost in Congress, a body that had already opposed handicapped consolidation and most of the administration's proposed funding cuts. In an August 18th press conference, several senators, including Democrat Kennedy of Massachusetts and Republican Stafford of Connecticut, requested that ED propose a regulations withdrawal. In the House more than fifty members cosponsored a resolution calling for the right to veto unacceptable finalized regulations, and nineteen California Congressmen requested that Terrell Bell extend the public comment period from 90 to 120 days,[102] a request accepted by the Secretary.

By the end of the public comment period on December 3, ED had received no fewer than 23,000 responses, which the SEP staff proceeded to analyze in a manner described as appearing "as complicated as the college admissions process, complete with i.d. numbers for each of the 23,000 comments."[103] In the meantime, Bell had withdrawn six of the most controversial of the regulatory changes for further study, which included alterations in "parental consent prior to evaluation or placement," redefining "the least restrictive environment" narrowing "related services" and modifying "qualifications of personnel."[104] At press time the Secretary had put on hold any revision of the proposed regulations and such alterations were not expected to surface before late summer of 1983.

The regulations supporting the education of the disadvantaged have faced far worse than those for handicapped children. As Chapter I of ECIA, Title I has, in effect, retained its categorical status, but the new Chapter I law, with its abbreviated rules, has punished the potency of the program. For example, two of Title I's most noteworthy features, the evaluation and parent involvement mandates, are components of Chapter I. Whereas formally these requirements were accompanied by specifics on program evaluation and advisory council construction, the new requirements mention only that "objective measurements and some accounting for sustenance be employed at least once every three years" and that a project be designed and implemented "in consultation with parents and teachers being served, including parents and teachers of children in private schools." Similar to the old law and regulations, the new governances target funds toward the "attendance areas... having the highest concentrations of low-income children," requires an eligibility criteria within such an agency based on educational need, and mandates that federal funds "supplement not supplant" local revenues.[105] Accordingly, we are still assured that children from low income families will receive a disproportionately greater share of the services, that schools will be guided in some form by the childrens' educational deprivation in determining eligibility, and that services will be rendered in addition to the regular school program. But the new legislation and regulations constitute little more than an abbreviated reference to the former Title I governances and localities are now licensed with considerably greater flexibility in constructing Chapter I programs.

Title I never required an IEP, but it did require that educators "identify in detail the precise educational needs of the children...," develop "educational objectives" for the program and spell out "types of services and instructional strategies to achieve those objectives." In addition to this planning, LEA's had to adopt an evaluation model to measure program impact that involved a regular pre- and posttesting of participants over a nine or twelve month period and a means of comparing the progress of Title I participants with nonparticipants. Perhaps the most noteworthy and least popular program regulations were those associated with parent involvement. In order "to encourage the involvement of parents in the planning, implementation, and evaluation of projects," the LEA typically had to have elected advisory councils with the majority membership composed of parents of project children. The councils received training "to carry out their responsibilities under the Title I project." Once established, the advisory councils were to be consulted on the various phases of project planning, be given specific information on the Title I law, and be provided copies of any report emerging from auditing or monitoring.[106]

Compliance with the aforementioned and other Title I regulations were under scrutiny of the LEA, which was required to monitor projects at least once every three years. Under Chapter I, districts are not only exempt from most regulations under what was formally Title I, but need not formally account for their compliance with the few existing requirements. Under Chapter I, there is no mention of state monitoring and LEA's are free to police their own activities.[107]

The failure to change the special education regulations or to fundamentally alter Title I is indicative of the difficulties the Reagan Administration has had in implementing education changes. Despite public interest in spending reduction, the diminished powers of Congressional authorizing committees and subcommittees long friendly to education, the emerging power of the budgeting and appropriations process under the tutelage of persons wishing to cut education, the political acumen and legislative lobbying of a persuasive president, the lack of unity of the Democratic Party, and despite the absence of any articulated widely accepted rationale for any federal involvement in education, the Reagan Administration has fallen far short of its goals of eliminating categorical programs and severely cutting educational funding.

There is also little question, however, that the deregulatory, consolidating, and budget reduction efforts of the Reagan Administration have left a significant impression on the educational order. The administration's challenging assault on the status quo and moderate success he has enjoyed have curbed the growth of federal involvement, generally simplified federal involvement with states and localities, and have been, perhaps inadvertantly, the impetus for important dialogue on devising a meaningful educational agenda for the 1980s.

REFERENCES

1. From an analysis of changing federalism by Guthrie, J.: The Future of Federal Education Policy, *Education and Urban Society, 14* (4):5ll–530, August 1982.

2. 1980 Political Platforms: The Democratic Education Platform. In Miller, R. (ed.): *Federal Role in Education: New Directions for the Eighties,* Washington, D.C., Institute for Educational Leadership, 1981, pp. 103–109.

3. Cannon, L.: Reagan. New York, NY, Putnam and Sons, 1982, p.329; *America's New Beginning: A Program for Economic Recovery.* The White House, Washington, D.C., February 18, 1981; *Summary Fact Sheet: A Program for Economics Recovery,* The White House, Washington, D.C., February 18, 1981, p.2.

4. Cannon, Reagan, p.321; *Congressional Quarterly Almanac, 1981,* Washington, D.C., Congressional Quarterly, Inc., 1981, 37:14,#21.

5. *Congressional Quarterly Almanac, 1981,* Washington, D.C., Congressional Quarterly, Inc., 1981, 37:21.

6. For analysis of this legislative process, *see* Schuster, J.: *Out of the Frying Pan: The Politics of Education in a New Era,* Phi Delta Kappan, 63(9):591–593, May 1982; *Congressional Quarterly Almanac, 1981,* Washington, D.C., Congressional Quarterly, Inc., 1981,37:89; Cannon, Reagan, p.333.

7. Cannon, Reagan, p. 333.

8. Cannon, Reagan, p. 371.

9. Cannon, Reagan, p. 372.

10. Reagan, R: Additional Reduction in Federal Spending. Delivered to the American people September 24, 1981. *Vital Speeches of the Day,* October 15, 1981, pp. 2–6.

11. *Congressional Quarterly Almanac, 1981,* Washington, D.C., Congressional Quarterly, Inc., 1981, 37:271–277.

12. See, for example, A.M. Advisory Memo Office, American Association of School Administrators, Arlington, VA, December 1981.

13. Reagan, R.: President Reagan's Report to the Nation on the Economy. Delivered to the American people February 5, 1981. Reprinted in *Congressional Quarterly Almanac, 1981,* Washington, D.C., Congressional Quarterly, Inc., 37:13–15E, 1981.

14. Reagan, R.: Address before joint session of Congress, February 18, 1981, Reprinted in *Congressional Quarterly Almanac, 1981.* Washington, D.C., Congressional Quarterly, Inc., 37:15–18E; *Summary Fact Sheet: A Program*

for Economic Recovery, The White House, Washington, D.C., February 18, 1981, p. 2.

15. *Fiscal Year 1982 Budget Revisions.* Washington, D.C., Office of Management and Budget, March 1981, pp. 63–64.

16. *Congressional Quarterly Almanac, 1981,* Washington, D.C., Congressional Quarterly, Inc., 1981, 37:257–258, 250–251.

17. *Congressional Quarterly Almanac, 1981,* Washington, D.C., Congressional Quarterly, Inc., 1981,37:250–251.

18. *Congressional Quarterly Almanac, 1981,* Washington, D.C., Congressional Quarterly, Inc., 1981, 37:256–263.

19. *Congressional Quarterly Almanac, 1981, Congressional Record,* Washington, D.C., Thursday, April 30, 1981, p. H1609.

20. *Congressional Quarterly Almanac, 1981, Congressional Record,* Washington, D.C., Thursday, April 30, 1981, p. H1607.

21. *Congressional Quarterly Almanac, 1981, Congressional Record,* Washington, D.C., Thursday, April 30, 1981, p. H1607.

22. *Congressional Quarterly Almanac, 1981,* Congressional Record, Washington, D.C., Thursday, April 30, 1981, pp. H1615, H1610–1611.

23. *Congressional Quarterly Almanac, 1981,* Washington, D.C., Congressional Quarterly, Inc., 1981, 37:256–266.

24. *Congressional Quarterly Almanac, 1981,* Washington, D.C., Congressional Quarterly, Inc., 1981, 37:265–266.

25. *Congressional Quarterly Almanac, 1981,* Washington, D.C., Congressional Quarterly, Inc., 1981, 37:265–266.

26. Weissman, S.: Reaganomics and the President's Men. *The New York Times Magazine,* October 24, 1982, pp. 26–29+.

27. Weissman, *Reaganomics and the President's Men.* p. 82.

28. *Congressional Quarterly Almanac, 1981,* Washington, D.C., Congressional Quarterly, Inc., 1981, 37:267–270.

29. Reagan, Additional Reductions, September 4, 1981, *Vital Speeches of the Day,* October 15, 1981, pp. 2–6.

30. *Congressional Quarterly Almanac, 1981,* Washington, D.C., Congressional Quarterly, Inc., 1981, 37:267–270.

31. *Congressional Quarterly Almanac, 1981,* Washington, D.C., Congressional Quarterly, Inc., 1981, 37:267–270.

32. Cuts in 1982 Spending as Spelled out by U.S. Education Department, *Education Times.* Washington, D.C., December 1981.

33. A.M. Advisory Memo, American Association of School Administrators, 1981.

34. *Congressional Quarterly Almanac, 1982.* Washington, D.C., Congressional Quarterly, Inc., 1982, 38:180–181.

35. From the coalition's publication, *Save Title I.* National Committee for Citizens in Education, Columbia, Maryland, 1982.

36. United States House Committee on Education and Labor, Hearing to consider H.R. 3645, 97th Congress, 15th session, May 28, 1981, pp. 44–109.

37. United States House Appropriations Committee hearings to consider fiscal year 1982 budget requests for DOL, HHS, Education Department & Related Agencies, 97th Congress, first session, October 22, 1981, pp. 1–187.
38. United States House Committee on Education and Labor, Sub-committee in Elementary, Secondary and Vocational Education, Oversight Hearing on Reading and Writing Achievement, 97th Congress, first session, May 7, 1981.
39. United States House Committee on Education and Labor, May 7, 1981, pp. 4–5.
40. United States House Committee on Education and Labor, May 7, 1981, pp.4–5.
41. United States House Committee on Education and Labor, Sub-committee on Elementary, Secondary and Vocational Education, Oversight Hearing on Title I, 97th Congress, 2nd session, March 23-25, 1982.
42. United States House Committee on Education and Labor, March 23-25, 1982, pp. 142–185.
43. United States House Committee on Education and Labor, March 23–25, 1982, p. 224.
44. United States House Committee on Education and Labor, March 23-25, 1982, p. 226.
45. Stickney, B.: *The Sustaining Effects Study: Implications for a Canceling Effect,* U.S. House Committee, March 23-25, 1982, pp. 240–242.
46. "Dear Colleague" letter from Augustus Hawkins and Carl Perkins, U.S. House of Representatives, Washington, D.C., May 12, 1982.
47. Rather, D.: CBS Evening News, January 22, 1982.
48. Coalition to Save Title I, Summary Minutes of December 15, 1981 meeting.
49. Coalition to Save Title I, December 15, 1981.
50. Report on Title I Day: A Big Success, Memorandum to the Title I Coalition from its Steering Committee, March 18, 1982.
51. *Congressional Record.* Washington, D.C., Thursday, May 20, 1982.
52. Reagan, R.: State of the Union Address. Delivered to a Joint Session of Congress January 25, 1983.
53. President Reagan Proposes Spending Curbs, Standby Tax to Repair Nation's Economy, *Congressional Quarterly Weekly Report, 41*(4):187-191, January 29, 1983.
54. Reagan, State of the Union Address, Delivered to a Joint Session of Congress January 25, 1981.
55. Budget Changes from Existing Policy; New Cuts in Social Programs Proposed by Administration, *Congressional Quarterly Weekly Report, 41*(5): 257-259; 307–309, February 5, 1983.
56. Reagan Seeks $13.2 Billion for Education "Self Help" Program for College Students, *Congressional Quarterly Weekly Report, 41*(5):289-290.
57. Reagan Seeks $13.2 Billion, *Congressional Quarterly Weekly Report, 41*(5): 289-290.
58. House Committee Approves Math/Science Aid Program, *Congressional Quarterly Weekly Report, 41*(6):349, February 12, 1983.

59. Deficit figures.
60. Stoffel, J.: Block Grants: A Bibliography, *State Government News*, April, 1982, Reprinted in *Block Grants*, Congressional Research Service, The Library of Congress, Washington, D.C., 1982, p. 69-72.
61. Educational Programs, *Congressional Quarterly Almanac, 1981*, op. cit., p. 500.
62. *Congress and the Nation: 1973-76*, 4: 401.
63. Osbourn, S.: Block Grants in the Omnibus Reconciliation Act of 1981 (P.L. 97-35): An Overview of their Characteristics, *Block Grants*, Congressional Research Service, The Library of Congress, Washington, D.C., 1982, p. CR5 6-25.
64. Education Consolidation and Improvement Act of 1981, p. 1.
65. *The Federal Education Project Newsletter*, December-January 1981-82, p. 1-2.
66. *The Federal Education Project Newsletter*, December-January, 1981, p. 1-2.
67. Education Consolidation and Improvement Act of 1981, p. 1-4.
68. Education Consolidation and Improvement Act of 1981, p. 1.
69. Education Consolidation and Improvement Act of 1981, p. 4-8.
70. Executive Order, Members Educational Block Grant Advisory Committee, A 26281, November 5, 1981; Colorado Application for Educational Block Grant Funds Under Title V, Public Law 97-35.
71. Partial Text of New York's State plan for block grants, reprinted in One State's Block Grant Plan: The New York Approach, *Education Times*, May 3, 1982, p. 4.
72. Executive Order . . ., November 5, 1981.
73. Elbers, G.: Why Federal Discretionary Programs Lost to Consolidation: A View from the Inside, *Education Times*, January 11, 1982, p. 2.
74. Interview with Arvin Bloom, Denver, Colorado, March 7, 1983.
75. Elbers, Why Federal Discretionary Programs, p. 2.
76. Elbers, Why Federal Discretionary Programs, p. 2.
77. The Educational Philosophy of John Ashbrook: Comments on the Education Block Grant by its Author, *Education Times*, May 3, 1982, p. 2.
78. See the *Federal Register*, April 27, 1979, p. 25148-25143; May 6, 1976, p. 18660-18673; June 29, 1979, p. 38364-38383; April 3, 1980, p. 22702-22727.
79. *See, for example, Application for Grants for Arts Education* (OE Form 449, 7/78); *Gifted and Talented Program* (OE Form 9048, 8/78); *Consumers Education Program* (OE Form 733, 9/79); *Basic Skills Improvement Program* (OE Form 295, 10/79); *Ethnic Heritage Studies Program* (ED Form 349, 10/80); *Community Education Program* (ED Form 453, 5/81).
80. *Application for Local Educational Agency Grants Under the Emergency School Aid Act,* (OE Form 116-1, 1979).
81. Application for Funds for Consolidation of Federal Programs for Elementary and Secondary Education, Chapter 2, ECIA, P.L. 97-35, Fiscal year 1984. Colorado Department of Education, Denver, Colorado, 1983.

82. From telephone interviews with Neil Shedd and Ann Short of the Division of Regulations, U.S. Department of Education, August 2-3, 1983.
83. Hamilton, B. and Yohalem, D.: The Effects of Deregulations, The Case of Handicapped Children, *Education and Urban Society,* 14 (4):399-423, August, 1982.
84. Hamilton & Yohalem, The Effects of Deregulations, pp. 399-423.
85. Hamilton & Yohalem, The Effects of Deregulations, pp. 418-419.
86. Hamilton & Yohalem, The Effects of Deregulations, pp. 403-407.
87. Hamilton & Yohalem, The Effects of Deregulations, p. 408.
88. Notice of Proposed Rulemaking for Regulations Implementing Part B of the Education of the Handicapped Act Factsheet, August 4, 1982, p. 1.
89. Administration sends Revised Handicapped Education Law to Congress, *Education Times,* March 2, 1982, p. 1.
90. Administration Sends Revised Handicapped Education Law to Congress, p. 1.
91. Notice of Proposed Rulemaking . . ., August 4, 1982, p. 2.
92. Notice of Proposed Rulemaking . . ., August 4, 1982, p. 2.
93. Secretary Bell quoted in Education Department unveils New Handicapped Regulations: Cites Reduced Compliance Burdens, *Education Times,* August 9, 1982, p. 1.
94. Assistance to States for Education of Handicapped Children. Proposed Rules, *Federal Register,* August 4, 1982, p. 33836-33860.
95. Assistance to States for Education of Handicapped Children, August 4, 1982, pp. 33836-33860.
96. Department of Education Statement for Public Hearings, Department of Education, Office of the Secretary, September 1982, p. 1.
97. Department of Education Statement for Public Hearings, September 1982, p. 1.
98. *Education Times,* February 1, 1982, p. 7.
99. Reprinted in *Education Times,* June 14, 1982.
100. Quoted in *Education Times,* August 30, 1982, p. 5.
101. Quoted in *Education Times,* August 30, 1982, p. 5.
102. Quoted in *Education Times,* August 30, 1982, p. 5.
103. Bell Announces Slowing of P.L. 94-142 Rulemaking Process, *Education of the Handicapped,* 9 (6): 1-2, March 23, 1983.
104. *See* Modification of Notice of Proposed Rulemaking, *Federal Register,* November 3, 1982, p. 49871-73; Assistance to States . . ., August 4, 1982.
105. Rules & Regulations, Chapter 1 of the Education Consolidation and Improvement Act of 1981. *Federal Register,* November 19, 1982, p. 52348-52849.
106. Rules & Regulations, Financial Assistance to Local and State Agencies to Meet Special Educational Needs; and Financial Assistance to Local Educational Agencies for Children with Special Education Needs. *Federal Register,* January 19, 1981, p. 5136-5236.
107. Telephone interview with Virginia Plunkett, Chapter 1 Consultant, Colorado Department of Education, October 19, 1983.

Chapter 4
THE CONSTITUTION AND THE SCHOOLS

Ever since its 1954 landmark school desegregation decision, the United States Supreme Court has come under strong attack from those who believe that educational policy should be determined by local school officials, not by federal judges. The 1962 school prayer ban added to those cries. In the last several decades, there have been a plethora of bills filed in Congress to restrict the authority of the federal judiciary and to prohibit the use of federal funds to litigate against those violating certain Supreme Court rulings. Similarly, there have been numerous proposals to nullify controversial Court decisions through new Constitutional amendments. For example, antibusing amendments have been frequently suggested, although generally such efforts have received insufficient support.

However, the 1980 election has given new life to the movement to limit the reach of the federal courts and to contract the impact of their earlier rulings. This chapter examines the Supreme Court rulings that seem to be at the heart of the current controversy. Since the issue is broader than the specific cases (but concerns the constitutional authority of the federal courts in general and the Supreme Court in particular), the debate over judicial activism and restraint is presented. From there, the chapter moves to a focus on the various measures proposed to limit the power of the federal judiciary and a few pending cases that might have profound impact if those limiting measures prove successful.

(The operation of the schools includes a wide range of activity. Thus, the courts have been called upon to adjudicate an equally wide range of cases including ones to determine who may attend, who may teach, what may be taught, what rights must be accorded

128

students and teachers, how must public funds be used, etc. Since the issues of racial integration and church-state interaction evoke the strongest emotions, they serve as the focus of the discussion in this chapter.)

Local Autonomy

Two nineteenth century cases set local autonomy boundaries that stood firmly until the last half of the twentieth century when the Supreme Court began to view constitutional rights as national, rather than local or regional, in nature. In 1819, the Court sided with Dartmouth College that it should be able to operate without governmental interference.[1] Eighty years later, the Court held that "separate but equal," the racial doctrine approved in the 1896 case of *Plessy v. Ferguson,* was applicable to the public schools, and that a school district that claimed to have inadequate resources was not obligated to provide fully equal education for blacks.[2]

School Desegregation

For all practical purposes, it was not until 1954 that the Court decided that the schools had to answer to a higher standard than that set by local officials. *Brown v. Board of Education* was landmark, not only in that it put an end to the constitutionality of "separate but equal" ("Separate educational facilities are inherently unequal," said the Court) but also in that it opened the schools to federal scrutiny in order to guarantee that the "equal protection" and "due process" clauses of the Constitution do not stop at the schoolhouse door.[3] The enforcement order, known as *Brown II,* called for school districts to make a "prompt and reasonable start" toward desegregation under the supervision of the local federal district judges.[4] The Court took this approach since it believed that the myriad of local problems and peculiarities could be best understood by jurists who had firsthand knowledge of the people and politics of the school districts in question. While making sense in the abstract, the order had the effect of thwarting the high court's desire to see desegregation proceed "with all deliberate speed": the fifty-eight federal judges who were to oversee the desegregation were products of the society that had created the practice, and, perhaps more important, were subject to substantial local pressure.

It took a series of additional Supreme Court actions, along with the Civil Rights Act of 1964, to put an end to racially separate schools. The pace of progress was painstakingly slow. In fact, by the tenth anniversary of the *Brown* decision, only one-tenth of 1 percent of the black children in the Deep South were attending classes with whites. Resistance in some places was violent. In Little Rock, for example, a small group of black children was stopped from entering Central High School by an unruly mob of whites, while the National Guard, with bayonettes fixed, maintained a centurion vigil in front of the school. On the premise that desegregating Central High would endanger the lives of the black children, city officials used the ugliness of that situation to forestall integration. The Supreme Court, in *Cooper v. Aaron,* found such a posture unacceptable.[5] It ruled that the government has a fundamental obligation to protect the constitutional rights of its citizens. Thus, the force of the law should be used to make desegregation safe, rather than to postpone the implementation of the plan.

Most instances of local delay were the result either of footdragging by state and local officials or of the passage of statutes that were clearly intended to thwart the Supreme Court's mandate. In Tennessee, for instance, several school boards rezoned attendance districts to remove racial requirements, yet permitted students to transfer out of schools in which they were in the racial minority. This had the effect of maintaining the original segregation and, thus, in 1963 was ruled unconstitutional by the Supreme Court.[6] The following year, the Court outlawed the underpinning of Virginia's "massive resistance" policy, the providing of tax credits and tuition grants for attendance at all-white private schools under the guise of "freedom of choice."[7] Said Chief Justice Earl Warren during the oral arguments, the policy merely gave black children the "freedom to go through life without an education."

The Court grew tired of official resistance and in 1965 stated, "delays in desegregating school systems are no longer tolerable."[8] Immediately thereafter it ruled "grade a year" plans unconstitutional.[9] Three years later, in another Virginia case, it finally put an end to "freedom of choice" plans, since in the matter at hand such a policy had resulted in 85 percent of the black children remaining in all black schools: school authorities could no longer allow students to choose among the public schools; they had an affirmative duty to act to put an end to segregation.[10]

It was the implementation of an active plan that resulted in a ruling that is at the heart of many of the current court-limiting proposals. In 1971, in its last unanimous school desegregation action, the Court upheld a federal judge's remedy for the segregation that remained in the Charlotte-Mecklenberg (N.C.) school district.[11] Richard Nixon's first Supreme Court appointee, Chief Justice Warren Burger, spoke for the Court in its acceptance of the use of mathematical ratios, which reflect districtwide racial proportions, as the foundation upon which a desegregation plan could be built. To do so would require school assignments to be based on race, a permissible tool as long as it was used positively to promote integration, rather than invidiously to promote segregation. Since the school district's neighborhoods were as segregated as its schools, it was not possible to integrate the school through a neighborhood approach. Said the Chief Justice in the *Swann* decision:

> All things being equal, with no history of discrimination, it might well be desirable to assign pupils to schools nearest their homes. But all things are not equal in a system that has been deliberately constructed and maintained to enforce racial segregation.

Thus, the Court held that "desegregation plans cannot be limited to the walk-in school" and that it was constitutionally acceptable for a federal judge to require the school district "to employ bus transportation as one tool of school desegregation." It did this in what some believe to have been a contradiction of Title IV of the Civil Rights Act of 1964 that prohibited any federal official or court from issuing "any order seeking to achieve a racial balance in any school by requiring the transportation of pupils or students from one school to another." However, the Court held that Title IV is "designed to foreclose any interpretation of the Act as expanding the existing powers of federal courts to enforce the Equal Protection Clause." Burger went on to state that the Act had no "intention to restrict those powers or withdraw from courts their historic equitable remedial powers" in instances of state-imposed segregation.

As written, the *Swann* decision affected only those districts where segregation had the official sanction of the state. Had the Supreme Court stopped there, court-ordered busing would only have been found in the Southern, Border and a few Western states. However, in 1973 in the *Keyes* case, the Court found the Denver public schools to be segregated despite the fact that the City of Denver had never officially permitted racially separate schools.[12] The majority opinion, written by Justice William Brennan, held that techniques such as the manipulation of school attendance zones and school site selection, combined with a neighborhood school policy that on its face appeared to be neutral, had resulted in the "deliberate racial segregation in the schools attended by over one-third of the Negro school population." Thus, it was the Court's view that Denver's de facto segregation was, indeed, *de jure.* Under the *Keyes* doctrine, any school system so segregated was as liable to court remedy as any school in the Southern and Border states.

Thus, busing orders and resistance to them spread throughout the North and West. As has been noted by Derrick A. Bell, Jr., this resistance

> belied the earlier belief that only ignorant rednecks would violently oppose a federal court order. We now know more clearly that many whites at any class level will oppose any school remedy . . . particularly if it threatens their status and prerogatives.[13]

At first, orders and opposition were centered in the cities. However, it quickly became apparent that if there were to be effective central city school desegregation, some big city school district plans would need to involve the independent suburban districts. To the delight of most suburban residents, however, the Court ruled that desegregation plans must be limited to those districts that had acted to bring about the condition to be remedied. Thus, in the *Milliken* case, the Court held that since Detroit's suburbs had not participated in the segregative acts that had resulted in Detroit's one-race schools, they could not be involuntarily included in the desegregation plan.[14] To the chagrin of some other suburban residents, the Court has, however, ruled that where there is suburban complicity, the remedy may involve the entire metropolitan area. Two instances where such plans have been implemented are Jefferson County (KY), which includes Louisville[15] and New Castle County (DE), which includes Wilmington.[16]

(Beyond busing, there is one additional school desegregation measure that is the focus of controversy emanating from a Supreme Court ruling. In 1974, in *Lau v. Nichols*, the Court held that special instruction must be provided to students whose native language is other than English, if there are substantial numbers of such students in the district.[17] While this case concerned Chinese-speaking children, it has been felt most strongly in school districts with sizable Hispanic populations.)

Church, State and the Schools

A second major area of involvement of the federal courts in educational matters has been in the First Amendment area of freedom of religion and the separation of church and state. Fundamental to American democracy is the concept of religious freedom embodied in the First Amendment: "Congress shall make no law respecting an establishment of religion or prohibiting the free exercise thereof." (The first portion of this statement is known as the "Establishment" Clause; the latter portion is known as the "Free Exercise" clause.) However, for good or bad, religion has never been completely separate from government and politics. The Supreme Court recognized this in the 1952 case of *Zorach v. Clauson* in which it stated, "we are a religious people whose institutions presuppose a Supreme Being."[18] Thus, decisions that have made religion private have been particularly controversial.

No case proves that point as well as *Engel v. Vitale*, the 1962 case that remains today as controversial as it was when announced two decades ago: a twenty-two-word nonsectarian prayer composed by the New York State Board of Regents for daily recitation in the state's public schools was ruled unconstitutional.[19] The majority opinion of the Court held that any prayer "composed by government officials as part of a governmental program to further religious beliefs" violates the constitutional prohibition against the "Establishment" Clause of the First Amendment. The fact that participation in the daily exercise was voluntary made no difference since "the power, prestige and financial support of government [had been] placed behind a particular religious belief" (i.e., praying in school).

The outcry from many prominent religious leaders was loud and immediate. Nevertheless, shortly thereafter, the Court followed with a ruling that invalidated a Pennsylvania law requiring the daily reading of a biblical passage. At the same time, it declared unconstitutional Baltimore's official practice (not required by state or local law) of daily Bible reading and recitation of the Lord's Prayer in the public schools.[20] Writing for the majority, Justice Tom Clark held that any activity by governmental authorities is unconstitutional if it seeks to promote or inhibit religion. The Court ruled similarly in 1980 when it overruled a Kentucky law that required the posting of the Ten Commandments in all public school classrooms.[21]

Schools are, however, permitted to teach *about* religion if they do so in a neutral manner. Not long ago, the American Civil Liberties Union and the American Jewish Congress attempted to end Christmas celebrations in the public schools. They claimed that such observances have gone beyond the permissible. When the Supreme Court declined to accept the case, it allowed a 2 to 1 decision of the Eighth Circuit Court of Appeals to stand; that court had found the schools in Sioux Falls, South Dakota were within the acceptable limits of the Constitution and were, in fact, less objectionable then than they had been several years earlier.[22]

One issue that has yet to reach the United States Supreme Court, but is likely to within the next few years, is the teaching of creationism in the schools. Creationists believe that the world was created some 6,000 to 10,000 years ago in the manner described in the Book of Genesis; included in this interpretation is the belief that Noah's Ark provided refuge from a worldwide flood. Creationists reject evolutionist theory as expressed by those who have built upon the research of Charles Darwin; they reject as inaccurate such evidence as provided by carbon-14 dating techniques that reveal ancient objects to be millions of years old. Promoting creationism have been a variety of groups on the Christian right including a number of television evangelists who claim that more than 50 million Americans watch their programs.[23] They are a growing force in America. One of the better known of this group, fundamentalist minister Jerry Falwell, recently captured the essence of the creationist movement:

> Textbooks have become absolutely obscene and vulgar. Many of them are openly attacking the integrity of the Bible. Humanism is the main thrust of the public school textbook. Darwinian evolution is taught from kindergarten age right through high school . . .. For our nation, this is a life-and-death struggle, and the battle line for this struggle is in the textbooks.[24]

To win the textbook battle, the creationists need only carry the day in a few key states, since decisions regarding textbook acquisition are made on a statewide basis in twenty-two states. A 1981 study undertaken by the Association of American Publishers, the American Library Association, and the Association for Supervision and Curriculum Development revealed that a textbook "prepared for Texas or California, the two largest adopting states, often becomes the sole edition available nationwide," as a result of the business generated by those states and the expense involved in preparing multiple editions.[25] Jessica Tuchman Matthews contends that "[p]ressure from creationists has already led school book publishers, many of whom follow a policy of avoiding controversy at whatever cost to their integrity, to alter texts far more than most Americans imagine."[26]

This national movement has an ally Ronald Reagan, who, during the 1980 presidential campaign, made creationism one of his issues,[27] and since his election, has consistently spoken out in its behalf.[28] Buoyed by presidential leadership, creationists have now proposed "equal time" legislation in more than forty states. Such measures would require that "creation science" be taught in public school biology classes alongside the theory of evolution.[29] Bills have been signed into law in Arkansas and Louisiana.[30] Further, school boards in Dallas, Texas; Columbus, Ohio; and Charleston, West Virginia have prescribed the teaching of creationism.[31]

Creationists have also taken the judicial route. In California, Kelly L. Seagraves, director of the Creation Science Research Center, filed suit in Superior Court on behalf of his children against the California Board of Education that had distributed a guideline for the development of science courses that

> espouses and promotes with factual delineation and factual emphasis the evolutionary theory of the origin of man and all plant and animal life, thereby holding and promulgating that the theory of evolution is the only credible theory of the origin of said life.[32]

Seagraves claimed that such a policy violates the religious freedom of persons who believe in creationism. He further held that by holding to the "dogma" of evolution, California was establishing the religion of "secular humanism" in the schools.[33]

Judge Irving H. Perluss avoided what was sure to become a major constitutional case by ruling on June 12, 1981, that the policy of the California School Board did not require that evolution be taught as dogma. In fact, he pointed to the Board's 1972 antidogmatism policy intended for textbook publishers as well as science teachers, and directed the Board to make sure that school districts clearly understood it.[34] While not the victory that Seagraves had sought, the Perluss ruling gave creationists an opening.

The federal courts had their first crack in recent years at this issue as a result of an "equal time" act signed into law in Arkansas on March 19, 1981.[35] The bill was introduced in the Arkansas General Assembly by Senator James L. Holsted, a "born again" Christian Fundamentalist. It proceeded through the legislative process in quick measure—no hearings were held in the Senate and a fifteen minute hearing was held in the House; floor debate was limited. Neither the state's Department of Education nor the Attorney General were consulted. Two months after enactment, the American Civil Liberties Union (ACLU) sued on the ground that the law violated the Establishment Clause of the First Amendment, that it violated students' and teachers' rights to academic freedom guaranteed by the Free Speech Clause, and that the vagueness of the act violates the Due Process Clause. Included among the plaintiffs were Christian and Jewish groups, parents, a high school biology teacher, the Arkansas Education Association, the National Association of Biology Teachers, and the National Coalition for Public Education and Religious Liberty.

Testimony presented during the trial indicated that Paul Ellwanger, a respiratory therapist from South Carolina, had drafted model "equal time" legislation, which ultimately became the "Balanced Treatment for Creation-Science and Evolution Science Act" (Act 590) in Arkansas. Letters, written by Ellwanger and introduced as evidence, indicated that he does not believe that creation science is a science, but that it is a religious crusade: "I view this whole battle as one between God and anti-God forces . . .." Yet, his letters stressed the need to mask the religious thrust in favor of an argument regarding the scientific search for truth.

Called to the stand to support Act 590 were a number of faculty from fundamentalist colleges; many were members of the Creation Research Society that requires as a precondition for membership that an oath be signed affirming the belief in the historical and scientific accuracy of the Bible.[36] One such witness, Dr. Norman Geisler of the Dallas Theological Seminary, stated his belief that Darwin's commitment to evolution elevated a theory to a religion, and that creation science, despite its inspiration by the Book of Genesis, is, therefore, no more religious than is evolution.[37]

The decision in this case—*Reverend Bill McLean* et al. *v. The Arkansas Board of Education* et al.—was rendered by U.S. District Court Judge William R. Overton on January 5, 1982. He held that

> The State failed to produce any evidence which would warrant an inference or conclusion that at any point in the process anyone considered the legitimate educational value of the Act. It was simply and purely an effort to introduce the Biblical version of creation into the public school curricula. The only inference which can be drawn from these circumstances is that the Act was passed with the specific purpose by the General Assembly of advancing religion.

He found that the Act's definition of creation science is "inspired by the Book of Genesis" and "is simply not science" since the concept of creation "depends upon a supernatural intervention which is not guided by natural law" and, thus, is not testable through scientific research. In drawing this conclusion, Overton cited creationist textbooks including *Evolution—The Fossils Say No!* that states:

> We do not know how the Creator created, what processes He used, for He used processes which are not now operating anywhere in the natural universe . . .. We cannot discover by scientific investigation anything about the creative processes used by the Creator.

Overton went on to criticize Act 590 for prohibiting, in the instruction of creationism, reference to religious writings (the mask called for by Ellwanger), since, he wondered, "How will a teacher explain the occurrence of a worldwide flood? How will a teacher explain the concept of a relatively recent age of the earth?"

To the contention of the State that the public school curriculum should reflect the subjects that the public wants taught, Overton responded

> The application and content of the First Amendment principles are not determined by public opinion pools or by a majority vote . . .. No group, no matter how large or small, may use the organs of government, of which the public schools are the most conspicuous and influential, to foist its religious beliefs on others.

Thus, he slammed the door on Arkansas's "equal time" law.

Since Arkansas Attorney General Steve Clark decided not to appeal Overton's decision, this case will not reach the Supreme Court. However, that opportunity may present itself as a result of Louisiana's "equal time" law. In that instance, a suit was filed on

December 2, 1981, by a group of creationists, and another the following day by the ACLU.[38] Or, perhaps, the Supreme Court case will arise from a future case based on a new model legislation drafted by Paul Ellwanger that he hopes will avoid many of Judge Overton's complaints.[39]

Protection of Religious Liberty

While the federal courts have acted to keep the practice of religion out of the operation of the schools, they have also served to protect the First Amendment rights of those who seek to fulfill the doctrines of their religion. In 1925, the Supreme Court voided an Oregon law that would have required public school attendance through the eighth grade by children between the ages of eight and sixteen.[40] The enforcement of such a law would have resulted in the closing of parochial schools. The Court ruled that states had the right to regulate education and to require attendance of children in an adequate school, but that they could not require that all children attend public schools.

Nearly half a century later, the Court went a bit further in its definition of adequate schooling. In the case of *Wisconsin v. Yoder,* the state's interest in developing an educated populous was balanced against the beliefs of a religious community.[41] Members of the Old Order Amish, a Christian group that attempts to maintain a pre-Industrial Revolution way of life, had been convicted of violating Wisconsin's compulsory school attendance law. They had withdrawn their children from school after the eighth grade (rather than at age sixteen) because they believed that the children at that point in their lives required preparation for the hard life of the Amish adult. The Amish established that all facets of their daily existence were directly tied to their religious beliefs, and the Supreme Court held that Wisconsin could demonstrate no compelling reason for infringing upon the Amish's unhindered practice of their religion. Thus, if any religious group is able to demonstrate that compulsory education laws interfere with the group's established religious approach to the preparation of its youth for responsible adulthood, the law must yield to the supremacy of the religious practice.

In December 1981, the Court supported the rights of another religious group. In an effort to maintain a strict separation of church and state, the University of Missouri at Kansas City adopted a policy prohibiting the use of university buildings and grounds for religious purposes. The university believed that to allow religious groups to use university property would have the primary effect of advancing religion. Noting that the university had a policy of providing space to all student groups regardless of their political or social outlook, the Court stated, "We are satisfied that any religious benefits of an open forum at UMKC would be incidental" since "an open forum in a public university does not confer any imprimatur of State approval . . . ."[42]

This decision is indicative of the distinction drawn by the Supreme Court between elementary and secondary education on the one hand, and higher education on the other since the 1971 case of *Tilton v. Richardson*.[43] This distinction is based on the belief that religion is less pervasive in most religiously affiliated colleges with a public mission (this, of course, excludes monasteries and wholly religious colleges) than it is in the lower levels.

Public Funds and Religious Education

Many communities and states have sought cooperative arrangements with religious schools. In part, these practices derive from an understanding that public school systems would need to grow larger if it became necessary to accommodate all of those children currently attending private schools. Such schools account for approximately 10 percent of elementary and secondary school enrollments;[44] 80 percent of these are in church supported schools.[45]

While the Supreme Court has permitted the use of public monies in support of the secular purposes of religious colleges and universities, it has drawn distinct lines around the purposes to which they can be used in parochial elementary and secondary schools. For example, the 1947 case of *Everson v. Board of Education of the Township of Ewing* upheld a New Jersey statute that authorized school districts to provide for the transportation of children to the public schools and to nonprofit private schools, including those that were religiously affiliated.[46] The Court held that the use of public funds to bus children to Catholic schools was acceptable under the Fourteenth Amendment guarantee that provides for the protection of life, liberty, and property. Just as church-related schools are entitled to police and fire protection and to water and sewer service, they are entitled to school bus service. Otherwise, argued the Court, the state's position would move from one that is religiously neutral to one that seeks to inhibit religion.

Based on *Everson*, the Court let stand a New York law that provides for the loan of public textbooks to parochial school children. In the 1968 case of *Board of Education v. Allen*, Justice Byron White found the statute to be "in conformity with the Constitution, for the books are furnished for the use of individual students and at their request."[47]

State neutrality is, however, breached if public funds are used to support the teaching of nonsecular subjects in the parochial schools. In 1971, the Court held as unconstitutional laws in Pennsylvania (*Lemon v. Kurtzman*) and Rhode Island (*Earley v. Dicenso*) that provided a state salary support for parochial school teachers who taught nonreligious courses.[48] In so doing, the Court established a three-pronged test to determine the constitutionality of public aid to students enrolled in church schools: (1) aid must be intended to promote a student's education, health, and safety, not to enhance religion; (2) the primary effect of the aid must be religiously neutral; (3) the aid program must be such that it can stand without excessive surveillance that would result in excessive government entanglement in the affairs of the church.

Two years later, three New York programs were invalidated in an action in which the Court held it improper for the state to subsidize tuition charged to low income students who wished to attend parochial schools, for the state to provide a tuition tax credit for nonpublic schools, and for the state to share in the capital costs of those schools.[49] In *Meek v. Pittenger* (1975), the Court once again permitted the loaning of public school textbooks to parochial schools, but ruled direct aid in the form of the provision of auxiliary services (counseling, testing, speech therapy, etc.) to be noncompliant with Constitutional prohibitions.[50] Said Justice Potter Stewart, "the potential for political entanglement [between church and state], together with the administrative entanglement which would be necessary to ensure that auxiliary services personnel remain strictly neutral and nonideological" compels an unconstitutional finding concerning this sort of support. However, in 1977, a badly split Court backed away from this position in the case of *Wolman v. Walter*. A majority of the Justices favored the provision of the same standardized and diagnostic testing services to parochial school children as are provided to public school children if the testing is

administered by public school employees. They permitted thera-
peutic services provided at public expense if provided by public
school employees at a site outside of the parochial school. Further,
they agreed to the public purchase of secular texts and reusable
workbooks for loan to parochial school students, but they balked at
the provision of instructional materials, audiovisual equipment and
transportation for field trips.[51] Two years later, the Court declined
to order the return of the instructional materials loaned by Ohio to
the parochial schools under the statute struck down by *Wolman*.[52]
The federal district court judge had earlier determined that the
process of returning the loaned items would require an entangling
relationship forbidden by *Lemon*; the Supreme Court agreed by
refusing to hear the appeal.[53]

The Court split again when it upheld, in a 5-4 decision, the
constitutionality of a New York law that provided up to $20 million
to nonpublic schools to support the paperwork, recordkeeping,
and other administrative costs associated with state-mandated
testing requirements. Writing for the majority in the *Regan* case,
Justice Byron White cautioned that, because the Court was so
divided, this case should not be used as a "litmus paper test to
distinguish permissible from impermissible aid to religiously oriented schools." Nevertheless, Justice Blackman called the decision "a
long step backwards," and Justice Stephens called for the rebuild-
ing of the "high and impregnable wall between church and state
constructed by the Framers of the First Amendment."[54]

Thus, while the three-pronged test of *Lemon* remains the
measure for constitutionality, the decisions of the Court are not
predictable in this area of public and to religious schools. Without
strong leadership by the Supreme Court, district courts have taken
conflicting positions, most of which have not been accepted for
review by the high Court.[55] As Justice White noted in the *Regan*
case, the nation is divided in its reaction to such programs, and the
Court reflects that division.[56]

Other Areas of Court Activity

It is fair to say that the range of activity associated with education
is a microcosm of daily life in America; that is, school districts hire
people, spend money, construct buildings, etc. Some court rulings
regarding public spending and public institutions apply to the
enterprise of education as well. Others focus specifically on

education. For example, the 1957 *Sweazy* case reaffirmed the premise of a faculty member's academic freedom.[57] While this led to a decision upholding the right to teach evolution, it did not lead to a ruling that academic freedom obviates the requirement for a faculty member to sign a loyalty oath in order to be employed at a public institution.

One case that had nothing to do with education, nevertheless has had profound impact on the rights of school children. In 1967, the Supreme Court ruled in the case of *In re Gault* that children must be accorded the same constitutional protections accorded to adults.[58] That decision led to several cases that established the premise in the schools. The 1969 *Tinker* case was landmark in its extension of freedom of speech to students in school so long as that expression did not "materially and substantially disrupt the work and discipline of the school."[59] Thus, it was acceptable for Tinker to wear a black arm band in protest against the Vietnam War. Student groups were also found to have the First Amendment right of assembly. A 1972 decision concerning the radical Students for a Democratic Society forbids a college or university from denying recognition to a student group "simply because it finds the views expressed by any group abhorrent."[60] This ruling enjoyed a recent round of controversy in the quest of gay student groups to receive official college recognition in order to be able to use college facilities for their functions.

The second landmark case in the area of student rights is that of *Goss v. Lopez*, a 1975 ruling requiring that students be accorded minimal due process prior to being severely disciplined in response to alleged misconduct; that case involved the suspension of nine students without being accorded a hearing or any other means to present their side of the story.[61] The due process requirement was extended beyond exclusion from the school to the matter of corporal punishment within the school in *Baker v. Owen* (1975),[62] but two years later the Court changed its mind. In *Ingraham v. Wright*, it held that since a student could file civil or criminal charges against school personnel who are excessive in carrying out corporal punishment regulations, it is not necessary for the student to be given a hearing prior to such punishment.[63]

Proposals to Limit Court Jurisdiction

The range of federal court decisions—school desegregation and busing, school prayer and the limits to public support for church schools, and the provision of faculty and students rights—have provoked tremendous controversy (although the debate in the latter area of student and faculty rights generally only rears itself in times of broader social and political strife). Efforts at the Congressional level to moot Supreme Court rulings, including those regarding education, have been present for as long as the Court has been issuing rulings.

There is no question that Congress has the power under the Constitution (Article III, Section 2, Paragraph 2) to limit the Supreme Court's appellate jurisdiction.[64] As stated by Alexander Hamilton in the Federalist Papers (No. 81), the Supreme Court's appellate jurisdiction is "subject to any exceptions and regulations which may be thought advisable" by Congress. This was recognized by the Supreme Court in an 1805 decision written by Chief Justice Marshall who stated, "an affirmative description of [the Court's] powers must be understood as a regulation, under the Constitution, prohibiting the exercise of other powers than those described." Similarly, in 1847, Chief Justice Taney noted that the Court "possesses no appellate power in any case, unless conferred upon it by act of Congress." This limitation was so well understood that no criminal cases reached the Supreme Court on appeal until 1891—after Congress gave the Court appellate jurisdiction in that area.[65]

Just as limits can be placed on the Supreme Court by Congress, they can be placed on the lower federal courts as well. Those courts were created under the authority granted to Congress by the Constitution; they were not mandated by the law of the land.[66]

Between 1953 and 1968, over sixty court-limiting initiatives were introduced in Congress, but as has been pointed out by Telford Taylor, "Congress, as a whole, has exhibited a most commendable restraint in this regard."[67]

The movement to limit the purview of the federal judiciary has picked up steam as conservatism has taken hold in American politics. Currently there are approximately twenty bills before Congress that would have the effect of trying the hands of the federal judges regarding one or another topic.[68] For example, North Carolina Senator Jesse Helms joined with Louisiana's J. Bennett Johnston to sponsor the Neighborhood School Act, which, if enacted, would limit busing orders issued by federal courts by requiring that no bus ride be longer than five miles or fifteen minutes in length. The proposal would also apply retroactively to existing court orders.[69] Such an approach directly complements the position taken by the Reagan Justice Department that announced, late in 1981, that it would no longer seek to desegregate an entire school district on the basis of segregation shown to exist in a portion of the district. As reported in the national press, Assistant Attorney General for Civil Rights William Bradford Reynolds stated, "We are not going to compel children who don't choose to have an integrated education to have one." He went on:

> Every kid in America has a right to an integrated education if he wants it. But I don't think that means the Government can compel an integrated education. I don't think there's anything in the Constitution that suggests it can, or any of the cases by the Supreme Court.

Nevertheless, he did cite a Supreme Court case and stated the Administration's intention to disregard it: "We will not rely on the *Keys* presumption, but . . . seek to limit the remedy only to those schools in which racial imbalance is the product of intentionally segregative acts of state officials."[70]

The Reagan Administration has also chosen to seek the reversal of the school prayer decision. In the 1962 school prayer case, *Engel v. Vitale,* it was revealed that only one child in four years in the school district where the prayer was challenged had asked to be excused from participating in the voluntary prayer. The Court recognized that a subtle form of coercion had removed the voluntary aspect of the exercise. Nonetheless, in the spring of 1982, President Reagan announced his intention to introduce an amendment to the Constitution that would permit voluntary school prayer.[71] Senator Helms has attempted to accomplish the same goal in a different way by tacking on to the federal appropriations act a measure removing the jurisdiction of the federal courts over school prayer. The effort, characterized by the New York *Times* as an "end run around the Constitution" and "a sneak attack on the Federal courts to remove them as a bulwark for religious liberty," was defeated as a result of a filibuster by liberal senators.[72]

One Senate initiative that proved to be more successful was a measure to bar the Justice Department from bringing suit against school districts with voluntary prayer or meditation practices. Even if such legislation were to be signed into law, it is unlikely that it would have major impact since most school prayer suits are brought by individuals, not by the Justice Department.[73] Still, this action represents another assault on the federal courts.

The Republican takeover of the Senate after the 1980 election resulted in liberal committee chairs being replaced by conservatives. One important change was in the Judiciary Committee where Strom Thurmond succeeded Ted Kennedy in the leadership role. A segregationist for most of his life, Thurmond has been an opponent of most Supreme Court desegregation and separation of church and state rulings. In the days following the Republican landslide, he talked boldly of turning back the clock in a number of areas.[74] One possibility is an effort to remove education from the purview of the federal courts.

The Judicial Activism—Judicial Restraint Debate

Court-limiting proposals are likely to gather serious support, and it will not come only from those who do not want their children bussed or who want prayers in the schools. Those who oppose many Supreme Court rulings do so because they believe that the Court has exceeded its constitutional authority; they see little in the Constitution that permits the Court to order school busing for racial balance or that prohibits voluntary prayer at the start of the school day. Persons holding this view espouse a philosophy of judicial restraint.

According to the Constitutional scholar, Charles M. Lamb, there are six fundamental notions of judicial restraint. First, it is the intent of the framers of the Constitution and the various statutes that should guide the judiciary, not the personal preferences of the sitting jurists. Second, justices should not substitute their own judgment for that of those in the executive or legislative branches except to point out when the strict bounds of law have been crossed. Third, whenever possible, judges should base their decisions on existing statutes rather than looking to the Constitution for answers. Fourth, only cases in which those bringing the suit are directly affected by a real, rather than projected, issue should be accepted by the courts. Fifth, judges should not issue advisory opinions. Finally, justices should not answer political questions.[75]

Persons who support judicial restraint believe that statutes and the Constitution should be strictly interpreted; they believe that judicial policymaking (or loose interpretation) is undemocratic.

They contend that it is the President and Congress, governors and legislatures, mayors and councils who are elected by a majority of the voters to fashion the laws to meet the current and emerging needs of American society. Federal judges, they point out, are neither elected nor are they intended to be lawmakers. Lino Graglia characterizes the permissibility of court activism harshly: "[i]f tyranny describes government in which the governors are not regularly subjected to the control of the governed, this system qualifies for the description."[76] His criticism is repeated by Thomas J. Higgins who sees a certain undemocratic arrogance by activist judges who assume "that the people do not understand the Constitution and will not respect it, but that [the] Court does understand it and will respect it."[77]

Not all critics of court activism hold such extreme positions, however. Louis Lasky, who served as law clerk to Justice Stone in the 1937-38 term of the Supreme Court and who helped to draft the decision that was the vanguard of the current activist era, has come to believe that there ought to be certain limits to judicial activity:

> The Court does revise the Constitution from time to time (exercising, to that extent, the prerogatives of a continuing constitutional convention)— and this is legitimate if, but only if, the Court submits to the restraint imposed by overriding principles and does not proceed on an ad hoc basis to implement the Justices' personal views of rational policy.[78]

Raoul Berger would disagree. He believes strongly in the premise of carrying out the intention of those who drafted the law. He cites the great Supreme Court Justice Joseph Story who believed that reference to the original intention of the framers provides, "a 'fixed standard' for interpretation, without which a 'fixed Constitution' would be forever unfixed."[79] He contends that proponents of judicial activism who look to the words of Justice Oliver Wendell Holmes as a "shibboleth of judicial law making" do so erroneously.[80] In a 1914 decision, Holmes wrote:

> [The] provisions of the Constitution . . . are *organic living institutions* transplanted from English soil. Their significance is to be gathered not simply by taking the words and a dictionary but by considering their origin and *the line of their growth.*[81] (emphasis added)

Not only does Berger believe the passage to have been improperly lifted from its context,[82] but he posits that "judicial power to revise the Constitution transforms the bulwark of our liberties into a parchment barrier."[83] One can conclude from Berger that the most appropriate way for a constitution or a set of statutes to evolve is not by decree from the bench but by amendment through the appropriate legislative process.

Obviously, such has not been the case. Since 1954, the Supreme Court has, according to Lasky, "engaged in constitutional innovation on a large and expanding scale."[84] Judicial activism has not been limited to the high Court, however. In fact, most has come from the district court judges who "do the nuts-and-bolts work of expanding the reach of judicial authority."[85] Nevertheless, it is to Earl Warren and his Court that judicial restraint proponents aim their barbs.

Let us look to the decisions on race and religion in the schools to demonstrate this point. The desegregation rulings were derived from an interpretation of the Fourteenth Amendment. Raoul Berger contends that the amendment's framers were quite clear in their enumeration of the rights they sought to protect from state discrimination; regretably the matter of integration was not one of them. Thus, he believes that the Court "has flouted the will of the framers and substituted an interpretation in flat contradiction of the original design: to leave...segregation...to State governance."[86] (This argument might go a bit too far, however, since during the *Brown* case the Court asked both sides to brief the issue of whether the framers and the individual state legislatures that passed the amendment had meant to preclude school segregation. The historical evidence presented in response did not convincingly resolve the matter and, thus, left the Court without clear guidance regarding intent.)[87]

Graglia is equally upset with the Court's use of the Fourteenth Amendment. He notes that while the Constitution contains approximately 7,000 words, most decisions of recent decades have been focused on

> a single constitutional provision, one sentence in the Fourteenth Amendment, and, indeed, on four words in that sentence: "due process" and "equal protection." The judges have in effect made of these four words a second Constitution, which is very different and in many ways a vastly more important Constitution than the one that came from the hands of the framers.[88]

The reliance on "due process" and "equal protection" came about as a result of the concern for equality and the desire to change social conditions at the heart of many of the decisions of the Warren Court. Unfortunately, as Bickel sees it, the Court

> all too often assimilated private behavior to government action; it not only forbade...discrimination at the hands of the state, or of any unit of government, but was keen to detect the hand of the state in private discriminations.[89]

Many believe the Warren Court's First Amendment decisions to be based on an erroneous view of constitutional history. Lasky, for instance, is among those who contend that the Establishment Clause prohibits Congress from establishing a national church, but does not preclude the states from doing so. He points out that ten of the thirteen original states had established religions, the last of which (that in Massachusetts) was not disestablished until 1833.[90] Thus, Lasky believes that it was the intent of those who drafted the First Amendment merely to prohibit religious persecution, not to remove religion from the public arena.[91] According to this view, placing a nationwide ban on voluntary prayer in the public schools would seem to go beyond the Court's authority. Rice concurs since his interpretation of the Constitution calls for such decisions to be made by the states. (Presumably, then, the Court would have the authority to uphold a state's ban on school prayer.) Rice argues that the Warren Court's stance on school prayer was based on "judicial fictions" that would shock those who framed the First Amendment.[92]

Carrying Forth a Judicial Tradition

Charles Lamb believes the activism of the Warren Court to have been atypical: with the exception of the Marshall Court and the laissez faire Courts of 1890-1936, most Supreme Courts have taken a posture of restraint.[93] Once Earl Warren was succeeded as Chief
Chief by Warren Burger, many expected the Court to return to restraint. However, it appears that such has not happened.

The judicial principle of *stare decisis* ("let the decision stand") generally requires future decisions to be based on passed decisions unless there has been a change in the law or unless the justices can cite an error in law made by their predecessors that would obviate the earlier ruling. This principle provides that stability and predictability to the law that transcends the personalities on the bench.

The Burger Court has often been a disappointment to political conservatives and to those favoring judicial restraint (not always congruent groups). But, as Caldiera and McCrone assert, activism is cyclical in nature. Activist decisions create a certain amount of uncertainty; litigants attempt to clarify this uncertainty through their suits; the courts try to provide added clarity through their decisions; sometimes more confusion results and the process continues until surety is restored.[94] Given the protracted length of time that it takes cases to reach the Supreme Court, such cycles extend over the course of many years.

Further, as Marvin Schick notes, it would be difficult as a result of the constraints of *stare decisis* for the Burger Court to turn back the clock. Instead, it can "refuse to move the clock ahead...by refusing to expand on precedents and by restricting the meaning, though not the applicability, of certain rights."[95] But, even that approach does not seem to describe Burger's Court. Lamb points out that it "has broadened some Warren decisions and has chipped away at others." Archibald Cox goes a bit further in his observation that the present group of justices "are not restrained by a modest conception of the judicial function but will be activitists when a statute offends their policy preferences."[96]

Two good examples of activism by the Burger Court have been cited by Donald Horowitz. In *Griggs v. Duke Power Company* (the case in which it ordered that tests given by employers to prospective employees could not be general or aptitude in nature, but must relate directly to the job in question), the Court ruled in opposition to "convincing legislative history to show that Congress intended the opposite result reached in [the case]". In *Lau v. Nichols,* the bilingual education case, Horowitz contends that

> [t]here is little in the language of Title VI [of the Civil Rights Act of 1964] that suggests it contemplates affirmative action to remedy linguistic deficiencies, and there is nothing in the legislative history that hints at such a purpose.[97]

Similarly, Abraham cites what he believes to be another travesty by the Burger Court. In the *Weber* case (the affirmative action matter in which the Court upheld the right of Kaiser Aluminum to reserve spaces for minority employees in a company training program), the opinion written by Justice Brennen acknowledged the statutory proscription against racial quotas in employment but allowed them to stand in this instance since they were being used to promote the spirit of nondiscrimination by providing minorities a chance for a better job. Says Abraham, "No wonder that well-organized segments of the public have urged limits to the Court's power. And no wonder that Congress is...tempted to strike back."[98]

That the politically conservative Burger Court has not reversed the activist trend has prompted Court observers such as Schick to comment that "nowadays all Supreme Courts are activist."[99] Tushnet believes that the courts have gone beyond mere activism to a position of governing since the patterns that emerge from court rulings have the same force as those that emerge from the enactment of new statutes.[100] This was not always the case.

In all of the years prior to the Warren Court, Supreme Courts only sought to restrain the actions of legislatures and executives that they believed to have transgressed the limits of statutory authority or constitutionality. Since the enforcement order that followed *Brown v. Board of Education*, the Court has imposed affirmative norms on the society.[101] After 1962, its interest in the realization of its rulings increased. As the Court began to develop a greater concern for those affected by the law, it began to be sure that its rulings included enforceable remedies for those who had been improperly treated, rather than merely prescribing the treatment.[102]

Anthony Lewis of the New York *Times* believes that such intervention by the Court is justified "when there is no other remedy for a situation that threatens the national fabric—when the path to political change is blocked."[103] But, retorts Henry Abraham, while such action may have been necessary to clear the path that "was blocked in the case of endemic racial segregation," the practice of employing judicial remedies such as school busing, racial pairing, racial quotas and affirmative action raises the question of whether the Court "has begun to overreach itself."[104]

The Legislative Process or the Judicial Process?

Many believe that remedies are best developed through the legislative process since legislatures have technical staffs to develop specific statutes. Horowitz, for one, argues that "courts are better equipped with the machinery to discover the past than to forecast the future."[105] That is, the adversarial process of a court hearing brings out the facts as both sides see them. The bench then makes a decision grounded in the law and based on the most convincing argument as to what actually happened. When a court moves to issue a remedial decision, Horowitz believes it does so without the adequate technical expertise to determine whether the remedy will accomplish the desired end.

Youngblood and Folse disagree. They note that judges have available to them law clerks and interns, librarians and up-to-date law libraries, and staff attorneys as well as the "ready ear" of law school faculties. Further, judges, as a result either of their earlier law practice or their particular interests once they reach the bench, develop expertise in specialized areas. For example, on the Fifth Circuit Court of Appeals, different justices have distinctive knowledge regarding admiralty and insurance matters, tax and securities law, administrative law, civil rights, and so forth.[106]

Lamb would agree with the observation made by Horowitz if it were limited to highly complicated questions such as those that arise in medicine or technology. However, as he points out, most of the rulings that Horowitz finds offensive are in the area of social policy, and, as he sees it

> Questions of social policy are quite another matter. Social policy issues usually are not technical; rather they require that policy makers reach value judgments on how they believe an issue should be resolved.[107]

Rebell and Block studied sixty-five federal court cases concerning education. They found that in forty-two of the cases, social fact evidence was presented and, that in each instance, the judges seemed to possess "reasonable working knowledge" of the concepts at hand.[108] Further, they found that judges often engage in greater analytical decision making than do legislatures who are enacting laws in the same topical areas.[109] These findings support Lamb's position.

However, it is true that not all social policy issues are easily resolved. For example, it may be apparent that a school district is racially segregated. The most effective approach to desegregating the system may not be as apparent, and may require complex solutions. Bickel would agree with Horowitz that the court is not the best place to resolve such a problem:

> in dealing with problems of great magnitude and pervasive ramifications, problems with complex roots and unpredictably multiplying offshoots— in dealing with such problems, the society is best allowed to develop its own standards out of its tradition....;

that is, through the political process, not the judicial process.[110]

Those who support the notion of judicial activism believe as does Stephen Wasby that "the government must be forced to act where it has neglected or refused to do so."[111] In the above example, the government permitted the segregated schools to exist. It is not enough for the court to tell the government to cease this practice. It is proper for the court to tell the officials how to bring about the desired condition since the officials have not previously acted to desegregate the schools. As Wasby puts it, "[w]ere the courts not to act, the disadvantaged would remain disadvantaged or would become more so."[112]

The Rebell and Block study indicated that the disadvantaged the court seeks to protect are minorities—racial, ethnic, sexual, religious, etc. In fact, 74 percent of their sample cases involved minorities.[113] Those who oppose the court protection of minorities contend that the framers of the Equal Protection and Due Process clauses never intended them to apply to such things as busing to achieve racial balance. However, others believe that it is often not productive to attempt to apply the intent of the framers to current problems. (Buses did not exist in the third quarter of the nineteenth century; thus, the framers of the Fourteenth Amendment could not have envisioned the mass transportation of students to remedy segregation in the schools.) As Walter Murphy puts it, the effort to determine intent "is based on the usually self-deceptive myth that there is such a discoverable entity as a single intent on particular matters." He believes that a constitution provides a "charter for governance...a set of authoritative statements about a society's basic goals." As such, it "has a spirit as well as a body" and, thus, is intended to be adaptable to new situations. He states that the "root problem of constitutional interpretation lies in the stubborn refusal of the real world to stand still so that immutable general principles can have immutable applications to human behavior."[114]

Ronald Dworkin agrees. He contends that the Constitution is not based on "simple majoritarian theory," that it was framed so as to shield individuals and groups from a possible tyranny of the majority. Thus, certain portions such as the Equal Protection and Due Process clauses were intended to provide a general concept of fairness, and, thus, were intentionally vague.[115] Dworkin asserts that although the Constitution does not state "in plain words" that

> segregation was so unjust that heroic measures are required to undo its effects... neither does it provide as a matter of constitutional law that the Court would be wrong to reach these conclusions. It leaves these issues to the Court's judgment.[116]

Balancing Competing Interests—Two Current Issues
The courts, in attempting to resolve the position of the government in matters in which there are competing interests, must balance the rights of the groups involved. A case in point is a school busing controversy in which the claims of whites that their children should be free to restrict their association to other white children from the neighborhood must be balanced against the claims of blacks for an equal education. The court must determine which right takes precedence; it then must place the government behind the realization of that right.[117]

While many would contend that this matter has been resolved by the Court in favor of the blacks' right to an equal education, there are several recent matters that lead one to believe that the issue is far from being settled. The first concerns the applicability of federal tax exemptions; the second concerns the use of federal tax credits. Both balance religious rights against rights of blacks to an equal education.

Since taxation is a form of regulation, churches have been tax exempt in fulfillment of the Free Exercise clause of the First Amendment. However, beginning with the administration of Richard M. Nixon, the Internal Revenue Service began to deny tax exemptions to religiously affiliated schools that discriminate against blacks. In 1971 this practice was challenged by several "segregationist academies," but the IRS was ruled to have acted within its authority.[118] In the twelve years that the policy has been in effect, 111 private schools in eleven southern states (the majority in Alabama, Mississippi and South Carolina) have seen their tax exemptions revoked.[119]

On October 12, 1982, the Supreme Court heard the arguments of Bob Jones University and the Goldsboro Christian Schools that their tax-exempt status had been unconstitutionally withdrawn by the IRS. The Goldsboro Christian Schools do not admit blacks. Bob Jones does, but prohibits its students from interracial dating and marriage. Both institutions claim a biblical basis for their policies. They contend that the First Amendment protects them from governmental action regarding these beliefs.[120]

Conflicting rulings were issued by the respective federal district courts that originally heard the cases brought by the two schools. In the Bob Jones case, the court found that the IRS had improperly withdrawn the University's tax-exempt status. In the Goldsboro case, a different court ruled that "[t]here is a legitimate secular purpose for denying tax-exempt status to schools generally maintaining a racially discriminatory admissions policy," and that the denial of tax exemptions to schools such as Goldsboro does not inhibit religion.[121] Arguing before the Supreme Court, William Bentley Ball (the attorney who successfully represented the Amish in the *Yoder* case) stated that while the theology of Bob Jones University "may not be yours, and it certainly is not mine," it would be an "egregious offense to religious liberty" for it to be required to relinquish its beliefs in order to qualify for a tax exemption.

Since Ronald Reagan had recently acted to revoke the IRS practice, the Supreme Court asked the Chairman of the NAACP Legal Defense Fund, William T. Coleman, Jr., to argue the government's case. Coleman countered the contention of the two schools by stating,

> Their argument is that because their racism is religiously based, they have a right to tax benefits denied to all others who cannot defend their policies on religious grounds.... When a fundamental public policy is violated a defense of religious belief is not available.[122]

In a major rebuke of the actions of the President, the Supreme Court ruled, on May 24, 1983, against tax exemptions for these discriminating religious schools. Writing for the 8 to 1 majority, Chief Justice Burger noted that

> charitable exemptions are justified on the basis that the exempt entity confers a public benefit...[Thus] the institution's purpose must not be so at odds with the common community conscience as to undermine any public benefit that might otherwise be conferred.

Since it was the view of the Court that "there can no longer be any doubt that racial discrimination in education violates deeply and widely accepted views of elementary justice," the educational institutions in question do not confer a public benefit and thus do not qualify for tax-exempt status.[123] Thus, those who seek to avoid desegregation by attending discriminatory schools will not be able to do so through the subsidy of the taxpaying public.

That is not to say, however, that the public schools are free from threat of tax incentives for private school attendance. Many states have enacted tuition tax credits for parents whose children attend private schools, and such proposals have received serious consideration by recent Congresses. The basis for such proposals is a desire to provide financial relief for persons being "doubly taxed." Parents who choose to send their children to nonpublic schools pay taxes that support the public schools but do not receive any direct benefit from their taxes; in addition, they pay tuition to the nonpublic school. Thus, they claim to be doubly taxed. To remedy this, they argue that they should be able to claim as an income tax credit the amount of tuition that they pay (or a portion thereof). They point out that if they all decided to send their children to public schools, those schools would become overcrowded, thereby driving up the amount of tax support required to run a quality school program. They contend that a program of tuition tax credits would keep both the public and nonpublic schools financially stronger than if tax credits were not available.

The cosponsor (with Daniel Patrick Moynihan) of one of the most prominent tuition tax credit bills introduced in Congress, Oregon Senator Robert Packwood, argues,

> A parent might perfer a private or parochial elementary school for a child because the school offers an enriched curriculum, smaller classes, tighter discipline or religious instruction.... Freedom to make that choice, however, should not be dependent on the degree of financial hardship one must suffer to attain the desired qualities in education.[124]

And hardship it is in many instances since the cost of tuition at many nonpublic elementary and secondary schools surpasses the tuition charged by public colleges and universities. Says Packwood, "Ever increasing tuition costs have made the freedom of choice in education an elusive goal that is slipping further from economic reality for many Americans."[125]

A certain portion of the attractiveness of a tax-supported private alternative to public education comes as a result of the general dissatisfaction with the outcomes of public funding in the full range of human service areas.[126] Proponents of tax credits recently received a boost from the noted sociologist, James Coleman, whose research indicated that children attending Catholic schools achieved significantly higher in vocabulary and mathematics than did children in public schools; results in reading were less consistent.[127] While the differences in scores can be accounted for by the different demographic concentrations of students in the public and nonpublic schools,[128] Coleman's message to parents comes forth loudly: send your kids to a nonpublic school and they will learn more.

Under the plan proposed in the spring of 1982 by President Reagan, parents would be able to receive a tax credit for 50 percent of the tuition and fees that they pay for each child in nonpublic school. This would be phased in over a period of three years such that the maximum credit would grow from $100 in the first year of the program's existence to $500 by its third year.[129] The annual cost of such a program would not be insignificant to the federal treasury: $1.9 billion once it is fully in place.[130]

This has prompted the National Education Association to point out that under such a plan, students in private schools would receive two and a half times the federal support provided to public school students.[131] Further, as is cited by David Breneman, families with children in private secondary schools had a median income in 1980 that was nearly 25 percent higher than those whose children attend public schools; thus credits such as those proposed by Senators Packwood and Moynihan and President Reagan would be regressive.[132]

If postsecondary education were to be eligible for tax credits, the cost would rise by at least $2 billion[133] and the total might exceed $5 billion.[134] There would also be a regressive element to the inclusion of postsecondary education since, as Breneman estimates, 45 percent of the credits would be used by 14 percent of all families, those whose adjusted gross incomes exceed $25,000, while less than 9 percent would be used by families with incomes of less than $10,000. Further, Breneman posits that it is "implausible" that a tax credit in the amount of half of the tuition up to a limit of $500 per year would have any influence on where a student goes to college.[135]

Arguments against tax credits were quick to follow President Reagan's April 1982 proposal. The *New York Times* ran an editorial saying that tax credits would "undermine the principle that government should finance education that is available to all." It feared that public funds would flow to "fanatic cults and blatant racists" whose aims are opposite to those of the national interest.[136] Similarly, the Philadelphia *Inquirer* was critical of the President for encouraging "the hegira from the public schools of the bright." It recommended, instead, that Reagan call "for further aid to the public schools."[137]

South Carolina Senator Ernest Hollings believes that it is the obligation of the government toward private schools "to leave them alone."[138] He fears that tuition tax credits

> would turn our nation's education policy on its head, benefit the few at the expense of the many, add a sea of red ink to the federal deficit, violate the clear meaning of the First Amendment of the Constitution, and destroy the diversity and genius of our system of public education.[139]

To the double taxation argument, Hollings wonders whether those who are not pleased with the local police should be given tax credits to hire private security guards.[140] Similarly, Breneman makes short of the double taxation claim by pointing out that logic would have tax credits extended to persons who prefer private clubs, parks, pools and golf courses to public ones.[141]

The argument against tax credits is aptly summed up by Bill Anderson who believes that such an approach would turn the public schools into "dumping grounds" for less capable students and those with learning disabilities, and would reduce the federal money available to the public schools due both to the lower head count in the public schools and the diminished federal treasury that would occur as a result of the credits. Further, since all current proposals call for nonpublic schools to be both accredited and nondiscriminatory in order to qualify for credits, the spectre of federal regulation of private schools is present. The supervision of such a system would surely cause an entangling relationship with religion.[142]

According to the Congressional Budget Office, approximately 5 million children attend nonpublic schools.[143] This represents about one in every ten school children, 58 percent of whom live in eight populous states.[144] Of the nearly 20,000 private schools, approximately half are Catholic and 5,900 more have other religious affiliations.[145] Thus, tuition tax credits would, in the main, serve to enhance religious schools, and, thus, might very well violate the Establishment and Free Exercise clauses of the First Amendment. Such was found to be the case by a federal district court in Ohio that ruled unconstitutional an Ohio tuition tax credit provision, and by the United States Supreme Court that overturned similar laws in New York and New Jersey.[146]

However, on June 29, 1983, the Court did a turnabout by a slim 5 to 4 margin when it upheld a Minnesota law that permits state tax deductions for tuition or other educational expenses paid by parents of children attending any public or private elementary or secondary school. The opinion in *Mueller v. Allen,* written by Justice William Rehnquist, stated that, despite the fact 95 percent of the 91,000 private school students attended religious schools,

> [A] state's decision to defray the cost of educational expenses incurred by parents, regardless of the type of schools their children attend, evidences a purpose that is both secular and understandable...a state's efforts to assist parents in meeting the rising cost of educational expenses plainly serves this secular purpose of insuring that the state's citizenry is well educated.

The fact that the Minnesota law provided an income tax deduction—one of many permissible deductions on the state income tax—rather than a tax credit (as was the case in the earlier New York instance) proved compelling to the Court's majority who ruled that such a provision met the three-pronged *Lemon* test and was, thus, permissible. This difference was one of only nuance to the four members of the Court who dissented from the opinion.[147] Nevertheless, it has permitted a conservative Court an avenue to respond to the growing dissatisfaction with the public schools without reversing a ruling that was only ten years old. *Mueller* may result in a change in the proposals made heretofore by tax credit proponents in the Congress. It most certainly will take its toll on the public schools.

Is the Court a Free Agent?

If there is a defiance of a ruling of the Court by governmental bodies, the Court must move to establish a firm foundation for its orders. As Derrick Bell demonstrates, the massive resistance that followed the *Brown* ruling led the Supreme Court, over the subsequent fifteen-year period, to issue decisions that countered defiance to the original ruling rather than obtaining compliance to it.[148] To accomplish this, points out David Keys, the Court's decisions blended politics and law. This has resulted in the provision of great discretion to the federal district court judge to fashion a remedy that makes sense in a specific locality and to those whose rights required protection.[149]

Thus, it is clear that considerations of political power rather than restrictions of constitutional intent provide the greatest restraints of judicial activism.[150] Miller believes that the Supreme Court serves as the role "leader in a vital national seminar that leads to the formulation of values for the American people;" in attempting to permit various minorities the ability to enjoy rights long denied them, the Court has been the vanguard of a "movement toward decency—toward stating affirmative principles of morality."[151] It must do this, however, within the political context, for if it gets out too far in front of the American citizenry, a limiting response will spring forth from the Congress. Robert Dahl is probably correct that it would not be possible for the Court to block for a sustained period of time the "major alternatives sought by the lawmaking majority."[152]

Are we at that point now? Probably not, but we may be close. The mood of the country today might not permit great advances in the tradition of the Warren Court. The Burger Court, however, does not attempt great advances in that tradition. Since it is comprised of more conservative justices and since it currently sits in a more conservative period, its more recent decisions have been modest and probably reflect (as has been the case throughout most of our history) a national consensus.

The danger to the Court (and, thus, to the Constitution), however, is that we are currently in an era of single-issue politics; that is, candidates are often elected to office based on their position on an issue of importance to a group of voters, who, because of their intense interest in that one issue, can swing an election. Most of those issues are conservative (cut public spending, prohibit abortion, put prayers back in the schools, etc.). Office holders and office seekers in times such as these tend to lean toward such positions, if only to block the emergence of a single-issue opposition candidate. Thus, despite the fact that a majority of the people might not want to put a curb on the activity of the federal courts, it is plausible that such a curb could result in response to a vocal minority of single issue voters, particularly if it is a well-financed bloc.

Protecting Fundamental Rights in Education

If proponents of measures to limit the authority of the courts over the schools are successful, what might be lost? The notions of removing the schools from the purview of the federal courts or of exempting certain aspects of school activity from court oversight are based on the premise that education falls within the powers left to the several states since in neither the original Constitution nor in the subsequent amendments is education specifically listed as an area of federal concern. Indeed, the federal courts have historically stood behind that principle. Prior to the *Brown* decision, instances of the federal courts overturning state or local education ordinances or practices were rare. In the post-*Brown* era, such instances have been more frequent. Yet in each case, a more basic constitutional principle has been at issue.

The school desegregation cases (including today's busing decisions) are grounded on the Fourteenth Amendment guarantee of equal protection under the laws (or in the case of the District of Columbia, the Fifth Amendment right to due process). Judges have ordered desegregation when plaintiffs have been able to prove that statutes or willful acts by official bodies have led to the separate (and, therefore, unequal) education of minority children. They have been careful to hold harmless from such orders school districts in neighboring communities if those districts were clearly noncomplicitous in the segregation of the schools. Thus, despite the fact that segregated housing patterns exist in Detroit and its suburbs, the suburbs were not required to share in the burden of the city's desegregation since they were independent school districts that did not officially participate in the de facto segregation of the Detroit schools. While it is obvious that the paucity of white students in Detroit will not allow its schools to be integrated without the inclusion of the suburbs, the Supreme Court has maintained its traditional posture of basing its decisions on the narrowest possible ground; since the suburbs did not deny equal protection, they may not be required to provide remediation. Again, desegregation orders are based on denial of equal protection.

Similarly, the Court has struggled in its various rulings concerning the interface between religion and the schools. The First Amendment protection of freedom of religion and the separation of church and state is one of our most basic principles. The Supreme Court found that requiring the Amish teenagers to remain in school was an unnecessary interference with religious freedom. Similarly, the posting of biblical passages and the recitation of prayers in school was found to interfere with the Constitutional rights of those who followed other religious practices or no religious practices at all. In its rulings regarding public financial assistance for those who choose to enroll in religious rather than public schools, the Court has held to the doctrine that financial support diminishes the separation between church and state; it has esablished a strict set of criteria to insure that public dollars are used only in conformance with the Constitutional requirement. By so doing, it has found it possible to charge the public coffers for certain expenses associated with parochial education, but not for all expenses.

The students' rights decisions have been based on the First Amendment guarantee of freedom of speech, and the Fifth Amendment guarantee of due process. Even there, however, the Supreme Court has not been one-sided. It has sought to insure that such basic rights as the ability to wear a political button (of reasonable size) and the requirement that one have the opportunity to refute charges leading to penalty not stop at the school-house door.

While the court-limiting proposals are surely based on the popular desire to put an end to court-ordered busing and to see a return of prayers to the public schools, it is clear that their impact might be more far reaching, for they would remove the national requirement in the schools for equal protection, due process, freedom of speech, freedom of religion, etc., and would, in their place, either allow the establishment of fifty independent standards for rights that currently form the cornerstone of our democracy or, alternatively, would provide for a national standard that would be as temporal as the majority in Congress.

The best protection against potential federal excess is not the removal of the schools from the authority of the federal courts, but the Supreme Court's tradition of moving slowly and acting narrowly. Fundamental civil liberties and civil rights can only be guaranteed if the law of the land is supreme over all of America including the schoolhouse. As a people, we can ill afford to void the Constitution in the facet of American life that needs it the most, education—the institution that is responsible for transmitting the American democratic tradition to those who will shape this nation's future.

REFERENCES

1. Trustees of Dartmouth College v. Woodward, 4 Wheat 518, 17 U.S. 518 (1819).
2. Plessy v. Ferguson, 163 U.S. 537 (1896); Cumming v. Richmond County Board of Education 175 U.S. 528 (1899).
3. Brown v. Board of Education, 347 U.S. 483 (1954).
4. Brown v. Board of Education, 349 U.S. 294 (1955).
5. Cooper v. Aaron, 358 U.S. 1 (1958).
6. Goss v. Board of Education, 373 U.S. 683 (1963).
7. Griffin v. County School Board, 377 U.S. 218 (1964).
8. Bradley v. School Board of City of Richmond, 382, U.S. 103 (1965).
9. Rogers v. Paul, 382 U.S. 198 (1965).
10. Green v. County School Board, 391 U.S. 430 (1968).
11. Swann v. Charlotte-Mecklenburg Board of Education, 402 U.S. 1 (1971).
12. Keyes v. School District Number l, Denver, Colorado, 413 U.S. 189 (1973).
13. Bell, D. *Race, Racism and American Law*. Boston, Little, Brown, 1980, p. 439.
14. Milliken v. Bradley, 418 U.S. 717 (1974).
15. Newburg Area Council v. Jefferson County Board of Education, 421 U.S. 931 (1974).
16. Evans v. Buchanan, 423 U.S. 963 (1975).
17. Lau v. Nichols, 414 U.S. 563 (1974).
18. Zorach v. Clauson, 343 U.S. 306 (1952).
19. Engel v. Vitale, 370 U.S. 421 (1962).
20. School District of Abington TP, Pa. v. Schempp, Murray v. Curlett, 374 U.S. 203 (1963).
21. Stone v. Graham, 449 U.S. 39 (1980).
22. Florey v. Sioux Falls School District, 102 S. Ct. 409 (1980).
23. Kincheloe, J.: The New Right Comes to School, Education and the Power of the Pious, *Principal*, 61 (3): 34-35, 1982.
24. Welch, I.D., Medieros, D. and Tate, G.: Education, Religion and the New Right, *Educational Leadership*, 39 (3): 204, 1981.
25. Zuidema, H.: Less Evolution, More Creationism in Text Books, *Educational Leadership*, 39 (3): 217, 1981.
26. Matthews, J.: The Creationist Threat to Science, *AAHE Bulletin*, 34 (6):

27. Kincheloe (1982), The New Right comes to School, p. 35.
28. Welch, Medieros and Tate (1981), Education, Religion, and the New Right, p. 205.
29. Parker, F.: Behind the Evolution-Creation Science Controversy, *College Board Review* (123): 18, 1982.
30. Sullivan, L.: The Arkansas Landmark Court Challenge of Creation Science, *College Board Review* (123): 12, 35, 1982.
31. O'Neil, R.: Creationism, Curriculum and the Constitution, *Academe* 68 (2): 21, 1982.
32. Flygare, T.: The Case of Segraves v. State of California, *Phi Delta Kappan,* 63 (2): 98, 1981.
33. Siegel, H.: Creationism, Evolution and Education: The California Fiasco, *Phi Delta Kappan,* 63 (2): 95-96, 1981.
34. Flygare (1981), The Case of Segraves, p. 99.
35. Rev. Bill McLean *et al* v. The Arkansas Board of Education *et al,* 529 F. Supp. 1255 (Eastern District, Arkansas 1982).
36. Sullivan (1982), The Arkansas Landmark, p. 33.
37. Sullivan (1982), The Arkansas Landmark, p. 16.
38. Edwords, F.: Creation Evolution Update, The Aftermath of Arkansas, *The Humanist,* 42 (2): 55, 1982.
39. Edwords (1982), Creation p. 55.
40. Pierce v. Society of Sisters, 268 U.S. 510 (1925).
41. Wisconsin v. Yoder, 406 U.S. 205 (1972).
42. Widmar v. Vincent, 102 S. Ct. 269 (1981).
43. Tilton v. Richardson, 403 U.S. 672 (1971).
44. Finn, C.: Public Policy and Private Education: The Case for Private Schools, *Compact,* 15 (3): 14, 1981.
45. Jensen, D. *Tuition Tax Credits: Constitutional and Legal Implications.* Palo Alto, Cal., Institute for Research on Educational Finance and Governance, Stanford University, 1981, p. 1.
46. Everson v. Board of Education of the Township of Ewing, 330 U.S. 1 (1947).
47. Board of Education v. Allen, 392 U.S. 236 (1968).
48. Lemon v. Kurtzman, Early v. Dicenso, 403 U.S. 602 (1971).
49. Committee for Public Education and Religious Liberty v. Nyquist, 413 U.S. 756 (1973).
50. Meek v. Pittenger, 421 U.S. 349 (1975).
51. Wolman v. Walter, 433 U.S. 229 (1977).
52. Wolman v. Walter, 100 S. Ct. 26 (1979).
53. McCarthy, M.: Church and State: Separation or Accommodation? *Harvard Educational Review,* 51 (3): 376-7, 1981.
54. Committee for Public Education and Religious Liberty v. Regan, 100 S. Ct. 840 (1980).
55. McCarthy (1980), Church and State, p. 393.
56. Committee for Public Education and Religious Liberty v. Regan, 100 S. Ct. 840 (1980).

57. Sweazy v. New Hampshire, 354 U.S. 234 (1957).
58. *In re* Gault, 387 U.S. 1 (1967).
59. Tinker v. Des Moines Independent Community School District, 393 U.S. 503 (1969).
60. Healy v. James, 408 U.S. 169 (1972).
61. Goss v. Lopez, 419 U.S. 565 (1975).
62. Baker v. Owen, 423 U.S. 907 (1975).
63. Ingraham v. Wright, 430 U.S. 651 (1977).
64. Lusky, L. *By What Right? A Commentary on the Supreme Court's Power to Revise the Constitution.* Charlottesville, Va., Michie, 1975, p. 29.
65. Rice, C.: Limiting Federal Court Jurisdiction: The Constitutional Basis for the Proposals in Congress Today, *Judicature,* 65 (4): 192-193, 1981.
66. Rice (1981), Limiting Federal Court Jurisdiction, p. 190.
67. Taylor, T.: Limiting Federal Court Jurisdiction: The Unconstitutionality of Current Legislative Proposals, *Judicature,* 65 (4): 204, 1981.
68. Kay, K.: Limiting Federal Court Jurisdiction: The Unforeseen Impact on Courts and Congress, *Judicature,* 65 (4): 185, 1981.
69. Administration Reinforces its Support of Department of Justice Busing Amendment, *Department of Education Weekly,* 3 (33): 4, 1982.
70. Pear, R.: U.S. Alters Policy on Desegregation, New York *Times,* November 20, 1981.
71. Lewis, A.: School Prayer Also Moves to the Fore Again, New York *Times,* May 9, 1982.
72. Prayer Was Not the Issue, New York *Times* (Editorial), September 26, 1982.
73. Roberts, S.: Senate Restricts Suits on Prayers in the Schools, New ⁻York *Times,* November 17, 1981.
74. Roberts, S.: Two Reagan Allies in Senate Press Their Own Aims, New York *Times,* November 7, 1980. New Republican Chairmen, The MacNeil/Lehrer Report (transcript), November 12, 1980.
75. Lamb, C.: Judicial Restraint on the Supreme Court. In Halpern S. and Lamb, C. (eds.): *Supreme Court Activism and Restraint.* Lexington, Ma., Lexington Books, 1982, p. 8.
76. Graglia, L.: In Defense of Judicial Restraint. In Halpern, S. and Lamb, C. (Eds.): *Supreme Court Activism and Restraint.* Lexington, Ma., Lexingon Books, 1982, p. 135.
77. Higgins, T. *Judicial Review Unmasked.* West Hanover, Ma., Christopher Publishing House, 1981, p. 138.
78. Lusky (1975), *By What Right?* p. 21.
79. Berger, R. *Government by Judiciary: The Transformation of the Fourteenth Amendment.* Cambridge, Ma., Harvard University Press, 1977, p. 365-6.
80. Berger (1977), *Government by Judiciary,* p. 382.
81. Berger (1977), *Government by Judiciary,* p. 382.
82. Berger (1977), *Government by Judiciary,* p. 382.

83. Berger (1977), *Government by Judiciary*, p. 364.

84. Lusky (1975), *By What Right?* p. 9.

85. Schick, M.: Judicial Activism on the Supreme Court. In Halpern, S. and Lamb, C. (Eds.): *Supreme Court Activism and Restraint*. Lexington, Ma., Lexington Books, 1982, p. 37-8.

86. Berger (1977), *Government by Judiciary*, p. 407.

87. Marcus, L. and Stickney, B. *Race and Education: The Unending Controversy*. Springfield, Ill., Charles C Thomas, 1981, p. 68-70.

88. Graglia (1982), In Defense of Judicial Restraint, p. 141.

89. Bickel, A. *The Supreme Court and the Idea of Progress*. New Haven, Conn., Yale University Press, 1979, p. 104.

90. Lusky (1975), *By What Right?* p. 168.

91. Lusky (1975), *By What Right?* p. 167.

92. Rice (1981), Limiting Federal Court Jurisdiction, pp. 195–196.

93. Lamb (1982), Judicial Restraint, p. 7.

94. Caldiera, G. and McCrone, D.: Of Time and Judicial Activism: A Study of the U.S. Supreme Court, 1800-1973. In Halpern, S. and Lamb, C. (eds.): *Supreme Court Activism and Restraint*. Lexington, Ma., Lexington Books, 1982, p. 123.

95. Schick (1982), Judicial Activism, p. 41.

96. Lamb (1982), Judicial Restraint, pp. 24–25.

97. Horowitz, D. *The Courts and Social Policy*. Washington, The Brookings Institution, 1977, p. 14-17.

98. Abraham, H.: Limiting Federal Court Jurisdiction: A "Self-inflicted Wound"? *Judicature*, 65 (4): 179-180, 1981.

99. Schick (1982), Judicial Activism, p. 37.

100. Tushnet, M.: Should Courts Govern? The Law of the Public Bureaucracy. In Gambitta, R., May, M., and Foster, J. (eds.): *Governing Through Courts*. Beverly Hills, Cal., Sage Publications, 1981, p. 66.

101. Bickel (1979), *The Supreme Court and the Idea of Progress*, p. 40.

102. Lusky (1975), *By What Right?* p. 276.

103. Abraham (1981), Limiting Federal Court Jurisdiction, p. 181.

104. Abraham (1981), Limiting Federal Court Jurisdiction, p. 181.

105. Horowitz (1977), *The Courts and Social Policy*, p. 264.

106. Youngblood, J. and Folse, P. III: Can Courts Govern? An Inquiry into Capacity and Purpose. In Gambitta, R., May, M., and Foster, J. (eds.): *Governing Through Courts*. Beverly Hills, Cal., Sage Publications, 1981, p. 29, 31.

107. Lamb, C.: Book Review of *The Courts and Social Policy*, *UCLA Law Review*, 26 (1): 247, 1978.

108. Rebell, M. and Block, A. *Educational Policy Making and the Courts: An Empirical Study of Judicial Activism*. Chicago, University of Chicago Press, 1982, p. 33, 57.

109. Rebell and Block, *Educational Policy Making*, pp. 208–209.

110. Bickel (1979), *The Supreme Court and the Idea of Progress*, p. 175.

111. Wasby, S.: Review of *The Courts and Social Policy*, *Vanderbilt Law Review*, 31 (3): 740, 1978.

112. Wasby (1978), Review of the *The Courts and Social Policy,* p. 740.
113. Rebell and Block (1982), *Educational Policy Making,* p. 42.
114. Murphy, W.: Constitutional Interpretation: The Art of the Historian, Magician, or Statesman? *Yale Law Journal,* 87 (8): 1770-1771, 1978.
115. Dworkin, R. *Taking Rights Seriously.* Cambridge, Ma., Harvard University Press, 1977, p. 133-134.
116. Dworkin (1977), *Taking Rights Seriously,* p. 132.
117. Dworkin (1977), *Taking Rights Seriously,* p. 199.
118. Green v. Connally, 330 F. Supp 1150 (DDC), affirmed 404 U.S. 997 (1971).
119. Taylor, S.: Ex-Tax Officials Assail Shift on School Exemption Status, New York *Times,* January 12, 1982.
120. Hook, J.: Justices Hear Arguments on Tax Exemption for Church Colleges that Show Racial Bias, *Chronicle of Higher Education,* 25 (8): 11, 1982.
121. Jensen (1981), *Tuition Tax Credits,* p. 31.
122. Greenhouse, L.: Justices Weigh Tax Status of Biased Schools, New York *Times,* October 13, 1982.
123. Bob Jones University v. U.S., Goldsboro Christian Schools, Inc. v. U.S. 103 S. Ct. 2017 (1983).
124. Packwood, B.: The Case for Tuition Tax Credits, *NASSP Bulletin* 65 (447): 80, 1981.
125. Packwood (1981), The Case for Tuition Tax Credits, p. 76.
126. James, T.: Tuition Tax Credits and the Pains of Democracy, *Phi Delta Kappan* 63 (9): 607, 1982.
127. Coleman, J., Hoffer, T. and Kilgore, S.: Cognitive Outcomes in Public and Private Schools, *Sociology of Education,* 55 (April/July):76, 1982.
128. McPartland, J. and McDill, E.: Control and Differentiation in the Structure of American Education, *Sociology of Education,* 55 (April/July): 87, 1982.
129. Bell Cites Benefits of Tuition Tax Credits: Education Groups Object to President's Plan, *Department of Education Weekly,* 3 (33): 2-3, 1982.
130. Sparling, V.: Tuition Tax Credits, *Today's Education,* 70 (4): 17, 1981.
131. Bell Cites Benefits...(1982), *Dept. of Education Weekly,* p. 3.
132. Breneman, D. *Where Would Tuition Tax Credits Take Us? Should We Agree to Go?* Palo Alto, Cal., Institute for Research on Educational Finance and Governance, Stanford University, 1982, p. 7.
133. Breneman (1982), *Where Would Tuition Tax Credits Take Us?* p. 4.
134. Hollings, E.: The Case Against Tuition Tax Credits, *NASSP Bulletin,* 65 (447): 79, 1981.
135. Breneman (1982), *Where Would Tuition Tax Credits Take Us?* pp. 3–5.
136. Private School Aid Is Still a Bad Idea, New York *Times* (Editorial), April 18, 1982.
137. Tuition Tax Credit Plan; Assault on Public Schools, Philadelphia *Inquirer* (Editorial), April 18, 1982.
138. Hollings (1981), The Case Against Tuition Tax Credits, p. 77.
139. Hollings (1981), The Case Against Tuition Tax Credits, p. 79.

140. Hollings (1981), The Case Against Tuition Tax Credits, p. 83.
141. Breneman (1982), Where Would Tuition Tax Credits Take Us? p. 8.
142. Anderson, B.: Public Schools Are Under Fire, But We Have Just Begun to Fight, *American School Board Journal,* 168 (9): 20, 1981.
143. Sparling (1981), Tuition Tax Credits, p. 17.
144. Finn (1981), Public Policy, p. 14.
145. Sparling (1981), Tuition Tax Credits, p. 16.
146. Jensen (1981), Tuition Tax Credits, p. 15. McCarthy (1981), Church and State, p. 380.
147. Mueller v. Allen, *U.S. Law Weekly,* 51 (49): 82-195, 1983.
148. Bell, D. *Race, Racism and American Law.* Boston, Little Brown, 1980, p. 440.
149. Kirp, D.: The Bounded Politics of School Desegregation Litigation, *Harvard Educational Review,* 51 (3): 396, 402, 1981.
150. Halpern, S.: On the Imperial Judiciary and Cooperative Institutional Development and Power in America. In Halpern, S. and Lamb, C. (eds.): *Supreme Court Activism and Restraint.* Lexington, Ma., Lexington Books, 1982, p. 240-241.
151. Miller, A.: In Defense of Judicial Activism. In Halpern, S. and Lamb, C. (eds.): *Supreme Court Activism and Restraint.* Lexington, Ma., Lexington Books, 1982, p. 177, 180.
152. Caldeira and McCrone (1982), Of Time and Judicial Activism, p. 104.

Chapter 5

IN THE NATIONAL INTEREST

F rom the earliest days of our national sovereignty, Washington's involvement with the schools has been driven by the sense that broad-based education is in the national interest. The education provisions of the Northwest Ordinances and the establishment of the military and naval academies set the basis for future federal involvement. That more people should be literate, that greater numbers should be able to conduct research (and apply its results), and that an educated populace keeps our country strong economically, socially, and militarily are fibers that are intimately woven into the fabric of our society. Consequently, when our nation was torn apart during the Civil War, the Morrill Land Grant Act was enacted to draw the resources of higher education to develop America's agricultural and mechanical capacity as well as to provide for military training at the colleges receiving support from the act. Similarly, the efforts of the twentieth century, including the establishment of the Reserve Officers Training Corps (1925), the inclusion of education provisions in the various emergency acts passed during the Great Depression and World War II, the G.I. Bill, the National Science Foundation Act, and the NDEA, all sought to keep America strong through improved education. The focus of the Kennedy-Johnson era on enhancing the life chances of the disadvantaged by providing them with quality educational opportunities carried forth this tradition, one that had the support (to varying degrees, of course) through the administration of Jimmy Carter.

Even as President Reagan has been attempting to pull the federal government out of the education arena, the belief of the American people in the importance of education remains strong. A September

1982 Gallup Poll that asked, "What would *best* guarantee a strong America in the Future?" found 84 percent selecting a "strong educational system," 66 percent a "strong industrial system," and 47 percent a "strong military."[1]

The public funds driven to education by such thinking have by many measures proven immensely successful. Harold Hodgkinson, Former director of the National Institute of Education, has asserted:

> In the last two decades especially, a key task of U.S. public schools has been to increase access for all youths, regardless of race, sex, or social class. Access to higher education has been a means of enhancing the quality of human life, and we now have data to support that common-sensical connection.

> Since 1947, the 'yield' of those going on to higher education has increased significantly. In 1954, 28 percent of those youngsters who had been fifth graders seven years earlier entered college. By 1977 that percentage had risen to 43 percent. Fifty-five percent of that earlier group of fifth graders graduated from high school; 74 percent of the group from the seventies did so. This represents a major achievement for the U.S. and a major improvement in quality of life for its citizens.

> Let us consider the matter of access in another way: In 1950 approximately 55 percent of white students graduated from high school, whereas 30 percent of black students graduated. Today 85 percent of white students and 75 percent of black students are graduating from high school. Moreover, various economists have estimated that between one-quarter and one-half of the increase in the U.S. gross national product over the last two decades can be attributed to the increased educational level of the workforce.[2]

Nevertheless, America is not delighted with the present state of educational affairs. According to a *Newsweek* poll taken in June 1983, 62 percent of American adults rated "The quality of public education" as a most important issue in 1984, a percentage tied with "protecting American jobs" and second only to "unemployment" (73%) in an eleven-item listing that included "the size of the federal deficit" (47%), "inflation" (59%), "defense spending" (51%) and "U.S. nuclear weapons policy."[3]

Discontent with education has been largely focused on alleged declining standards in the public schools, and, thus, has led to an interest in supporting private schools, giving the impression that private schools have emphasized scholastic excellence to a greater extent than public schools. During 1981, this view gained some credibility from the research of James Coleman and his colleagues who concluded, in their paper *Public and Private Schools,* that generally private high schools are superior to public high schools in producing pupil learning. (Coleman's paper was one of five commissioned by the National Center for Educational Statistics to analyze data generated by *High School and Beyond,* a 1980 multiyear investigation of 58,728 pupils in 1,016 high schools.) Largely because this research has had important political implications (an outcome aided and abetted by Coleman because of his endorsement of some form of tuition tax credits), there have been numerous rebuttals and impassioned debate over the validity of the findings.[4] Much of the scientific criticism has focused on methodological problems, the most serious of which is Coleman's inability properly to control for motivational effects or whatever zeal for education may prompt parents to send their children to private schools. In the words of Yale economist Richard Murnane, "Clearly one must ask: is (high achievement scores of private school pupils) a result of differences in the quality of education provided by the schools or is the result of differences in the skills, motivation, and parental support possessed by the children who attend these schools."[5]

While Coleman's conclusions are somewhat less than persuasive, his findings should hardly come as a surprise, given their congruency with much of the school effectiveness research in public education. Principally, Coleman and his colleagues concluded that the academic environment of a school, its organization, its scholastic requirements and its intellectual experience are associated with pupil learning and that these variables are more prevalent in private schools. Ronald Edmunds in Detroit, and Michael Rutter in London found similar disparities in climate and academic emphasis to explain differences respectively in low and high achieving public elementary and secondary schools.[6] Consequently, is it Chester Finn's argument that "...methodological disputes ought not divert attention away from the critical policy questions raised by the study's findings? *Why* are favorable learning environments found proportionately more often in private than in public schools? What are the constraints on public education that keep it from equaling if not surpassing private education? What causes such constraints and how might they be eased or eliminated?" Or in summary,

"...how to produce in more public schools the kinds of favorable learning environment that is today more commonly encountered in private schools."[7]

The initial response of the Reagan Administration was to state that the answers were best determined at the local level. Thus, it sought to pull the federal government out of the school finance and school regulation business.

But during the first year of Reaganomics, when Congressional cuts in human services *exceeded* Reagan's requests by some $3 billion, education was not cut the way the President wanted. According to Congressional Aide Jack Jennings, "The Democrats raised hell about what the President wanted to do...and through the process of hearings and publicity, word did get out about what some of these educational cutbacks could do." Jennings continued:

> But it was the Republicans in the House and in the Senate who really saved education from the degree of cutbacks the President wanted. He wanted 25 percent in elementary and secondary education in general, and he only got about 12 percent. He wanted 25 percent in vocational education. The Congress only gave him about 16 percent in terms of real dollar cutbacks at the federal level.
>
> The President wanted a 50 percent cutback in the school lunch program. He got about 33 percent.
>
> He got a third of the programs eliminated, not half, as he wanted.
>
> And, as I said, the people that you have to thank are Sen. Stafford from Vermont; the conservative Republican congressman from Ohio, John Ashbrook; Sen. Weicker of Connecticut; and some of the other Republican congressmen and senators. They are the ones who really diverted the President's cuts in education to the degree that they were diverted.[8]

Fiscal Problems at the State Level

Regardless of the bypartisan Congressional balking, the federal education budget did represent a significant retreat from the trends of the recent years. And while it may have been based on a philosophical premise that certain governmental efforts are best carried out by state and local authorities, it came at a time when the lower levels of government found themselves unable to afford the continuation of existing services, never mind taking on greater responsibility for some programs that had been the beneficiary of federal concern. Even though a majority of the nation's governors apparently endorsed the concept of new federalism (more state discretion in spending federal funds), most point to the precarious fiscal conditions of the states as the basis for their worry about inadequate federal funding for social programs they are to take over.[9] To illustrate the point, a National Conference of State Legislators survey published in January 1983 found nineteen states would end FY'83 in debt and another twelve projected only miniscule balances. An analysis of the survey by Congressional Quarterly Weekly Report, reinforces the pessimism:

> For FY'83, only six states expect a balance of more than 5 percent of their annual expenditures, traditionally considered a minimum prudent balance needed to meet any unexpected decrease in tax revenues or emergencies.
>
> To avoid financial ruin, over the past two years at least 42 states have been forced to adopt fiscal measures ranging from increased taxes to budget cuts.[10]

An analysis of the NCSL report by economist Kathleen Adams extends the pessimism.

> States will undoubtedly adjust either their expenditure or their taxation plans in order to avoid deficits. Because state spending has already slowed in nominal terms and has actually declined in real terms, further budget reductions are likely to reduce service levels significantly. The alternative - for the states to raise tax burdens - may be both politically difficult and insufficient to outweigh the effects of a continuing recession and deepening federal cuts. The end result for most states is likely to be continued deficit problems, significant reductions in state-provided services, and a passing along of further cuts in federal aid.[11]

The fiscal ills afflicting most states have significant implications for educational financing, caused in part by the reductions in federal aid. Between 1975 and 1980, the average annual growth rate of federal aid to state elementary and secondary education was 11.2 percent, in striking contrast to the 31 percent decline in federal aid during the 1981–82 school year. Interestingly, education is one state service that also grew impressively from 1975 to 1981 with an 11.2 percent annual growth rate matching that of the federal increase. During the 1982–83 school year, however, the state aid growth rate in education was cut to 6 percent, which was compensated for in part by a doubling of revenues from local sources.[12]

If cuts in federal education spending continue and if the state fiscal condition and education aid to the localities continue their downtrend, there will be little choice but to cut services or increase local taxes. According to Adams,

> Some states, such as Pennsylvania, are seriously considering the use of local income tax for financing school districts, but their alternative does not appear to be a national trend. Increases in local property taxes are the most feasible option for financing K-12 education. But, with property tax rates limited by state law in many states, local-option sales and income taxes and user fees become attractive alternatives. Reductions in education services are the other option.[13]

At the postsecondary level, an Education Commission of the States survey conducted in late 1981 found state educational leaders projecting state aid to higher education to be less than the inflation rate and thus a decline in real dollars. Thus, higher education may face the same dilemma as elementary and secondary education: either increases in local costs (largely family tuition payments) or reduced services.[14]

Categorical Aid versus Block Grants

At the same time that the Reagan Administration has sought to withdraw funds from education, it has also attempted to move from categorial aid to block grant approaches with reduced federal regulation. Throughout much of the 1960s and 1970s, educational liberalism was aided and abetted by what political scientist Frederick Wirt describes as proliferation of local groups, blocked by LEAs, who turned to state and national government for assistance. According to Wirt, these local groups, racial, professional and lay school constituents, had similar features. Each was stifled locally, turned to larger government and, in so doing, rallied public opinion.[15]

If the local groups seeking greater federal involvement served to perpetuate educational liberalism, they are precipitated, probably unknowingly and seemingly indirectly, in its decline. Typically, the major benefactors of federal assistance were not the usual tradition coalitions (teachers, administrators, board members) that had long dominated local education. According to Berkeley's James Guthrie, support of these groups had not been critical or mandatory to a growing federal role because of significant public endorsement of governmental involvement. It is Guthrie's observation that "interest groups bypassed at one or another stage in the policy process simply await a subsequent opportunity to reassert their influence."[16] The "get even" attitude was augmented by the Federal Programs' resultant creation of additional interest groups, representing people long denied equal access to the political process. Typically, these federally created groups took the form of advisory councils or committees. Guthrie's analysis:

> Consequently, each of the highly publicized federally sponsored education programs came, over time, to be something of a solar system, within which the program itself served as a major body around which orbited a number of newly created satellites. These satellites, whatever their degree of size of professionalization, seldom recognized the gravitational pull exerted by conventional association bodies such as school board, administrator, or teacher associations. On the contrary, in that last group frequently espoused federal aid that was more general than categorical, the first group maintained its sovereignty all the more. The outcome was a weakened and less cohesive galaxy of interest groups than would otherwise probably have been the case.[17]

One of the apparent ironies of federal involvement in education is that those programs that are most popular and most adopted by the states and localities are the ones that become the most difficult to reduce federal aid. Citing vocational education as an example, William Clune discussed this phenomenon:

> Unfortunately, when programs become widely adopted they also develop strong constituencies. Therefore, when the federal government is least needed because it has become popular, the political difficulty of terminating the program may be very great. It is probably the programs whose objectives are still politically unpopular that receive the most vociferous criticism. In other words, while the idea of the federal government as an innovator (and while withdrawing once the program is established and widely adopted) in education sounds attractive in the abstract, practically speaking the role may involve the federal government in perpetually unpopular actions.[18]

The strong constituencies have generally been drawn from such nontraditional groups as the National Advisory Council for the Education of Disadvantaged Children, the National Welfare Rights Organization, and the Lawyers' Committee for Civil Rights Under the Law. Mainstream organizations such as the National School Boards Association, the National Education Association, and the American Association of School Administrators, while hardly in opposition to federal aid, have not taken the leadership in efforts to broaden categorical programs.

The Danger in Deregulation

And at the same time that these mainstream groups have taken the backseat in supporting categorical programs, they have often been at the forefront of the pleas for deregulation. Of course, this should come as no surprise, for it was precisely the apathy and reluctance of the mainstream groups to serve the underprivileged in our society that provided much of the impetus for federal intervention in the first place. If the local school districts had provided remedial services for underachieving youth, offered quality education to retarded citizens and the handicapped, initiated desegregation efforts, promoted racial and sexual equity, and so forth, there would have been little need for the federal government to make laws, construct programs, and enforce rules to protect the rights of the less fortunate. In order to provide greater equality of educational opportunity to those whom state and local education officials had been unwilling to serve properly, it was necessary to increase federal spending and impose federal regulations.

Following a comprehensive critique of recent federal education program deregulation, law professor William Clune has concluded that "while many deregulatory type adjustments may be possible and desirable, the idea of costless wholesale deregulation is almost exclusively associated with criticisms of the *goals* of federal intervention rather than with means." Accordingly, Clune contends that "Deregulation in education represents a fundamental reexamination of policy."[19] Although the regulations associated with civil rights compliance, education of the handicapped, and affirmative action may be excessive and duplicative, it is Chester Finn's observation in his book *Scholars, Dollars and Bureaucrats* that, even in higher education, "...anyone who seeks to mitigate the effects of government regulation on colleges and universities had best recognize at the outset that it is not a struggle between the academy and bureaucracy, but between parts of the society that want change and parts that resist changing."[20]

Economist Steven Barro has reviewed much of the research on state and local usage of federal education aid that is not accompanied by specific mandates. He points out that before Title I ESEA was legislated, compensatory education was operating in only three states, and poor and/or minority children often received fewer district funds than did the average child. During the early years of

Title I, it was discovered that substantial amounts of Title I revenues were being used for general district expenses or being used to supplant local funds.[21] Examples of such misuse included the hiring of Title I nurses to serve an entire school as well as the building of swimming pools not otherwise affordable by the school district.[22] As a consequence, in the early 1970s, Congress passed legislation that significantly tightened the directions for use of Title I funds by requiring that the funds supplement, not supplant, local effort, and that revenues expended by a district in non-Title I schools be "comparable" to expended monies in Title I schools.[23] Barro offered further evidence on the local usage of federal money by summarizing the empirical work related to this subject:

> Nearly all such studies have found that a large fraction of external aid tends to be substituted for the local district's own revenue. Thus, only a portion of the grant money (most estimates are in the range from one-third to two-thirds) translates into net local expenditure for *any* purpose.[24]

There is compelling evidence that deregulation may result in the redeployment of federal dollars from the areas of greatest need to the areas of greatest population. For example, Title I has targeted a greater amount of its revenues toward the central cities since the problem Title I sought to address is greatest there. In 1977, the central cities, which comprised only 25 percent of the American population, received 42.3 percent of the national Title I funds, while the suburbs, in which 61 percent of Americans lived, received only 34.7 percent of the Title I monies.[25] An analysis of educational consolidation and deregulation by political scientist Marilyn Gittell found that when states have discretion in the expenditure of federal revenues, they tend to favor suburban areas. In 1977, the Congressional Budget Office reported that the suburbs and central cities received respectively 43.5 percent and 36.1 percent of state discretionary federal dollars.[27] According to Gittell, further research on general revenue sharing "reported that 44 percent of all units of government felt that the revenue-sharing money had been used to help avoid tax increases!"[28]

Because the Education Consolidation and Improvement Act of 1981 does not require a careful accounting of block grant expenditures, there is a paucity of hard data on how school districts are using their block grant money. Surveys conducted at the national and state levels, however, suggest that nearly one-half of all Chapter 2 funds are being used to purchase library resources, textbooks, instructional materials, and equipment, and that only a miniscule percentage is being targeted at disadvantaged populations.[28] Although it is the observation of Allen King, deputy director of the Division of Elementary and Secondary Education at ED, that many states feel that the federal government should be more concerned about audits, most state and local officials "like the flexibility" permitted by block grants.[29] According to preliminary returns from another ED survey, the states appear to like the reduction in administration and paperwork associated with Chapter 2.[30]

It should come as no surprise that block grants are more popular than categoricals. They are not targeted at the less fortunate groups in our society, a population to which most schools had not been unduly receptive before the advent of federal programs with specific mandates. Block grant philosophy is congruent with what political scientist Frederick Wirt describes as "The first rule of governmental politics..., the maximization of external funding and the minimization of external control." In Wirt's words, "Each lower level would like the higher level to put money on a stump quietly (say about midnight), then turn and march away smartly, while the locals grab the money and run off in the darkness."[30] Then, those left with the money can spend it as they see best, which often is defined in parochial or political terms.

Despite the growing federal financing of education in recent years, the distaste for external control has contributed to separateness and fragmentation having been perhaps the dominate trait of federal involvement in education at both the collegiate and lower levels. That separateness, fragmentation, and debate over the appropriate federal role will continue as a part of our life in education is highly probable, given the nature of our federal system. It is Wirt's conclusion "...that the interactions of local units with other levels in education cannot be frozen into a pattern of either total local or total national control." Wirt continues that "Some people fear or hope for one or the other outcome, but the reality is more fluid, dynamic, and messy. Federalism is not written on tables of granite. Against that background, we cannot expect a permanent solution to the question of who will govern in a multi-level society."[31]

If Wirt's analysis is correct, it is unlikely that the Reagan administration's attack on Washington's involvement in education will culminate in a negation or even significant reversal of the federal involvement of recent years. Given the "fluidity" of federalism, we have born witness in the early eighties to a muscular exercise by the states and localities to equalize multilevel governance. Apparently, a significant segment of the population believes that the federal government has excessively involved itself in some matters and probably views President Reagan as a checking of power of the first tier of federalism. The second and third tiers, representing (respectively) the states and localities, have asserted their power to maintain a certain equilibrium in what is now viewed as a multilevel educational system.

A Nation At Risk

This phenomenon may have run its course at least as far as education is concerned, and the unknown initiator may have been the Reagan Administration itself. Capitalizing on the malaise surrounding the quality of American schools (as evidenced by declines on the SATs, the inability of many high school graduates to pass simple basic skills tests, etc.) and the apparent fall-off in world influence of American technological achievements, in April 1981, Education Secretary Terrell Bell appointed a National Commission on Excellence in Education (NCEE) to undertake an examination of the cause of the decline in educational quality. Released two years later the Commission's report, *A Nation at Risk: The Imperative for Educational Reform,* has had profound impact in raising our national consciousness.[32] Typifying the public response to the NCEE report and education may be an Associated Press quoting of an Oregon community relations official: "I've been in education for 20 years, and nothing has had this much effect, even more than Sputnik."[33]

Using such language as "If an unfriendly foreign power had attempted to impose on America the mediocre educational performance that exists today, we might have viewed it as an act of war," the NCEE report has captured a mood by sounding an alarm. It suggests that a principal cause of the recent decline in America's international stature is the inadequacy of an educational system that typically requires less schoolwork than other nations and offers at the secondary level a curricula that has been "homogenized, diluted, and diffused to the point that they no longer have a central purpose." Accordingly, the commission found a "cafeteria-style curriculum in which the appetizers and desserts can easily be mistaken for the main course." Regretfully, "this curricular smorgasbord, combined with extensive student choice, explains a great deal about where we find ourselves today." Most students do not complete such components of the "New Basics" as intermediate algebra, calculus, and geography; far too much time and credit involves courses in remedial English, mathematics, physical and health education, out of school work experience and personal-service and development. "In many schools, the time spent learning how to cook and drive counts as much toward a high-school diploma as the time spent studying mathematics, English, chemistry, U.S. history, or biology." In higher education, the commission found that one-fifth of the colleges and universities have open admissions for state residents, thereby putting little pressure on many high school students to perform well or to take demanding courses. Even among the more selective colleges and universities, approximately a quarter to a third reported a decline in general level of selectivity and a reduction in high school courses required for admission.[34]

Pointing to the facts that the Japanese make more efficient automobiles, that the South Koreans now have a steel mill that is the world's most efficient, and that the unparalleled excellence of American machine tools is being seriously challenged by West Germany, the Commission called for fundamental changes in American education. Developments such as these are indicative of a redistribution of the skilled workers around the globe.

> Knowledge, learning, information and skilled intelligence are the new raw materials of international commerce and are today spreading throughout the world as vigorously as miracle drugs. Synthetic fertilizers and blue jeans did earlier. If only to keep and improve on the slim competitive edge we will retain in world markets, we must rededicate ourselves to the reform of our educational system for the benefit of all—old and young alike, affluent and poor, majority and minority. Learning is the indispensable investment required for success in the 'information age' we are entering.[35]

The recommended reforms spelled out by the commission included the requiring of all diploma-seeking high school students to be versed in the "Five New Basics," which should involve successful completion of "(a) four years of English; (b) three years of mathematics; (c) three years of science; (d) three years of social studies; and (e) one-half year of computer science. College-bound students should also take two years of foreign language." The institutions of higher education were urged to raise admission requirements, zeroing in on standards that assure that potential students have proficiency in the five basics. The Commission also recommended a lengthened school year (from the current average of 180 days to 200 or 220), more assigned homework, better instructional management to maximize learning time, increased salaries and longer contracts for teachers, and a performance-based reward system for classroom instructors.[36]

In addressing the federal role, the nonpartisan commission appeared to endorse the major thrust of recent federal educational involvement by recommending the federal protection of civil rights; that "the Federal government, in combination with states and localities, should help meet the needs of key groups of students, such as gifted and talented, the socioeconomically disadvantaged, minority and language-minority students, and the handicapped." In total, "these groups include both national sources and the nation's youth who are most at risk." The Commission also appeared to go somewhat beyond the current state by noting not only that "the federal government has the primary responsibility to identify the national interest in education" but recommended that "it should also help fund and support efforts to protect and promote that interest." In addition, the federal government should be "supporting teacher training in areas of critical shortages or key national needs,...collecting data, statistics, and information about education generally,...supporting curriculum improvement and researching teaching, learning, and management of schools,...and providing student financial assistance and research and graduate training."[37]

Initial Reaction

Public discontent with education has been tapped and nurtured by the report and the political debate surrounding it. In the June 1983 *Newsweek* poll, the vast majority of the sample supported the report recommendations that more English, math, and science be taught (89%), that merit pay be employed to attract and maintain better teachers (80%), and that competency tests be given to those entering the teaching profession (90%).[38] Responding to such dissatisfaction, at least twelve states have already toughened high school graduation requirements and several others have raised admission requirements at institutions of higher education. During the 1982-83 school year, New York City and Washington, D.C., have, respectively, begun mandating nightly homework and planned an extension of the school year from 180 to 192 and the school day from 6 to 7 hours.[39] Following the NCEE release, Mississippi Governor William Winter stated that "The report will make it easier for our state to go forward in education,"[40] which has involved the Mississippi legislature considering twenty additional school days and increasing state school aid by $69 million.[41] Alarmed by the fact that only 27 percent of its ninth grade students passed a state–mandated minimum competency math test, Prince George's County, Maryland plans to increase math instructional time, introduce a special computer program, and increase the teacher training of an estimated 12 to 14 percent of its math teachers who are uncertified to teach the subject.[42] Colorado, which began in 1982 requiring prospective teacher passage of minimum competency tests in language and mathematics (failure rate: 39% for language, 52% for math), has responded to the NCEE report by "Some legislators implying that if there were severe deficiencies in test scores or concise requirements, then perhaps the legislature or State Department of Education should adopt certain minimums or requirements that would go far beyond the current standards," according to school district administration leader Ray Kilmer. Regrettably, "Such actions could potentially move away from local control and toward a state curriculum."[43] Requirements constituting a "state curriculum" are already firmly established in Texas and Virginia, states boldly moving in that direction. Virginia Superintendent of Public Instruction S. John Davis has proposed what is described as a "sweeping overhaul by the state's public school curriculum," which includes requiring more science and math and a special "advanced studies" college preparatory program. Virginia's Governor Charles B. Robb is not only generally endorsing Davis' recommendations, but is pushing the State Board of Education to adopt most of NCEE's recommendations.[44] One of these recommendations is higher salaries for public school teachers and university faculty (a 10% raise in each of the upcoming fiscal years), which will cost the state $250 million, on absolutely essential expenditures, according to his aides, to adequately address the educational needs of the state.[45]

Obviously, such efforts will not be brought to fruition without increased educational spending. The American people appear ready to meet this challenge. When the *Newsweek* poll asked, "Do you favor more funds for public education and teacher training?", a plurality of 45 percent said, "Yes, even if it means higher taxes." When asked from where the money should come, the percentage pointing to state and local services (30%) approximated the percentage checking Washington (31%).[46]

President Reagan, however, has continued to speak out against additional spending, implicitly from any source. In an address to the annual meeting of the National Congress of Parents and Teachers in June 1983, Reagan insisted that "We have an educational problem because we're not getting our money's worth for what we spend," not because we're "not spending enough."[47] In a weekly radio address on June 25, 1983, Reagan pointed out that despite increased federal funding, SAT scores have declined and chastised the "noisy debate" created by Democrats on increasing federal aid to education. And then in an overture to the NCEE, Reagan said that the commission "talked of something that could translate into more money: better pay for better teachers to attract the brightest and the best to choose teaching as a career." Continued Reagan, "Do what is done in every other profession and business: offer merit pay raises for those who earn and deserve them...Let's ignore the noisemakers and set sail."[48]

A Renewed Federal Role

But set sail on what course? The Democrats will surely point to a federal pullback as part of the problem in education. And they may well strike a responsive chord, for if the nation is indeed "at risk" and if people feel the nation's schools should shoulder part of the blame, then they will expect the nation as a whole to begin coming to grips with the problem. Those who do not support an increased federal role may find themselves in political trouble. In fact, there is some evidence that such a transformation may already have begun. Shortly before the release of *A Nation At Risk*, 100 Republicans joined 248 Democrats in House passage of the Emergency Mathematics and Science Education Act by the overwhelming margin of 348 to 54.[49]

While this one vote cannot conclusively hail the commencement of a new period of federal involvement with the schools, it is indicative of Washington's historical approach to dealing with national problems (in this specific instance, a shortage of qualified math and science teachers)—the provision of money for specific programs intended to bring about specific results, not the mere handing over to the states of federal money to enhance their ability to deliver the services they believe most appropriate to the state.

In instances where it was the absence of national policy that caused a national problem—no national policy exists regarding the basic skills necessary for functioning in our society, regarding moving from one grade to the next, regarding high school graduation standards, regarding the issues of teacher supply, competence and pay, and so forth—a national policy might well emerge. Coming at a time such as this when the conservatives are in control of the government, such a policy has the potential to reorder, in a fundamental way, the governance of American education. A liberal attack on the ability of localism to provide for uniformly acceptable education would be expected; a conservative move to such a position in the name of the national interest could signal the start of a transformation that could loosen the historic grip of local school boards and local teachers groups over the American educational system. While such a change would not happen overnight or without a major national debate, it is a clear possibility. Given our long-standing fear of federal control of education, it is more likely that the focus of the governance shift would be from local to state authorities rather than to Washington. Both elected and appointed officials in Washington might become less hesitant to make themselves known than has been the case since federal social programs began to find themselves in disfavor.

Whether or not this scenario occurs, it is likely that federal participation in education will outlive the Reagan Administration's desire for a return to the days of a simpler America. Since education is so closely tied to the national interest, there will always be a prominent federal role in that enterprise. Look at the results: Because we had land grant colleges, we improved our agricultural and technological output; because we enacted the G.I bill, we have strengthened the educational background of our workforce; because we have compensatory education, we have begun to witness a narrowing of the achievement deficit; because our executive, legislative, and judicial bodies have sought to desegregate our classrooms, to protect the civil rights of our citizens, and to more equally distribute educational resources, we stand today a more humane society; because of federal support of innumerable research ventures, we know a good deal more about the limits to and effectiveness of schooling.

We have a rich foundation on which to build, and we should continue to explore carefully that foundation as we address the challenges and uncertainties of education's national course.

REFERENCES

1. *The Gallup Poll, Public Opinion 1982.* Wilmington, Delaware, Scholarly Resources, Inc., 1983.
2. Hodgkinson, H.: What is Still Right with our Schools. *Phi Delta Kappan,* 64 *(4):* 231-35, December 1982.
3. A Newsweek Poll: The Issues. *Newsweek,* June 27, 1983, p. 4.
4. See, for example, "Report Analysis: Public and Private Schools," *Harvard Educational Review,* 51 *(4),* pp. 481-545, November 1981, for diverse viewpoints of seven social scientists plus a reply to the critics by Coleman and his collegues.
5. Murname, R. J.: "Evidence, Analysis, and Unanswered Questions." *Harvard Educational Review,* 51 *(4):* 483-489, November 1981.
6. Edmonds, R.: Effective Schools for the Urban Poor, *Educational Leadership,* 31 *(1):* 22, 1979.; Rutter, M., et al.: *Fifteen Thousand Hours: Secondary Schools and Their Effects on Children,* London, Open Books, 1979.
7. Finn, C.: Why Public and Private School Matter. *Harvard Educational Review,* 51 *(4):* 510-514, November, 1981.
8 Jennings, J.: A Political View of the Federal Education Budget: Review and Implications by a Top Democratic Aide. *Education Times,* May 17, 1982, p. 2.
9. Governor's Creativity Tested in Budget-Balancing Efforts, *Congressional Quarterly Weekly Report,* 41 *(10):* 513-515, March 12, 1983.
10. Governor's Creativity Tested, p. 513.
11. Adams, E. K.: The Fiscal Condition of the States, *Phi Delta Kappan,* 63 *(9):* 598-600, May 1982.
12. Adams, E. K., The Fiscal Condition, pp. 598-600.
13. Adams, E. K., The Fiscal Condition, pp. 598-600.
14. Adams, E. K.: A Changing Federalism: The Condition of the States and the Effect on Education Finance, *Education Times,* June 1, 1982, p. 7.

15. Wirt, F.: Federal School Policy in the 1980's: Historical Givens and Alternative Futures, Overview Paper Prepared for the School Finance Project, Washington, D.C., The National Institute of Education, July 31, 1981.

16. Guthrie, J. W.: The Future of Federal Education Policy, *Education and Urban Society*, 14 *(4):* 511–530, August 1982.

17. Guthrie, J. W., The Future of Federal Education Policy, p. 521.

18. Clune, W. H.: The Deregulation Critique of the Federal Role in Education, Institute for Research on Educational Finance and Governance. School of Education, Stanford University, April 1982, p. 17.

19. Clune, W. H., The Deregulation Critique, p. 3.

20. Finn, C.: *Scholars, Dollars and Bureaucrats.* Washington, D.C., Brookings Institute, 1978, p. 140.

21. Barro, S. Federal Education Goals and Policy Instruments: An Assessment of the 'Strings' Attached to Categorical Grants in Education. In Timpane, M. (ed.) *The Federal Interest in Financing Education.* Cambridge, Massachusetts, Ballinger Publishing Co., 1978, pp. 229–85.

22. Hearings before the Select Committee on Equal Educational Opportunity of the United States Senate, Ninety-Second Congress, Part 17, Delivery Systems for Federal Aid to Disadvantaged Children, Washington, D.C.: U.S. Government Printing Office, 1971, pp. 8674–8719.

23. Barro, Federal Education Goals, pp. 229–85; Stickney, B., and Plunkett, V.: Has Title I Done Its Job? *Educational Leadership.* 39 (5): 378– 83 February 1982.

24. Barro, Federal Education Goals, pp. 229–85.

25. Gittel, M.: Localizing Democracy Out of Schools. *Social Policy,* 12(2): 4–11, September-October 1981.

26. Gittel, M., Localizing Democracy Out of Schools, p. 6.

27. Gittel, M., Localizing Democracy Out of Schools, p. 7.

28. Chapter 2 of the Education Consolidation and Improvement Act of 1981: How LEA's Plan to Use Their Block Grants, U.S. Department of Education, April 1983.

29. From a telephone interview with Allen King, Deputy Director of the Division of Elementary and Secondary Education, U.S. Department of Education, July 22, 1983.

30. Reduction of Administrative Burdens and Paperwork, U.S. Department of Education, 1983. Wirt, Federal School Policy in the 1980's..., p. 11–12.

31. Wirt, Federal School Policy in the 1980's..., p. 12.

32. The National Commission on Excellence in Education, *A Nation At Risk: The Imperative for Educational Reform.* Washington, D.C., April, 1983.

33. "U.S. Towns are Grading Education," an article reported by the Associated Press, The Colorado Springs *Gazette Telegraph*, June 26, 1983, PA-6.

34. *A Nation at Risk*, p. 15, 18, 20–2.

35. *A Nation at Risk*, pp. 6–7.

36. *A Nation at Risk*, pp. 25–26, 29–30.

37. *A Nation at Risk*, pp. 32–33.

38. "The Politics of Education: What the Public Thinks." *Newsweek*, June 27, 1983, p. 61.
39. "To Stem the Tide of Mediocrity." *Time*, May 9, 1983, p. 62–3.
40. "U.S. Towns..." op. cit.
41. "To Stem a Tide..." op. cit., p. 63.
42. Wynter, L.: 75% of 9th Grade Fails P.G. Math Skills Exam. *The Washington Post*, May 27, p. 1 +.
43. This information and quotation was gathered from Raymond Kilmer, former president of Department of General Administration, Colorado Association of School Executives, at a meeting of the Pikes Peak Board of Cooperative Services, Colorado Springs, Colorado, May 10, 1983, and from a telephone conversation June 28, 1983.
44. Isikoff, M.: Tougher Virginia School Standards Urged. *The Washington Post*, May 27, 1983, p. 1 +.
45. Isikoff, M.: Robb Seeks Big Raise in Teacher Pay. *The Washington Post*, May 27, 1983, p. 1 +.
46. "The Politics of Education, p. 61.
47. The information and Reagan quotation excerpted from "Teacher Unions are Courted and Castigated," by Gene I. Mareoroff, in *The New York Times*, June 26, 1983, p. EY9.
48. Reagan, R.: Radio Address to the Nation, June 25, 1983.
49. "House Passes Math/Science Education Bill." *Congressional Quarterly Weekly Report*, 49(4): 474–75, 480, March 5, 1983.

INDEX

A

Abraham, Henry J., 149, 150
Adams, John, 6
Adams, John Quincy, 6
Adams, Kathleen, 172
Advisory Commission on Intergovernmental
  Relations, 61, 62
Advisory Committee on Education, 28
Affirmative action, 15, 149-150
Agriculture Act of 1954, 28-29
Alabama, 9, 15, 27, 153
Alaska, 5
Alcohol and Drug Abuse Education Act, 111
Allen, James A., Jr., 43
American Association of University Profes-
  sors, 46
American Association of School Administra-
  tors, 101-102, 174
American Civil Liberties Union, 134, 136, 138
American Council on Education, 16, 33
American Federation of Teachers, 47
American Institutes for Research, 68
American Jewish Congress, 134
American Library Association, 75
American School Board Journal, 68
Anderson, Bill, 157
Arkansas, 130, 135, 136-138
Ashbrook, John, 115-116, 171
Atkin, J. M. and House, E., 29

B

Bailey, Stephen K., 45
Baker v. Owen, 142
Ball, William Bentley, 154
Bankhead-Jones Act, 9
Barnard, Henry, 38, 39
Barro, Steven, 175
Bell, Derrick A., Jr., 132, 158
Bell, Terrel H., 51-52, 82, 103, 106, 119, 120-
  121, 178
Berger, Raoul, 146-147

Bethell, Tom, 68
Bickel, Alexander, 148, 151
Bilingual education, 37, 68, 102, 111, 113,
  132-133, 149
Blackman, Harry, 141
Blaine, James G., 25
Blair, Henry W., 25, 26
Block grants, 33, 89-90, 102, 109-117, 173,
  177
Bloom, Arvin, 115
Board of Education v. Allen, 140
Bob Jones University, 154-155
Bok, Derek, 62
"Boll Weevil" Southern Democrats, 90, 91
*Bradley v. School Board of City of Rich-
  mond,* 130
Breneman, David, 156, 157
Brennan, William, 132, 147
Brown v. Board of Education, 128, 129-130,
  147, 150, 158, 160
Brown II, 129
Buchanan, James, 7
Burger, Warren, 131, 148, 149, 150, 154, 159
Burnside, Ambrose, 9
Bussing, 35, 69, 128, 131, 139, 143-144, 145,
  150, 152, 153, 161

C

Caldiera, Gregory and McCrone, Donald,
  149
California, 29, 135-136
Cannon, Lou, 91
Career education, 112
Career Education Incentive Act, 111
Carter, Jimmy, 3, 37, 44, 46, 47, 49, 50, 51,
  52, 60, 61, 77, 78, 79, 94, 168
Carter, Launor, 104-105
Categorical aid, 8, 16, 25, 31, 32, 34, 62, 89-
  90, 99, 109, 110, 113-122, 173
Catholic Church/Catholic Schools, 23, 24,
  25, 30, 33, 41, 49, 156, 158

187

Chapter I, Education Consolidation & Improvement Act of 1981, 108, 111, 121-122

Chapter 2, Education Consolidation & Improvement Act of 1981, 108, 111-117, 121-122, 177

Children's Defense Fund, 120

Children's Defense League, 117

Chisholm, Shirley, 48-49

Chicago Sun Times, 50

Church, Frank, 88

Church and state, 23, 31, 32, 33, 38, 39, 41, 133-141, 148, 153-155, 161

Civil Rights Act of 1964, 15, 30-31, 35, 70, 129, 131, 149

Civilian Conservation Corps, 28

Clune, William, 174, 175

Coalition to Save Title I, 102-103, 106

Cold War, 11-12, 29

Coleman, James, 66, 67, 71, 156, 170

Coleman, William T., Jr., 154

Colorado, 113, 116-117, 131-132

Commission on National Aid to Vocational Education, 19

Commission on the Emergency in Education, 26

Committee for Public Education and Religious Liberty v. Nyquist, 140

Committee for Public Education and Religious Liberty v. Regan, 141

Community education, 116

Community schools, 112

Compensatory education, 32, 33, 37, 90, 102, 175, 184

Comprehensive Employment & Training Act of 1973, 109

Congressional Budget Office, 157, 176

Congressional Quarterly Weekly Report, 81-82, 172

Connecticut, 38

Conrad, C. and Cosand, J., 18

Cooper v. Aaron, 130

Cottle, Thomas, 70

Council on Exceptional Children, 120

Court-limiting measures, 142-145, 159-160

Cox, Archibald, 149

Creationism, 74-75, 134-138

D

Dahl, Robert, 159

Dartmouth College Case, 129

Davis, S. John, 181

Deaver, Michael, 92

Delaware, 132

Democratic Party Platform (1980), 76, 89

Deregulation of programs, 116-123, 175-178

Desegregation, 15, 30-31, 33, 34-35, 114, 128-133, 142, 144, 145, 147, 152, 160, 184

Domenici, Peter, 92

Donnelly, Harrison, 81-82

Due process clause, 136, 147, 152, 153

Dworkin, Ronald, 152-153

E

Earley v. Dicenso, 140

Education Amendments of 1972, 16-18, 34, 35

Education Amendments of 1980, 18, 37

Education Consolidation & Improvement Act of 1981, 108, 111-117, 121-122, 176, 177

Education Commission of the States Survey, 173

Education of the handicapped, 22, 93, 107, 111, 117-121

Education Professions Development Act, 14-15

Educational land grants, 4, 5, 7-8, 9, 10

Eisenhower, Dwight D., 42

Elbers, Gerald, 114-115

Elementary and Secondary Education Act of 1965, 30-34, 37, 43, 47, 111

Elementary/Secondary Education, 23-37, 49, 96

Ellwanger, Paul, 136-138

Emergency School Aid Act, 34-36, 37, 114, 116

Enarson, Harold, 63

Engle v. Vitale, 128, 133, 144

Environmental Protection Agency, 63

Equal Employment Opportunity Commission, 64

Equal Protection Clause, 131, 147, 152, 153

Equal Rights Amendment, 77-78, 79

Equal Time Laws, 135, 137-138

Equality of Educational Opportunity Survey, by James Coleman, et al., 66, 67, 72

Erlenborn, John N., 49, 82

Establishment clause, 133, 136, 148, 158

Ethic heritage programs, 112, 114

Evans v. Buchanan, 132

Everson v. Board of Education of the Township of Ewing, 139-140

F

Faculty rights, 142, 143
Falwell, Jerry, 134
Federal Emergency Relief Administration, 27
Federal Register, 63, 114, 116
Federal Security Agency, 42, 46
Fifth Amendment, 160, 161
Finn, Chester, 43, 170-171, 175
First Amendment, 133, 136, 137, 138, 141, 142, 148, 153, 161
Florey v. Sioux Falls School District, 134
Florida, 27, 70
Follow through, 89
Follow Through Act, 11, 117
Forbes, Roy, 103-104
Ford, Gerald, 44, 48, 103, 190-110
Fourteenth Amendment, 139, 147, 152, 160
Frankel, Max, 68
Free Exercise Clause, 133, 153, 158
Freedom of Choice Plans, 130
Freeman, Roger, 67
Free Speech Clause, 136

G

Gallup Poll, 60, 70, 75, 88, 169
Garfield, James A., 38, 39
Gay rights, 142
Geisler, Norman, 136
George-Barden Act, 20
George-Deen Act, 20
George-Ellzey Act, 20
George-Reed Act, 20
Gittell, Marilyn, 176
G. I. Bill, 11, 21, 168, 184
Goldsboro Christian schools, 154-155
Goodlad, John, 69
Goss v. Board of Education, 130
Goss v. Lopez, 142
Grade-a-Year Plans, 130
Graglia, Lino, 146, 147
Gramm, Phil, 91, 96-97
"Gramm-Latta" substitutes for the budget, 96-97, 98
Grant, Ulysses S., 24-25
Green v. County School Board, 130
Great Depression, 27-28, 40, 42, 168
Griffin v. County School Board, 130

Gifted and talented education, 116
Griggs v. Duke Power Company, 149
Guaranteed student loan, 90, 97
Guthrie, James, 173-174

H

Hamilton, Alexander, 6, 143
Hamilton, Bette, 117-118
Hance, Kent, 91
Handicapped children, 36-37, 157
Harpers Magazine, 68
Hart, Gary, 106-107
Hatch Act, 9
Hawaii, 5
Hawkins, Augustus, 98, 104, 106
Head Start, 67, 68, 111, 113
Healy v. James, 142
Heftel, Cecil, 45
Helms, Jesse, 143, 144
Higgins, Thomas J., 146
High School & Beyond: A Native Longetudinal Study for the 1980s, 170
Higher education, 6, 7-18, 30, 37, 39, 49, 139, 175
Higher Education Act of 1965, 13-14, 15, 16, 111, 112
Higher education amendments of 1968, 15
Higher Education Facilities Act, 12-13, 14
Hoar, George F., 24
Hodgkinson, Harold, 169
Hollings, Ernest, 157
Holsted, James L., 136
Hoover, Herbert, 20, 39
Hoover Commission, 109
Hoover Institute, 67
Horowitz, Donald, 149, 150, 151
House Appropriations Committee, U.S. House of Representatives, 101
House Budget Committee, U.S. House of Representatives, 96
House Education & Labor Committee, U.S. House of Representatives, 64
House Subcommittee on Elementary, Secondary & Vocational Education, U.S. House of Representatives, 61, 103-104
Housing & Community Development Act of 1974, 109
Howe, Harold, 33
Howe, Helena, 46
Hufstedler, Shirley, 51

I

Illinois, 29
Illiteracy, 24, 25, 26, 38, 39
Impact aid, 90
Indian education, 101, 117
Indiana, 9
Individualized Educational Programs (IEPs),
    118-119, 121
Ingraham v. Wright, 142
In re Gault, 142
Internal Revenue Service, 153-154
International Education Act, 14

J

Jackson, Andrew, 4, 25
Jefferson, Thomas, 6, 23, 38
Jennings, Jack, 61, 171
Jensen, Arthur, 67, 68
Johnson, Andrew, 39
Johnson, Lyndon B., 12, 13, 15, 18, 30, 31,
    32, 34, 37, 43, 44, 63
Johnston, J. Bennett, 143
Judicial Activism - Restraint, 145-162

K

Katzenbach, Nicholas, 15
Kennedy, Edward M., 120, 145
Kennedy, John F., 13, 15, 18, 21, 30
Kentucky, 5, 132, 134
Keppel, Francis, 31, 70
Keyes, David, 159
*Keyes v. School District Number 1, Denver,
    Colorado*, 131-132, 144
Kilmer, Raymond, 181
King, Allen, 177
Korean War, 11

L

Lamb, Charles M., 145, 149, 151
Lamm, Richard, 113
Lanham Act, 28
Laskey, Louis, 146, 147, 148
Latta, Phillip, 96-97
Lau v. Nichols, 132-133, 149
Lawyers' Committee for Civil Rights under
    the Law, 174
Lemon v. Kurtzman, 140, 141, 158
Lewis, Anthony, 150

Library of Congress Congressional Research
    Service, 110
Lincoln, Abraham, 7
Local control of education, 3-4, 20, 32, 38,
    39-40, 46, 49, 50, 51, 128, 137
Louisiana, 135, 137, 143
Loyalty oaths, 142

M

Madison, James, 6
Maine, 5, 25, 38
Marshall, John, 143, 148
Marshner, Connaught, 75
Maryland, 133
Massachusetts, 3-4, 23, 24, 27, 148
Massive resistance, 130, 158
Matching grants, 10, 13, 14, 20, 25-26, 40
Matthews, Jessica Tuchman, 135
Mayville, William V., 8
McGill, William, 63
McGovern, George, 88
McGuire, Willard, 77
McIntyre, James T., Jr., 46
Meek v. Pittenger, 140
Metric education, 112
Michel, Robert H., 90
Michigan, 23, 132, 160
Miller, Arthur S., 159
Milliken v. Bradley, 132
Minnesota, 158
Mississippi, 24, 27, 29, 153
Missouri, 138-139
Modern Language Journal, 68
Mondale, Walter, 3, 77
Monroe, James, 6
Moral Majority, 74
Morrill Act, 7, 8, 9, 168
Morrill, Justin, 7, 9
Morrill II, 9-10
Mort, Paul R., 8, 19-20
Moynihan, Daniel Patrick, 17, 63-64, 96, 155,
    156
Mueller v. Allen, 158
Murname, Richard, 170
Murphy, Walter, 152
Murray v. Curlett, 133

N

NAACP, 33
NAACP Legal Defense Fund, 154

A Nation at Risk: The Imperative For Educational Reform, National Commission on Excellence in Education, 178-182

National Advisory Committee on Education, 20, 39-41

National Advisory Council for the Education of the Disadvantaged, 174

National Assessment of Educational Progress, 103-105

National Center for Educational Statistics, 170

National Commission on Excellence in Education, 83, 178-182

National Conference of State Legislature, 172

National Conservative Political Action Committee, 74

National Defense Education Act (NDEA), 12, 21, 29-30, 42, 168

National Education Association, 25, 33, 36, 44, 45, 49, 50, 51, 76-78, 79, 156, 174

National Education Improvement Act, 21

National Institute of Education, 34

National P.T.A., 102

National Resources Planning Board, 42

National School Boards Association, 120, 174

National School Lunch Act, 28

National Science Foundation, 11, 29, 47, 162, 168

National Science Foundation Act of 1950, 11, 111

National Survey on School Finance, 27

National Welfare Rights Organization, 174

National Youth Administration, 10, 28

Neighborhood School Act, 143-144

Nelson Amendment, 10

Nevada, 27

Newburg Area Council v. Jefferson County Board of Education, 132

New Hampshire, 15, 25

New Jersey, 27, 36, 139-140, 158

New Right, 74-75

Newsweek Poll, 169, 180-181, 182

New York, 4, 9, 29, 113, 133, 141, 158

New York Times, 50, 68, 69, 144, 150, 157

1975 Title XX Amendments of the Social Security Act of 1935, 109

Nixon, Richard M., 15, 16, 18, 34, 43, 48, 60, 67, 70, 109-110, 131, 153

North Carolina, 27, 131, 145

Northwest Ordinances, 5, 23

O

Office of Civil Rights, U.S. Department of Education, 64

Office of Federal Contract Compliance Programs, U.S. Department of Labor, 64

Office of Management and the Budget, The White House, 64, 100

Ohio, 4-5, 135, 141, 158

Old Deluder Act, 3

Omnibus Crime Control & Safe Streets Act of 1968, 109

Omnibus Reconciliation Act of 1981, 98, 110, 112

Oregon, 5, 138, 155

Organized labor, 25, 33, 49

Osbourn, Sandra, 110

Overton, Willam R., 137-138

P

Packwood, Robert, 155, 156

Paradis, Wilfred, 49-50

Parent involvement, 122

Park, J. Charles, 74

Partnership for Health Act of 1966, 109

Pell, Clairborne, 109

Pennsylvania, 9, 36, 133, 140

Pennsylvania Association of Retarded Citizens v. Commonwealth of Pennsylvania, 36

Perkins, Carl, 64, 65, 98, 106, 107

Perluss, Irving H., 135-136

Philadelphia Inquirer, 157

Pickering, Timothy, 4-5

Pierce, Legrand W., 24

Pierce v. Society of Sisters, 138

Plattner, Andy, 81-82

Plessy v. Ferguson, 129

Powell, Adam Clayton, 13, 21

Pro-family movement, 74

Program for Economic Recovery, 89, 94-95

Proposition 13, 60

Public and Private Schools, by James Coleman, et al., 170

Public Works Administration, 28

Q

Quayle, Daniel, 82

R

Racial discrimination, 15, 23, 26, 27, 30-31, 33, 34-35, 41, 128-133, 147, 150, 160
Rather, Dan, 106
Ravitz, Diane, 72
Reagan, Ronald, 42, 52, 61, 76, 79, 80, 81, 82, 88-95, 98-102, 107, 110, 115, 117, 122-123, 135, 144, 154, 156, 157, 168, 171, 177-178, 182
Reagan, by Lou Cannon, 91
Rebell, Michael A. and Block, Arthur R., 151, 152
Rehnquist, William, 158
Republican Party Platform (1980), 76
Reserve Officers Training Corps (ROTC), 10, 168
Reuss, Henry, 97
Rev. Bill McLean et al. v. The Arkansas Board of Education et al., 136-138
Reynolds, William B., 144
Rhode Island, 9, 140
Ribicoff, Abraham, 21, 44-45, 46
Rice, Charles E., 148
Robb, Charles B., 181
Robinson, Donald L. 46
Rogers v. Paul, 130
Roosevelt, Franklin D., 28, 42, 79, 93
Rosenthal, Benjamin, 48
Rubin, Lillian,
Rutter, Michael, 170
Ryor, John, 45

S

Savage, David, 50
Schick, Marvin, 149, 150
Scholars Dollars & Bureaucrats, 175
School Assistance Act of 1961, 30
School District of Abington TP, Pa. v. Schempp, 133
School prayer, 107, 128, 133-134, 142, 144-145, 148, 159
Scott, Robert, 63
Seagraves, Kelly L., 135
Segregationist academies, 153-154
Senate Appropriations Committee, 100
Senate Budget Committee, 95

Senate Judiciary Committee, 72
Senate Labor & Human Resources Committee, 109
Sex discrimination, 17, 22
Sex equity, 117
Shanker, Albert, 47-48
Single issue politics, 159-160
Sloan Commission on Government and Higher Education, 64
Smith-Bankhead Act, 21
Smith-Hughes Act of 1917, 19, 20, 40
Smith-Lever Act, 10
Smith-Towner Bill, 39
Smithsonian Institute, 7
Social policy rulings, 151-152
South Carolina, 136, 153, 157
South Dakota, 134
Special Education Programs, U.S. Department of Education, 119-120
Stafford, Thomas, 120, 171
St. James, Fernand, 98
State of the Union Address, 1981, 80
State of the Union Address, 1983, 107
Stephens, John, 141
Stewart, Potter, 140
Stickney, Benjamin D., 105
Stockman, David, 90, 99
Stone, Harlan Fiske, 146
Stone v. Graham, 134
Story, Joseph, 146
Student financial aid, 10-11, 12, 14, 16-17, 18
Students for a Democratic Society, 142
Students' Rights, 142, 143, 161
Sustaining Effects Study, Systems Development Corporation, 104-105
Swann v. Charlotte-Mecklenburg Board of Education, 131
Sweazy v. New Hampshire, 142
Systems Development Corporation, 104

T

Taft, Robert A., 28
Taney, Roger B., 143
Tax cuts, increases, 99-100
Tax exemptions, 153-154
Taylor, Telford, 143
Teacher centers, 112
Teacher Corps, 112
Tennessee, 5, 130

Tenth Amendment, 6

Texas, 5, 32, 135

Thomason, Jo, 120

Thurmond, Strom, 145

Tilton v. Richardson, 139

Time Magazine Poll, 88

Tinker v. Des Moines Independent Community School District, 142

Title I, ESEA, 67, 68, 69, 81, 93, 94, 99, 101, 102-108, 111, 113, 121-122, 175-176

Title II, Elementary & Secondary Education Act of 1965, 112

Title IV, Elementary Secondary Education Act of 1965, 112, 115

Title VII, ESEA, 68

Today's Education, The Journal of the National Education Association, 77

Tuition tax credits, 107, 153, 155-158

Tushnet, Mark, 150

U

United States Steel Workers v. Weber, 149-150

Urban League, 102

U.S. Bureau of Education, 39

U.S. Constitution, 6, 19, 25, 33, 131, 133, 143, 144, 145, 146, 147, 148, 152-153, 160, 161, 162

U.S. Department of Education, 3, 37-52, 65, 76-77, 80-82, 103, 111, 114, 119-121, 177

U.S. Department of Health, Education, and Welfare, 36, 42-48

U.S. Department of Justice, 64

U.S. Office of Education, 33, 39, 42-43, 114

V

Van Buren, Martin, 7

Vermont, 5

Vietnam War, 15, 18, 34, 142

Virginia, 130

Vocational education, 19-22, 30

Vocational Education Act, 21

Vocational education program, 111, 117

W

Wallace, George, 15, 70

War Manpower Commission, 11

Warren, Earl, 130, 147, 148, 150, 159

Wasby, Stephen, 152

Washington, George, 6

Washington Post, 50, 69, 91

Weeks Act, 20

Weicker, Lowell, 171

Welfare clause, 6, 19, 25

West Virginia, 5, 135

Weyrich, Paul, 74

White, Andrew D., 8-9

White, Byron, 140, 141

White House Conference on Education, 30

Widmar v. Vincent, 138-139

Williams, Harrison, 36

Winter, William, 181

Wirt, Frederick, 173, 177

Wisconsin, 138

Wisconsin v. Yoder, 138, 154, 161

Wolman v. Walter, 140-141

Women's Educational Equity Act, 111

Works Progress Administration, 27-28

World War I, 26, 39

World War II, 10-11, 20, 168

Wyman, L.H., 15

Y

Yohalem, Daniel, 117-118

Youngblood, J. Craig and Folse, Parker C. III, 151

Z

Zorach v. Clauson, 133